El Lazarillo

A GUIDE FOR INEXPERIENCED TRAVELERS

EL LAZARILLO

DE CIEGOS CAMINANTES

desde Buenos-Ayres, hasta Lima con sus Itinerarios segun la mas puntual observacion, con algunas noticias utiles á los Nuevos Comerciantes que tratan en Mulas; y otras Historicas.

SACADO DE LAS MEMORIAS QUE

hizo Don Alonso Carrió de la Vandera en este dilatado Viage, y Comision que tubo por la Corte para el arreglo de Correos, y Estafetas, Situacion, y ajuste de Postas, desde Montevideo.

POR

DON CALIXTO BUSTAMANTE CARLOS Inca, alias CONCOLORCORVO *Natural del Cuzco, que acompañó al referido Comisionado en dicho Viage, y escribió sus Extractos.*

CON LICENCIA.

En Gijon, en la Imprenta de la Rovada. Año de 1773.

CONCOLORCORVO, *b. ca. 1706.*

El Lazarillo

A Guide for Inexperienced Travelers between Buenos Aires and Lima · 1773

TRANSLATED BY

Walter D. Kline

INDIANA UNIVERSITY PRESS

Bloomington 1965

UNESCO COLLECTION OF REPRESENTATIVE WORKS

LATIN-AMERICAN SERIES

This book has been accepted in the series of translations of Latin-American Literature sponsored by the United Nations Educational, Scientific and Cultural Organization (UNESCO).

)

TRANSLATOR'S PREFACE

The present translation is based on the 1942 edition of *El Lazarillo de ciegos caminantes* (Ediciones Argentinas Solar, Buenos Aires). An attempt has been made to preserve the charmingly awkward and unpolished style of the eighteenth-century author. However, for the sake of clarity liberties were taken with long and complicated sentences in which the structure tended to obscure the meaning. Some Spanish terms appear in the text, either to add flavor or because they defy translation; these are defined in the Glossary of Spanish Words. In a few cases where all dictionaries and informants were of no help, the meanings of specific words were inferred from the context.

Judicious cutting and editing have been done to spare the reader the tedium of passages which added little to the work; such omissions are indicated in the text by points of ellipses. Footnotes appear when their presence might enhance interest and understanding. The mileage tables, occurring at the beginning of each chapter in the original edition, have been moved from the text to the appendix.

If some passages appear perplexing, and if mules and mudholes are multitudinous, full credit is due the author and not the translator or the editor, whose supplies of synonyms and patience were frequently frustrated!

W.D.K.

CONTENTS

ILLUSTRATIONS

FOREWORD

The literary products of the former possessions of Spain in
the New World far exceeded in quantity and quality those of
the Atlantic colonies of England in North America. No British
historian of English letters is likely to include any prose or
versified work composed in the former American dependencies
as a significant—much less a classic—contribution to the literature of the mother country. Chroniclers of Castilian literary
expression, on the other hand, whether Spanish or Spanish-
American, are pleased and even proud to recognize many works
created in the former overseas realms of Spain as worthy elements of the great patrimony of Spanish genius. The writings
of the conquistadors for instance, notably *The True History
of the Conquest of Mexico* by the soldier-chronicler, Bernal
Díaz del Castillo (1494 or 1495-1584), a realistic narrative in
unvarnished prose, have acquired the status of classics, as
have Alonso de Ercilla's (1534-1594) epic of the conquest of
Chile, *La Araucana*, rated the best historical poem in Castilian,
and Father Diego de Hojeda's (1571-1615) *La Cristiada*, composed in Peru and accepted as the best religious epic in the language. If these masterpieces were the work of transplanted
Spaniards who sought careers in the New World, there were
also Creole or American-born writers of Spanish descent whose
contributions are also highly esteemed and have a respected
place in the literature of the mother country. Such are, for
example, the Mexican-born dramatist, Juan Ruiz de Alarcón
(1580-1639), now recognized as one of the greatest playwrights

of Spain's Golden Age of literature, and Sister Juana Inés de la Cruz (1648-1695), who lived out her days in a Mexico City convent, whose lyric verse is considered the most inspired of her time in the Spanish-speaking world.

There is a curious lack, however, in colonial Hispanic American literature of any true novel during the three centuries of Spanish rule even though works of this character poured into Spain's overseas realms by the thousands. But if an authentic novel is missing in pre-Independence Spanish America, examples of what might be called "prose with novelistic elements"—sometimes as readable as genuine novels—were numerous. Foremost among works in this peculiar form of literary expression is the eighteenth century *El Lazarillo de ciegos caminantes* (Guide for Blind Travelers), an animated description of an extended journey in South America from Montevideo in present-day Uruguay to Lima in Peru by way of the Argentine and Bolivian cities of Buenos Aires, Córdoba, Salta, Potosí, Chuquisaca [Sucre], and Cuzco. This lively narrative—possibly inspired by the immensely successful *A Voyage to South America* (1748) of two adventurous Spanish scientists, Jorge Juan (1713-1773) and Antonio de Ulloa (1716-1795), which was translated into many European languages—humorously combines didactic elements with satiric comments on types and mores of contemporary South American society.

The geographer, sociologist, and folklorist as well as the historian will glean interesting data from the pages of this odd work, while the reflection of nature, folk verse quoted, and the lively dialogues suggestive of the earlier Spanish picaresque tradition presented with the sardonic humor of a Francisco de Quevedo, the great Spanish satirist of the seventeenth century, will appeal to the general reader as well as to the student of literature. The novelesque character of this unique work (recently translated into French) adumbrates the later Spanish American novel. The Indiana University Press is rendering a decidedly useful service in bringing before the English-speaking public at this time this faithful rendition of the original work.

IRVING A. LEONARD

University of Michigan

INTRODUCTION

El Lazarillo de ciegos caminantes was first published in Lima in 1775-1776 under the colorful pseudonym "Concolorcorvo." The actual place and date of publication had been altered presumably to protect the author's true identity from his Spanish superiors, and only recently, after considerable research over the last half century, have scholars been able to confirm its true author as Don Alonso Carrió de la Vandera (or Bandera).[1] This curious travelogue—which smacks of the picaresque genre established by the sixteenth century Spanish work of similar title—reveals much about the character of its creator and may perhaps best be introduced with a sketch of the "Inspector's" life in the New World.[2]

Although Argentinians and Peruvians have long considered *El Lazarillo* a literary monument representative of their colonial eighteenth century, it is not an indigenous work. Nothing is known of the family background of Don Alonso Carrió whose

[1] The genesis and history of *El Lazarillo* have been studied by José J. Real Díaz in an article which forms the introduction to a recent edition of the work (ed. Juan Pérez de Tudela, *Biblioteca de Autores Españoles*, Vol. CXXII: *Relaciones histórico-literarias de la América Meridional* [Madrid, 1959], pp. 245-277.) By means of important documents Real Díaz proves Don Alonso Carrió to be the sole and undisputed author of *El Lazarillo*.

[2] My introduction owes much to Marcel Bataillon's "Introduccíon á Concolorcorvo y su itinerario de Buenos Aires á Lima" (*Cuadernos Americanos*, Año XIX, CXI, 197-216). This excellent study, originally prepared as an introduction to a French translation of *El Lazarillo* sponsored by UNESCO, summarizes previous research on this work.

name suggests Catalonian origin. He was born in Gijón, in Asturias, about 1715, arrived in Mexico at the age of 20, and moved to Lima in 1746, where he married and fixed his residence. During the years 1750 and 1757, under the reign of Fernando VI, he distinguished himself in various government and military positions of importance in and about Lima.

Under Carlos III of Spain, the Company of Jesus, whose missions in South America constituted a spiritual and economic power without precedent, was expelled in 1767. The religious were to be transported to Europe under close watch but treated with care and respect. Don Alonso Carrió offered to convoy the repatriated missionaries. In 1768, after having delivered the Jesuits to the authorities in Cádiz, Carrió went to the Court to solicit recompense for his services. His several efforts, including a published account of his services distributed in high places, proved unsuccessful. He was 55 years old, had sacrificed everything to make this voyage and felt somewhat bitter. All that remained for him to do, it appeared, was to return to Lima, where he had been respected for 24 years, with no tangible sign of royal esteem.

In May of 1771 the "Tucumán" landed at Montevideo, where Carrió discovered that another ship carrying his few possessions had been lost. Again he pleaded for a suitable appointment. This last request suprised the officials in Madrid. It seems that he had already been recommended to the Viceroy of Peru. The recommendation was renewed. In lieu of a lucrative post, Carrió had obtained a confidential mission. On January 12, 1771, the Marquis de Grimaldi had appointed him Inspector of the postal route between Buenos Aires and Lima. Viceroy Amat had been notified and along with this notice went a recommendation for a permanent position in Lima at the conclusion of the inspection tour.[3]

Marquis de Grimaldi's reform of the mails was part of the

[3] Walter B. L. Bose, the erudite historian of the mails in South America, has made a study of this tour of inspection.

Bourbon movement to accelerate centralization of power in the Spanish monarchy, a movement already begun under the Catholic kings by the recuperation of important concessions made to members of the nobility. The office of Chief Postmaster of the Indies, which the Carvajal family had held since 1514, was returned to royal supervision in 1768. In the future this office would be administered publicly as a principal branch of the Post Office.

Although Carrió had been charged only with the inspection and reorganization of the land mails from Buenos Aires to Lima, he felt that his mission had already begun on board the "Tucumán." Unfortunately, however, only a fragment of his *Nautical Journal,* if indeed he kept a complete one, has come down to us.[4]

Don Alonso's superior was Don José Antonio de Pandó, appointed General Administrator of Mails in the viceroyalty of Peru by the King. Pandó had begun his inspection in Cartagena in 1769 and had reached Bogotá, where he fell ill; he did not complete the first phase of his tour to Lima until 1772. Don Domingo de Basavilbaso, General Administrator of the Mails in the Rio de la Plata, had tried unsuccessfully to reach Pandó, and it was probably owing to his complaints to Madrid that a new Inspector was appointed to complete the tour, from Buenos Aires to Lima. Carrió and Basavilbaso, both dedicated men of action, quite naturally formed a poor opinion of Pandó, who, jealous of his prerogatives and misled by his adviser in Lima, did little but oppose Carrió's reforms all the way from Buenos Aires to Lima. Carrió, in turn, antagonized Pandó to the point that the Court, although generally favorable to Carrió, grew weary of polemic and ordered the Viceroy of Peru to end this

---

[4] *"El Lazarillo de ciegos caminantes* y su problema histórico" (*Labor de los Centros de Estudios,* XXIV, 219-287), published by Mr. Bose in La Plata in 1941, discusses the correspondence of Basavilbaso concerning this mission. Bose discovered other correspondence pertinent to the mission, which was studied by André Saint-Lu in the Indies Archive in Seville and transmitted to M. Bataillon.

dispute that was proving detrimental to the interests of the Crown. In subsequent affairs the Court was not favorably disposed toward Carrió, about whom nothing is known after 1778.

This tense situation undoubtedly influenced the conception and odd manner of publication of *El Lazarillo*. Carrió falsely identified "Concolorcorvo" as Don Calixto Bustamante Carlos Inca, a descendant of the Incas, who actually existed. Don Calixto had come from Chile and presented himself to Basavilbaso with a forged letter of recommendation. In spite of this deceit Don Calixto was accepted to accompany Carrió on his tour. He was included prominently (although condescendingly and humorously) as the *lazarillo* or secretary—even co-author —probably as much because of his character and personality as the author's. Carrió also invented a false place of publication (Gijón) and a false date (1773) for his strange travelogue. Subsequent correspondence accompanying shipments of his book to Spain helps to clarify these mysteries.

While Bataillon is certainly correct in holding that *El Lazarillo* is not primarily a picaresque novel, there are clearly some important elements in the work that are characteristic of the picaresque. If this *Lazarillo* is not a direct continuation of its celebrated ancestor, it does develop at some length the primary picaresque themes of hunger and vagabondage and shows some evidence of anti-clericalism and delight in scabrous details. The autobiographical aspects plus what little is known of the spurious "crow-colored" author are all picaresque traits in themselves.

It is probably the picaresque details in the text of *El Lazarillo* that most interest the literary scholar and amuse the general reader.[5] Following the conventions of the genre, Carrió has Concolorcorvo explain the latter's origins in terms that cast suspicions on his legitimacy. After implying that his mother

[5] A lengthier study of these picaresque details may be found in "Some Picaresque Elements in Concolorcorvo's 'El Lazarillo de ciegos caminantes'," *Hispania*, XLVI:2 (May, 1963), 323-327.

was dishonest, Concolorcorvo proceeds to impugn the honor of other female relatives. Mocking his master, he says that he is of a mind to aspire to the post of dog-chaser at the cathedral in Cuzco—so that he may enjoy ecclesiastical immunity—and hopes that publishing this record of his trip will help him attain his post. Concolorcorvo has only the vaguest recollections of his native Cuzco, his modest home and family, all abandoned at a very tender age, for reasons that remain a mystery to the reader. Here is the typically rough sketch of a picaresque hero, or anti-hero; the rest of the work, with a few additional details about his person, is filled with the physical and moral observations of Concolorcorvo and his master.

In his Prologue, Concolorcorvo dedicates his work, tongue in cheek, to those with whom it deals: the *pícaros*—some bandits, others *gauderios*; the travelers, who presumably will be served largely by *lazarillos* from the first group; and also, "lazy persons of sedentary exercise," particularly from abroad. For the benefit of the travelers, much space is devoted throughout the work to the procurement of abundant, healthful, and tasty provisions. From the beginning, numerous anecdotes warn against the thievery and cunning of peons and guides; but if the *pícaro* uses his wits, the traveler had better accept this with good grace, for to travel comfortably he must treat his *lazarillos* well.

Concolorcorvo is ironically careful to ingratiate himself with his Spanish readers, treating them with exaggerated humility and allowing each to choose the courteous flourish that most suits him. He is not afraid, however, to point out the weaknesses of the Spanish, which included prodigality and provincialism. He calls attention to their distrust of history and historians, including their great Mariana. Whatever its shortcomings, history is a study to which the wisest men of all ages have applied themselves, and Carrió in writing his book hopes to serve as *lazarillo* or source reference to historians, as well as *lazarillo* or guide to inexperienced travelers. The fact that *El Lazarillo* was also to serve as a report to government officials, who might later see fit to help him, was doubtless not the least of Carrió's considerations. Thus, there appears to be a succession of *mozos* and *amos* (servants and masters), all engaged in one form of peregrination or another to satisfy some ambition.

Montevideo, Buenos Aires, and evirons are described as a land of plenty, a heaven for all manner of carefree idlers, including those of the animal world. Prominent among the human inhabitants are the *gauderios*, whose predatory customs Carrió describes at some length. The quantities of beef consumed and wasted—waste is a frequent preoccupation of the very practical author—are prodigious. But we are also shown the *gauderios* of Tucumán in their rustic idyls. A humorous pastoral concludes with four somewhat bawdy *coplas*, verses composed by a passing friar, and Carrió assures us that they are as good as those of any Arcadian, ancient or modern. He pauses for a moment to lament the morals of these people, who could be so happy if they followed Christian precepts more closely. Immigration here should be encouraged, he further recommends, but with better distribution of land to eliminate the squatters who refuse to try to improve their lot for fear of being dispossessed or forced to pay higher rents. These ideas are repeated at length in rambling descriptions of the wretched way in which the *gauderios* live in the midst of abundance, how much they waste of what is abundant, how in part through laziness they lack many commodities, how matters might be improved for them and the kingdom, and other assorted digressions.

The various participants in the mule trade afford additional glimpses of those who live by their wits in this land of plenty. The herd owners must exercise constant vigilance against all sorts of tricks, some of them more or less legal. Since hard work is poorly compensated, cunning and thievery are commonplace. In order to ingratiate themselves with their masters, for example, foremen sometimes manage on a dark night to mix their poor, tired mules with a herd of fat, fresh animals; when the

mules are re-sorted, the foreman of the poor herd cannot fail
to improve his master's lot. Others cast doubts on the quality or
soundness of mules to be purchased so that their masters may
obtain them at a better price. Then there is the greedy, unscrup-
ulous Indian who rents his badly used and presumably badly
trained mule to the unsuspecting Spanish traveler; the mule
takes the first chance to return to his home. The Indian hides
the equipment that it carries and denies any satisfaction to the
Spaniard. These are tricks of the common people, but many
of the more privileged seem to behave in similar fashion with
far less justification.

Several anecdotes present a realistic and generally humorous
view of religion and the religious. It is difficult to tell, however,
which is the greater corruptor in the author's opinion—the
Indian or the Religious. The two are often found in close asso-
ciation, as for example in the description of the miraculous
tree of the festival of the Dulce Nombre de María in Guamanga.
Carrió deals harshly with both groups in many serious passages, especially in the later chapters. For the benefit of both
the Indians and the Spanish, all Indians must be hispanized,
and Carrió is undisguisedly glad to be free of the Jesuit missionaries, who Christianized some Indians but sheltered them
from the Spanish to preserve virtues that he says the not-so-
noble savages never had.

Throughout *El Lazarillo* it is generally the Indian who is
shown in the poorest light. If an occasional note of compassion
appears, it is condescending in tone. The Indian is of value only
when he allows himself to be completely domesticated, re-
nounces the heritage of his own people, identifies himself with
and serves the Spaniard, as Concolorcorvo serves Carrió. But
the typical Indian, unfortunately, has too much of the *pícaro*
in him and cannot serve continuously. If these shifty people
experience difficulties, it is their own fault. Carrió's faith in
colonialism is strong and both he and the alleged author, the
Inca Concolorcorvo, maintain the justification of the Spanish

against the Indians to the end. The Indian is not, and cannot hope to be, the equal of the Creole, nor does the thought really ever occur to Carrió, whose chief concern is with administrative and technical progress in the colonies. (It is unfortunate that Carrió seems not to have been destined to reap the rewards for which he worked so diligently.) Contact with the Spanish, however, gives the Indian, even the pure Indian, the necessary civilization to be socially acceptable as Concolorcorvo is accepted by Carrió. He has presumably reached the peak of all good fortune, much as Lazarillo de Tormes before him.

While *El Lazarillo* has many merits, its artistic value must not be exaggerated. Carrió, a writer by chance, had sufficient respect for literature, both classical and modern, to judge his book poorly written; he knew Virgil, Ovid, Cervantes, Gracián, Quevedo, Mariana and other chroniclers, Descartes and Fénélon, at least by name. His education, like that of all his cultured contemporaries, was humanistic. From it he had acquired a taste for ideas and moral observations, plus a small store of mythological allusions and Latin quotations. He also knew some French, as well he might under a Bourbon dynasty. There are numerous passages in Carrió's work that reflect the picaresque moralists of the seventeenth century, but others anticipate the nineteenth-century regionalists. His true master among the Spanish seems to be Feijóo, the Benedictine professor, critic, and natural scientist. Since descriptions of nature were exceptional in his day, it is not unlikely that he was also familiar with the French *philosophes* and Buffon in particular. Carrió does not believe in dwelling on documents of the past; it is present reality, especially in America, that most interests him. He knows the American scene intimately, both in general and in particular, and therefore understands perhaps better than Feijóo the latter's remarks on Creoles and Spaniards. Whatever its literary qualities, the greatest value of *El Lazarillo* is documentary. It is the only detailed account of such a journey known to date.

The difficulties in reading this work for the average hispanist, as for the translator, are due in part to the fact that the author writes in American Spanish for the guidance and entertainment of Spanish Americans. Carrió is perfectly familiar with the indigenous vocabulary, e.g., Quechua, designating everyday things and sometimes disconcertingly assimilated into Castilian. In addition, his prose style is careless. The technical nature of many passages dealing with woodlands and roads, the mails, local administration, and the dissertation on mules are certainly not easy for modern readers; but these concrete matters took precedence over theoretical or stylistic preoccupations for a man of Carrió's position. Carrió's prose is at times further burdened by a somewhat pompous vocabulary characteristic of an official. Characteristic, also, is the admittedly excessive length of this work by a conscientious functionary, perhaps over-eager to shame the apparently indifferent Pandó in the eyes of the Court. Sometimes, as in his calculation of percentages, Carrió is obscure. But the system of keeping peons and Indians indebted and therefore in virtual slavery is, alas, neither obscure nor outmoded. The civilizing and presumably beneficial ends of the Conquest are well worth the means to Carrió (as they are to some of our contemporaries today).

To paraphrase Carrió's words to Concolorcorvo, whatever the outcome of *El Lazarillo*, he has gained much by spreading his name throughout the dominions of Spain. For although Don Alonso failed to achieve success in the colonial administrative system by the publication of this record, he gained more enduring fame with his unique travelogue, which remains interesting and rewarding after almost 200 years to the historian, the student of literature, and the casual reader.

RICHARD A. MAZZARA

Franklin and Marshall College

El Lazarillo

A GUIDE FOR INEXPERIENCED TRAVELERS

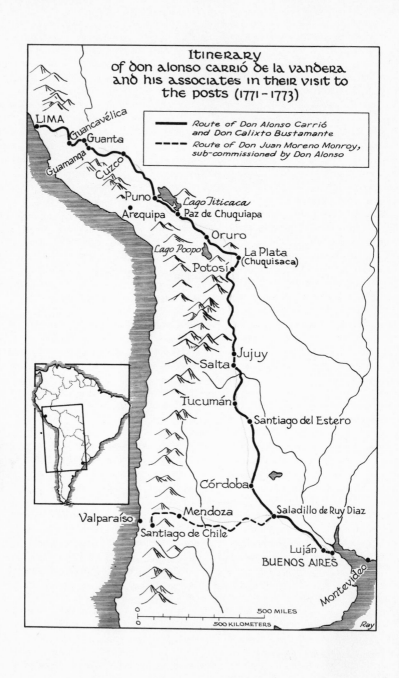

ITINERARY
of don alonso carrió de la vandera
and his associates in their visit to
the posts (1771-1773)

—————— Route of Don Alonso Carrió
and Don Calixto Bustamante
- - - - - - - Route of Don Juan Moreno Monroy,
sub-commissioned by Don Alonso

LIMA
Guancavélica
Guanta
Guamanga
Cuzco
Puno
Arequipa
Lago Titicaca
Paz de Chuquiapa
Oruro
Lago Poopo
La Plata
(Chuquisaca)
Potosí
Jujuy
Salta
Tucumán
Santiago del Estero
Córdoba
Mendoza
Saladillo de Ruy Diaz
Valparaíso
Santiago de Chile
Luján
BUENOS AIRES
Montevideo

500 MILES

500 KILOMETERS

Ray

PROLOGUE

AND DEDICATION TO THOSE TREATED HEREIN

JUST as weighty writers, such as Mr. Lead, and even those of a lighter vein, e. g., Mr. Cork, direct their lengthy prologues to wise, prudent, and pious men, perhaps to be exonerated from their criticism, I, inasmuch as I am a fish between two waters, that is, neither as ponderous as the first group nor of as little weight as the second, direct mine to people who are commonly called rowdies or querulous sorts, whether they use the sword, carbine, or pistol, or are adept with the bolas, horn cup, and lasso. I speak, finally, to the tired, thirsty, and dusty travelers, detaining them a short time,

> By way of epitaph
> On their sepulcher,
> Pantheon or cenotaph.

Although my principal purpose is to address travelers, I shall not refrain from speaking occasionally to the lazy persons of sedentary exercise, and particularly to those from across the sea, wherefore I beg the men from those shores to overlook all those matters in the kingdom which may be better omitted because of their notoriety.

It is well-known here that we half-breeds respect the Spaniards as sons of the Sun, and thus I have not the courage (although I am descended from royal blood in a line as straight as a rainbow) to threaten my readers with the lack of respect customarily shown by the more contemptible writers; therefore, when the title *señor* or *caballero* does not serve the purpose, I put a V so that everyone might accord himself the treatment which he deserves or which his fantasy dictates.[1]

Of course the dust-covered, thirsty, and tired gentlemen undoubtedly know that couriers and inns or posts are as old as the world, because, to my way of thinking, they are a natural institution, as anyone who chooses to reflect at all will agree. I observed that in the Court in Madrid some persons admired the grandeur of our Monarch, because when he journeyed to his country residence, his first Secretary of State had at his side two couriers from his staff, prepared at any time to make an unexpected trip of importance in the interests of the Crown. The inspector told these timid admirers, new and inexperienced in the ways of the *grand monde,* that the king was a poor *caballero,* because just any lady, courting or courted in the Court, and in other large cities as well, had at least a dozen couriers and post runners, and that there was not a lady in Lima who did not dispatch daily three or four extraordinaries to the homes of her relatives and acquaintances for the sole purpose of inquiring whether they had spent a good night, if the baby had cut its teeth, if the wet nurse had lost her supply of milk, and other impertinent matters. A certain young lady, he added, living on Aldabas Street, charged a courier who resided on the other side of the bridge, that on his way home he should take a message for her to the Bourbon general, and another to the prior of Monserrate, and that without losing his way he should go to the very last garden in the narrow lanes of Matamandinga and bring her a tulip, because only there were they of excellent quality.

The posts are so called not only because they are resting places, but also because they have changes of horses to expedite the celerity of trips. This service is very useful to the State for sending and receiving important news with speed; private in-

[1] The letter V could be the initial letter of *Vuesamerced, Vuecencia* and other possible titles of address which the reader might choose to insert into the text.

dividuals may also utilize it for their business, with the necessary licenses granted by royal decree in postal ordinances to assure that those traveling with the post are not delinquents, but persons free from all suspicion. The seriousness with which this matter has been treated in Spain is shown by the fact that when the Prince of Asturias, first-born son of the august Philip II, asked to join the post, he was, in due time, given an official notice by the postal director forbidding it, giving as reason the evil to the kingdom which could result from a thoughtless trip.

The posts, I repeat, serve not only for serious matters but also for the convenience and diversion of curious travelers who wish to see the great fiestas and other functions presented in the large courts. Those occasioned by the wedding of a great prince do not move curious people, until they are about to begin. The *Gazettes, Mercuries,* and other newspapers keep announcing the great preparation and the gathering of important princes and noblemen, with their magnificent retinues, which, with the assemblage of several nations, make the fiestas more specious.

Spaniards are reputed to be the least curious people in all of Europe, without considering that they are the ones who have the least opportunity due to their country's location at the extreme of the continent. The temperament of the Spaniards cannot be subjected to the frugalities of the French, Italians, Flemish, or Germans, because the Spaniard, with 200 doubloons in his pocket, tries to compete with a man from these nations carrying 2,000, not condescending to make his own curls or to take lodging in a cabaret, eating merely a trifle at midday and a portion of calf meat with a salad at night. On the other hand, men of propriety scorn these curious spectacles, fearing that their sons might associate with heretics and return to their homes imbued with impious maxims against their religion and the State.

The posts are of much service for these unexpected diversions, and although they are costly in themselves, they save much money by the brevity with which the trips are made. None but a stupid fellow would doubt the great pleasure experienced in seeing the principal courts of Europe, especially if two or three friends from one country, or with the same language and similar temperaments, get together; and even though one does not truly comprehend the grandeur of those courts and the kingdoms on these accelerated trips, such as those of one spring, summer, or part of an autumn, they suffice to formulate a valid idea, so that just any charlatan may not deceive us.

Those who have a martial spirit are eager, and rightly so, to behold and scrutinize two great armies opposed in battle, especially if crowned heads or royal princes are in command. The proponent of the innoculation of good judgment says that the grandeur of the French reached such an extreme in this century that all that was lacking was for them to hang tapestries in the trenches, perfume the powder, and enter their quarters in the summer to refresh themselves with lemonade.[2] There is no doubt that these armies in battle probably occasion notable joy. The Court is more manifest there. The battle tents of the King, princes, and grandees are comparable to great palaces. It is very pleasurable to hear and see the different manners whereby the various nations, of which a large army is composed, ingratiate themselves, and likewise those of the contenders. I make note only of the lack of distinguished members of the fair sex, because to each grandee or general official is accorded scarcely one gesture of a fan. The other officers, who are the Adonises of this century, find themselves obliged to pay court to the female sutlers.

In this extended kingdom there are really no curious men, for we have never seen a resident of Cuzco go by post to Lima for the sole purpose of seeing the prodigious four P's,[3] or of

---

[2] This statement, and others which appear in the text, reveal that the author was familiar with the works of Voltaire and perhaps the French Encyclopedists.

[3] An anecdote concerning the 4 P's of Lima is related in Chapter XXVII.

person is struck
the person of a v
There are unple
thing is put in ord
so that the master
the necessary sup
travel with celerity
or the postilion put
that passengers ma
pleasure, I advise th
from one inn to rea
and even to Potosí, t
some places; so I cou
saddlebags with a goc
this necessity but also
to good use the morse
chile, tomatoes, onion
rice, provisions for fou
napkin, along with son
the lack of vinegar, wh
or is so bitter that it rui
With these provision
parboiled meat, two stev
than an hour; to this one
at the inns and are four
The inspector has no tru
the ham and sausage cra
thirst which demands que
to indigestion and then to
extended trip from Buenos
and precautions that I scar
three times, but it is true
more than 8 leagues; by te
already traveled 5 or 6 leagu
only with preparing the mea

communicating with, and listening to the witty sayings of *Juan de la Coba*, just as we have never known a man from Lima to go to Cuzco to see the Rodadero and the Inca fortress, or to talk to *Coxo Nava*, a man who is in reality very unusual, since according to my countrymen, he maintains a mule on just one olive.

As a matter of fact, there are no fast post trips except those between Buenos Aires and Jujuy, since these are done on horseback and in flat country; all the rest in this great viceroyalty utilize mules, usually mischievous and in bad condition, which is like traveling on all fours. Nevertheless, a message could reach Buenos Aires from Lima, a distance of 946 leagues, in less than 36 days if the runs were shortened, because one man alone cannot travel more than three days without sleep and rest. The longest and most difficult run would be that from Lima to Guamanga, but with good pay for couriers and postmasters, it would be made possible, and even more so the trip from there to Cuzco, La Paz, and Potosí. The runs from the latter town to Jujuy, and from this city to San Miguel del Tucumán, are somewhat more doubtful because of their length, the possibility of the swelling of rivers over which there are no bridges, and some rather annoying stretches of road.

In spite of the fact that the majority of the posthouses are crude and the pack mules bad, in no other part of the world is it more advantageous to travel by post than on this road. Some residents of Tucumán use their own mules, principally as mounts. These, although they may be excellent, cannot endure over two or three successive trips, of 10 leagues each, because in many parts there is nothing to eat, and they must be turned into pasture lands at a distance where they are maimed or stolen. Others prefer to traverse the unpopulated areas with muleteers, trusting in the supplies carried by them and good tents for protection at night, as well as the care given their merchandise and the provisions made for crossing rivers and dangerous slopes.

The i
happeni
owners (
more sec
is very r
a bundle
when the
of the her
cargo is p
has no oth
bundles. H
livery of tl
the world;
importance,
dured by the
place, the lat
tween Lima a
many volunta
must take all
are the most e:
stocks of wine
about breaking
wine, brandy, d
ing some liquoi
accident was oc
with another or
the help of the v
inexperienced or
will pursue whei
or in some cordil
go in search of ot
the connivance of
selves obliged to
on the tent, which
protection. The foc

the inspector, would secure our animals and go in search of grass and water; with these precautions and four hours of rest, the mules would arrive at the inn with spirit. The cargo would depart an hour later, and the Indian guides left, after collecting the leftovers. Another servant, with one of us, would go out to the farms in search of a new supply of fresh meat and eggs for supper, which were prepared more slowly, while meat was parboiled for the main meal of the following day.

In this manner extended trips become more tolerable. Anyone wishing to travel further should do what a certain traveler did with his Indian guide. At the first shrine which he encountered, he performed his worship and, taking a draught from his bottle, he gave the same to the Indian who was driving a pack animal, which he then made double its pace.

He arrived at another of the shrines, which are usually at junctions of roads or on the crests of hills. When he saw the cross, the Indian approached it, saying to the Spaniard, "*Caimi*, cross," and he stopped the cargo mule until the Spaniard drank and gave him a second swallow. Finally they came to a pampa of 4 leagues' extension, and finding himself somewhat fatigued in the middle of it, the Indian said, "*Caimi*, Señor Spaniard," removing his hat to worship it and giving the jug a kiss. But the Spaniard, seeing no such cross, was obliged to ask the Indian, "Where was the cross? I did not see it." The Indian wiped the sweat from his brow with his right hand and hastily raised his arms to heaven saying, "*Caimi*, Señor." The Spaniard, who was a good sort, took such pleasure in the astuteness of the Indian that he doubled his ration, and the Indian was so grateful that as soon as they reached an inn, he reported the kindness of the Spaniard to the other *mitayos*, whereupon there was a great dispute the following day over who was to accompany the Spaniard.

The inspector informed me several times that he had never been wanting for supplies in the more than 36 years that he had been traveling, almost without interruption, through both Americas. Although he held the position of inspector of couriers and posts, he seated the postmasters at his table, even if they were Indians, and the first care of the morning was to count the amount earned in carriage and to pay, before his eyes, the *mitayos* who were to lead the pack animals and any other Indians who served to bring water or wood. Their work was quickly rewarded; thus everyone was pleased. The news spread from post to post, and he never lacked anything in the time he traveled as a private individual, always overlooking the avarice of the Indians and the tricks of the poor people. I should like to ask travelers, both Europeans and Americans, what fruits they reap from their arrogance? I believe they accomplish nothing more than being poorly served and exposing themselves to painful insurrections. Any postmaster can outwit a passenger, detaining him three or four days, because the former has an excess of pretexts, whether well or badly founded.

On the other hand, the pay is not half what such strenuous work deserves; a mule with a guide at 1½ reales a league costs barely 35 pesos, and one can make a trip from Lima to Cuzco, which is the most difficult route due to the roughness of the road, without exhaustion in a fortnight, sleeping under a roof every night. A mule driver who often takes 80 days, except for other contingencies, charges 30 pesos for a regular load of 12 *arrobas*, in which the passenger saves 5 pesos, but they do not compensate for the delay of more than two months. The honesty of the postal system, and its resulting great utility to the public, is best discernible in the carriage of a load of merchandise from Castilla. When taken by muleteers this costs 300 pesos for the same trip which costs 279 by post, because for ten loaded miles four *mitayos* are sufficient, each earning one-half real per league, and even if the passenger merchant distributes 21 pesos as reward for the best and fastest service, he gains the following advantages:

The first is that of transporting his cargo without risk of robbery, inasmuch as he travels with it all day, and at night it is locked in a room at the inn.

The second is the speed of the trip, and the third, which is the most important to small merchants, is that of being able to make sales en route. For example, they can sell some products in the Jauja valley, in Atunjauja, Là Concepción, and Guancayo, to which three towns came the priests, who are not the most despicable customers, from both sides of the river. If one chooses to go from Atunjauja to Tarma, it may be done with a muleteer or a private individual from one of the two towns, or by making arrangements with the postmaster, giving him something extra, in which I guarantee that nothing will be lost since in Tarma, because of the herd, there are many showy people who, although they can easily supply themselves in Lima with belts, cambric, and laces, do not refuse to pay a

higher price for those things which they see before their eyes;
wherefore I am of the opinion that all these trifles should be
carried in chests with two lids so that the goods may be arranged in them for the trip and, in case the sale should be
somewhat large, two or three bundles of tightly-woven Brittany
cloth or chambray may be unpacked, which is easily done, thus
saving carrying charges. Anyone who goes from Atunjauja to
Tarma should ask that he be taken to La Concepción and from
this town to Guancayo, although he pays the post as if he were
going to Guayucachi.

Although Guancavélica is usually well-stocked with provisions, a few trifles never fail to be lacking, which are sold at
greater value in these parts than in larger cities. Some things
are also sold in Guanta, from which one passes quickly to
Guamanga, where some products are bought by the canons
and priests for their own use and that of their households. The
resident merchants buy only on credit, and they usually want
to pay, or at least so they propose, with sewing baskets covered
with pressed cloth and gilded, trimmings for chairs, leather
goods and shoe soles, boxes of sweets and *magno* fruit, along
with other odds and ends, as they may be called, since there is
no one who has profited from their exchange. One must not get
involved with these small merchants, because if one pays as
much as 200 pesos, the affair becomes endless and reaches
1,000.

Some things may be sold in Andaguaylas and Abancay, the
only two large towns between Guamanga and Cuzco. The inspector is of the opinion that one should not enter Cuzco with
the idea of selling products at a high price, but for the purpose
of sacrificing them at an inferior price. He considers it more
certain to take them to the fair at Cocharcas, where the situation is sized up by small merchants, who are prepared not to
lose a sale from the first day the fair opens, since he has observed that every day the prices diminish. These remarks are
useless and could even be detrimental to the big merchants

who go to Cuzco, Paz, Oruro, or Potosí, where they have volu-minous business and want complete stocks; but it would always be best for these merchants to hand over their entire large cargo of wools, linens, and saleable goods to the common muleteers and take with them, on the post trip, the textiles made of gold and silver, silks and articles of greater value, filling no more than ten mules which the postmasters can provide with little delay.

The leagues are computed as best they can be, following the common measure of the kingdom, to which we should conform, as happens everywhere in the world. If some post is computed at too few or too many leagues, for the convenience of the pub-lic, it will in no way alter the total number of leagues on the present royal road, because those added to the one will be re-duced from the next. On the trips to Arequipa and Piura with cargo it is always wise, even necessary, to travel with resources, and to carry a tent and be satisfied, as far as meat is concerned, with that which may be found in transit, because it spoils from one day to the next, due to the heat and humidity of the air; it is on these two roads that salted meats are most detrimental to the health, because there are many pools of saltpetrous and offensive water, and much imbibing, of whatever it may be, is noxious; the least harmful is the drinking of brandy, in moderation.

The opposite happens in the harsh tablelands where the air is extremely dry, when all the heat, going to the stomach, im-pedes respiration and causes a kind of nausea like that suffered by sailors, which is remedied only by drinking cold water and eating chicken or beef broth soups, with sufficient chile; this seems extraordinary but the practice is in favor here, as among the common people in the Mexican empire, to cure indigestion with nothing more than eggs fried in water and salt, with a quantity of ground chile, corresponding to our *ají* and the Spanish *pimentón*, which is used in excess only in meat dishes of pickled pork and some fish that are indigestible and dry by nature.

The travelers eating *chuño*, dried and fresh potatoes, cheese, *zapallo* or calabash, with small pieces of cured mutton accompanied by herbs, are certain to suffer indigestion because their greatest excess is drinking a bellyful of milk at some farm which in two hours is converted into a passing torment of water and wind for them. My prologue is not concerned with them but rather with the crude Spaniards, both European and American, who, trusting in their robustness, eat, for lunch, dinner, and supper, ham, smoked sausage, blood pudding, stuffed suckling pig, onions and chiles pickled in vinegar, large and small capers, and all kinds of seafood found on the beaches. A portion of veal, leg of lamb, well-basted turkey or chicken, with considerable garlic, fruit and Parian cheese, which is usually quite salty, all give sufficient reason for the wineskin to be emptied, and for these vigorous travelers to stretch out to sleep under the branches in hot areas, and with no protection other than a sheet and blanket to cover their bodies in cold regions.

If doctors were as they are painted by some, they would use no other prescription than this to promote their own interests and those of their confreres, the apothecaries, a group that the parish priests could join with gratification. Rare is the passenger coming to this capital by way of the coast of Arequipa who does not make a contribution to medical and botanical science. Those coming through the valleys contribute less, because they make application of the mountaineers' methods, and although they eat goat, they rid themselves of it along the highways, and arrive in the capital without the necessity of paying *lanzas* and annates of a half year to the doctors, surgeons, and apothecaries; and the parish priests in this capital can put little hopes in the taxes on the high cross and the sepulcher, wherefore the alms priests have no source of income other than the promises of masses said for the successful crossing of the formidable rivers.

The mountaineers, and I speak now of mestizos, are more adept at roguery and malice than people from the coast. One of them, newly arrived, went with two companions to a convent of nuns, one of the most cloistered in the capital, and calling the mother superior, prioress, abbess, countess, or whatever she was, to the locutory, he told her that he had offered to give to an obedient convent alms of 1,000 sheep from a large group he was bringing from Pasco to Jauja. The good governess, or prioress, thanked him for the preference he showed for her community, and hastily provided them with a table filled with foodstuffs, of which each confrere took a dozen, in accordance with the mountain custom. The good mother invited them to eat the following day in the locutory, but the mountaineers fled to avoid a scene, made themselves invisible, and left the good prelate to the ridicule of all the nuns, because the thousand sheep went to Camel de N. which paid 10 reales a head for them, with excise. Be careful of tricky mestizos, for they are worse than gypsies, although in a different way.

I am an Indian pure and proud, except for the malpractices of my mother, for which I do not stand security. Two cousins of mine are preserving their virginity, to their sorrow, in a convent in Cuzco, where the King our lord supports them. I have in mind to try for the post of beadle of the Cuzco cathedral in order to enjoy ecclesiastical immunity, and my having written this itinerary will serve me well in this, for although in the eyes of God and of my conscience I wrote it with the help of the neighbors who whispered in my ear in idle moments, and of a certain friar of San Juan de Dios who inserted the introductory remarks and the Latin phrases, at least I had a large part in having paraphrased what the inspector said to me in a few words. Imitating his style, I included some jocularity for the diversion of the travelers for whom I wrote it in particular. I realize that the essense of my itinerary could be reduced to 100 pages in octavo. The inspector cut it to less than one quarter of the present length, as can be seen from my writing in the rough draft, which I have in my possession, but this kind of short narrative does not instruct the public who have not seen these vast countries, and it is necessary to give attention to what is contained therein, without violating the truth. The greatest cosmographer of the kingdom, Doctor Don Cosme Bueno,[4] has given, at the conclusion of his annual *Pronósticos*, a general idea of the kingdom, proceding by bishoprics, a work truly useful and vital for making a complete history of this extensive viceroyalty.

If the time and erudition which the great Peralta[5] wasted in his *Lima fundada* and *España vindicada* had been devoted to the writing of a civil and natural history of this kingdom, I have no doubt that it would have acquired more fame, adding luster and splendor to the entire monarchy; but the majority of men are inclined to know first the events transpiring in the most distant countries, completely neglecting those taking place in their own land. I do not mean by this that Peralta did not know the history of this kingdom, and I only condemn his choice because of what I have heard from wise men. One afternoon when the inspector and the rest of his company arrived at the country home of a gentleman from Tucumán, we noticed that he spoke in an unusual fashion and asked strange questions. On the table he had four books, very worn and with loose bindings: one was the *Viaje*, the trip to China by Fernán Méndez Pinto; another was *El teatro de los Dioses*; the third was the short history of Charlemagne and his twelve peers from France; and the fourth, *Guerras civiles de Granada*.[6] The inspector, who

[4] Cosme Bueno. An eighteenth-century Peruvian physician and scientist who served as royal cosmographer from 1757 to 1798, during which years he published annually *El conocimiento de los tiempos*—works filled with statistical and meteorological information, also known as *Almanaques* and *Pronósticos*.

[5] Pedro de Peralta Barnuevo (1663-1743). A Peruvian scientist, mathematician, historian, and poet whose best-known works are those mentioned here: *Lima fundada* (1732), a baroque epic poem about the founding of Lima, and *Historia de España vindicada* (1730).

[6] *Viaje* is apparently a Spanish translation of *Peregrinação* by Fernão Mendes Pinto (1509-1583), a Portuguese traveler who recorded in this work his experiences of 20 years of wandering through China and Japan. *El teatro de los Dioses* cannot be identified but is assumed to be a seven-

had read these works with great delight in his youth, leafed through them, praised the library, and asked the man if he had read any other books, to which the good man replied that he knew these from memory and reviewed them every day, so he would not forget the events recorded, because one ought to read only a few books, but good ones. Observing the folly of this fine man, the inspector asked him if he knew the name of the present king of Spain and the Indies, to which he replied that it was Charles III, because he had heard this name mentioned in the title of the governor, and he understood that he was a fine gentleman of the cape and sword. "And the father of this man, what was his name?" asked the inspector. To this he responded, without perplexity, that everyone could know this just by logical reasoning. The inspector, remembering what another erudite from France had answered, urged him to give the name, and without hesitation, he said it was Charles II. He knew nothing about his own country beyond 7 or 8 surrounding leagues of it, and all this information was so incorrect and confused that it seemed like delirium or daydreams.

I was going to continue with my prologue when the inspector took it into his head to read it; he told me it was very appropriate for the work, but that if I prolonged it more, he would say of it:

> The architect lacks in ability
> If the portico larger than the building be.

---

teenth-century moralistic work. The short history of Charlemagne could be either of the following: *Historia del Emperador Carlo Magno y delos doze pares de Francia* by Nicolás de Piamontes (1589), or *La historia del Emperador Carlo Magno en la qual se trata de las grandes proezas y hazañas de los doze pares de Francia* (1699?), author unknown. *Guerras civiles de Granada* in two parts (1595, 1604), also known as *Historia de los bandos de Zegríes y Abencerrajes* by Ginés Pérez de Hita (1544-1619). The work deals with the fall of Granada and the war against the Alpujarra Moors (1568-1571). Although proposing to be a history, its idealistic portrayal of the Moors, exaggeration, and free use of fantasy have caused it to be classed as an historical novel.

or another similar saying:

> A country house on the mountain wide,
> Magnificent façade, but a hovel inside.

"I do not think, Don Alonso, that my prologue deserves this censure because the house is large and extensive." To this he replied:

> *Non quia magna bona, sed quia bona magna.*

I paid little attention to the Latin, because the inspector was only trying to tell me that he knew a sentence from Tacitus; with it I conclude, putting my finger in my mouth, the pen in the inkwell, and the inkwell in the corner of my room, until another trip presents itself, if beforehand I have not given my last farewell to my readers.

Part One

 I FUERA CIERTA
la opinion comun, ò
llamese Vulgar, que
Viagero, y Embuste-
ro, son synonimos, se
debia preferir la lec-
tura de la Fabula, á la
de la Historia. No se
puede du dar con ra-
zon que la general extractò su principal fon-
do de los Viageros, y que algunas particu-
lares, se han escrito, sobre la fé de sus relaciones. Las Cifras de los Peruleros en
Quipus, ó ñudos de varios colores: Los
Geroglificos, ò Pinturas de los Mexicanos:
La tradiccion de unos, y o tros, vertida
en Cuentos, y Cantáres; y otros mo-
numentos, corresponden (acaso con mas
pureza) á nuestros roidos Pergaminos, car-
comidos Papeles, Inscripciones Sepulcra-
les, Pirámides, Estatuas, Medallas, y Mo-
nedas, que por su antiguedad no mere-
cen mas crédito: Por que así como no es-
torvan las Barbas para llorar, no impiden

B   las

CHAPTER I

Canendo et ludendo refero vera.

IF the common, or shall we call it popular, opinion were true, that the words traveler and liar are synonymous, then the reading of fables should be preferred to that of history. It cannot be doubted, and with justification, that history in general drew its principal sources from travelers, and that certain historical works have been written which accept the accounts of travelers as authoritative. The statistics recorded by the Peruvians on their *quipus*, or multicolored knots, the Mexican hieroglyphics or paintings, and the traditions of one or another peoples, translated into stories, songs, and other memorials, correspond (and perhaps more purely) to our worn parchments and moth-eaten papers, sepulchral inscriptions, pyramids, statues, medals and coins. The latter are no more worthy of merit because of their age, for just as a beard does not prevent one from weeping, neither do white hairs keep him from lying. These and other endless numbers of devices have been utilized in the writing of all ancient and modern histories. Scholars rank the first-mentioned in the category of fable, and the second they compare to the predictions of astrologers, but with the difference that the latter, since they hold conference with the gods, announce the future, while writers of modern history, being able to consult only mortals, set forth no more than events of the past.

Granted, then, the uncertain nature of history, I say again that the reading and study of fables ought to be preferable inasmuch as, being the offspring of free and unfettered imagination, they offer more inspiration and pleasure. The hero whom they present is generally of illustrious lineage, agile, robust, assiduous, and of agreeable appearance. He is thrust fearlessly into dangerous encounters. He is indicted for his carelessness, and at times it is punished by some adverse event, so that he may triumph out of honor and not fear. He is never forsaken nor lost from sight. In those encounters and undertakings in which human strength does not suffice, he turns to divine succor by means of the four main cards in that celestial deck.

Juno and Venus, rivals for the favor of the shepherd of Ida, pursued opposite interests, each trying to sway in her direction the thundering Jupiter, who, as a steadfast republican, longed for neutrality; but desirous of placating the two coquettes, he hurled his thunderbolts first to the right, then to the left, in the height of combat, so that the victory remained indecisive. The implacable Juno humbled his greatness, imploring Eolus that he blow, be becalmed, or become enraged. The cross-eyed one commanded Mars just as Proserpine did to a poor devil. Pallas did not leave the forge of the lamed ironsmith until she saw shields and swords tempered to her satisfaction, and the wise goddess did not hesitate to transform herself into a withered and wretched old man so that she might serve as tutor and manager of Penelope's only son. Finally, the principal hero of the fable triumphed, placing him in the immortal holy temple of sweet fame.

One should not be much surprised that the gods of heathendom take interest in the progress of mortals, inasmuch as, being descendants of earth, it is natural that they should be related to, or have a bond with, the heroes of fables, or at least they will be moved by the love of the fatherland from which they derive their origin. What is to be admired is that the devils, rich as well as poor, who are held in such bad repute by the dead and the living, open their underworld to these heroes, permitting them access, *fort bien,* as the French say, to the headquarters of Pluto and Proserpine without any resistance from

the strict Rhadamanthus and the greedy Charon. But what
causes most amazement is the benignity of the god of the
underworld in having permitted the exit of the sons of Ulysses
and Apollo. At times I wonder about the motive which Orpheus
must have had for searching in Hades for his wife, inasmuch
as she died exhibiting authentic characteristics of a martyr to
the cause of purity; and why Telemachus sought his father in
Elysium, it being manifest that he was a villainous hero. But it
is not licit for mortals to question the lofty judgments of the
gods.

Nevertheless, from the marvels narrated by the fabulists, we
see that in all ages and in all nations the wisest men have devoted themselves to history. There is no doubt that some have
been labeled as flatterers and even mercenaries; but there are
others so candid that they do not excuse their parents and
friends, making manifest their defects while extolling the good
qualities of their most bitter enemies. We are all in accord on
the incertitude of history because there is no one who does not
read with pleasure the praises made of his nation, vituperating
anyone who speaks of it with contempt or indifference. In all
of Europe our historian Mariana[1] is reputed for his accuracy
and candor, and even so, many from among us regard him as
suspect of disaffection toward our nation. The latter, so given
to the invention of witty absurdities, honored Mariana with the
epithet commonly given to the inmates of Lupa[2] because in
speaking of his ancestors, he labeled them as uncivilized people

[1] Juan de Mariana (1535-1624), moralist, theologian, political theorist,
and historian, whose 30-volume *Historia de España* is a monument to
Spanish historiography. Its purpose was to eulogize Spain, but since the
author believed it the historian's duty to tell the truth at all cost, to
praise right and condemn evil, some have found him more of a critic
than a eulogist.

[2] The reference is to the eighth and ninth circles of Dante's *Inferno*
in which the poet placed the shades of those guilty of the sins of Lupa,
the Wolf. Among the inmates of these circles are the flatterers as well as
the traitors to their country and to their kindred.

speaking a crude and unpolished language. I doubt that the mountaineers of Asturias, Galicia, and Navarre were more refined, but we shall pass this remark on to Mariana in exchange for the pleasure we shall have in hearing the defense of the Biscayan commoners.

Travelers (and here I come in) are, with respect to historians, just as guide boys are to the blind. The latter always solicit skillful youths to direct their steps and to supply them with necessary tidbits for composing the songs with which they entertain the public and assure themselves a living. Historians, of a higher order, collect the memoirs of travelers most distinguished for their talent and veracity. I make no pretext of placing myself among these because my observations have been reduced to giving to inexperienced travelers an idea of the royal road from Buenos Aires to this capital, Lima, with a few remarks which may be useful to travelers and of some succor and comfort to persons destined for positions in this vast viceroyalty, and for this reason the title given to this little treatise will be *El Lazarillo: A Guide for Inexperienced Travelers.* But enough of exordium; let us begin our task.

I have said in my *Nautical Diary*[3] that 84 days after having left the mouth of the Coruña River in His Majesty's mail vessel *El Tucumán,* we cast anchor on the weedy sand of the best cove in the Paraná River. At daybreak of the following day, while the launch was being readied, I took leave of the officers and crew with joyful sadness, particularly at leaving the witty commander, whom I called aside and asked confidentially, and under word of honor, that he give me his opinion concerning the vagrant island of Samborombón. What he told me was veri-

---

[3] The *Diario náutico* is Alonso Carrió's account of the voyage (Feb. 17—May 11, 1771) from La Coruña to Montevideo where he was to begin his commission as Postal Inspector. Two extant manuscripts of the work are in the Archivo General de Indias bearing the title, *Extracto del viaje que hizo la fragata nombrada el Tucumán, Correo de S.M. desde la bahía de La Coruña hasta el puerto de Montevideo.*

fied when the wind left us motionless between the islands of
Tenerife, Gomera, Palma, and Fierro; that was, that the island
in question could not be seen except in times of grape vintage,
although his countrymen climbed to the summits of Tenerife.
I asked again that he tell me what he knew about the reason
for calling that fantastic island Samborombón, and he promptly
replied that he had not seen the name of such a saint in the
Spanish calendar, nor had he ever known an islander, or any
foreigner with whom he had sailed, with such a name, wherefore he was convinced that doubtless the name was a hodge-
podge like that which Dismas said to Gestas. I embraced him
a second time and, bowing again to the officers, I availed myself
of the manropes for descending into the launch since in these
small vessels the accommodation ladder is not used. The sailors
began to row at the water level and used poles to drive the
prow to a little more than 1 *vara* from the hard sand, to which
one descended by means of a short gangplank. From the beach
to the town is a short distance, the ascent of which is made
without exertion, and situated on the level ground is the
newest city with the name of

Montevideo

a crude word, or at least an adulterated and corrupted form of
the Castilian *Monteveo*, the Portuguese *Monteveio*, or the Latin
Montemvideo. Because of its beautiful cove and other features,
its settling was begun in the year 1731, more or less, by Don
Bruno de Zabala, with 14 or 15 families which were brought by
Don Domingo de Basavilbaso on the ship of Don Francisco
Alzaibar from the island and city of La Palma, one of the
Canaries. The acting governor, in the absence of the incumbent,
Brigadier Don Agustín de la Rosa, was the Field Marshal Don
Joaquín de Viana, who had formerly been Governor with gen-
eral acceptance. It has a fortress, serving as a citadel, which
threatens collapse because of its poor construction. A long

stretch of beach is protected by a thick mud wall crowned by good and heavy cannons. In addition to the regular garrison, the regiment of Mallorca and the volunteers of Catalonia are to be found in the fortress and in the military post of San Carlos. The commander of the port, with two frigates and a small armed boat, was the captain José Díaz Veanes; the administrator of mail on land and sea, Don Melchor de Viana; and the auditor, Don Joaquín de Vedia y la Cuadra, men of esteem and good character; there was also an official who helped in the loading and unloading of vessels, all receiving salaries proportionate to the profits.

It is said that the residents of this city and its common land number 1,000. The priests preceding the present one did not keep a public registry, a failing which extends throughout all of Tucumán. In the year 1770, 170 persons were born in this city and its common land, while only 70 died, giving proof of the healthfulness of the country and the lack of fecundity among the women, if we fix the number of residents at 1,000. It is most certain that the married persons do not exceed 300, and the remaining large number is composed of many fugitives from sea and land, and some drones who, with the abundance of food, establish stores with very little money, in order to conceal their idleness and contraband activities, which are not very frequent these days due to the great zeal of the present governors of Buenos Aires.

One must also discount from the aforementioned number of residents the many lazy Creoles, known with great propriety as *gauderios*, whom I shall discuss later. In this city and its extended countryside there is only one priest, whose benefice yields 1,500 pesos yearly; he has one assistant and five resident clerics, but he enjoys no synod established by the King. There is a convent of San Francisco, with eight priests and six lay brothers, whose sustenance is provided by a farm containing a flock of sheep and a small number of cows, without which they would be unable to subsist in a country of such abundance, in which bread, meat, and fish are given gratuitously, and in abundance, to the idlers; therefore I believe that the products of the farm are destined only for the church, along with some other unusual things which are not given as alms.

The principal source from which the farmers make their money is the hide of bulls, calves, and cows which they sell there regularly for 6 to 9 reales, depending on the size. From the number of hides which are shipped to Spain, one cannot draw conclusions about the great slaughterings which take place in Montevideo and its environs, and in the area of Buenos Aires, because one must take into account the vast quantities which are sent surreptitiously to Portugal, and the large number which are wasted in this country. The roofs and walls of all huts are made of hides, as are the vast corrals in which cattle are enclosed. The majority of the hampers in which merchandise is transported and provisions carried are of crudely-worked leather. In the carts which travel back and forth between Jujuy, Mendoza, and Corrientes, a sizeable number is lost because they rot and shrivel so much, due to the sun, so that it is necessary to replace them after a few days of use; and finally, they are utilized for many other purposes, which it would be prolix to relate. It is estimated that every year the flesh of 2,000 oxen and cows is lost, serving only as food for animals, birds, and insects, without taking into account the considerable number stolen by Indians from the pampas and other regions.

The general director of mails had intended to take advantage of a large part of this meat to provide the royal armadas, in place of the sizeable quantities which are brought to Spain from the north. The costs having been computed, it was found that a hundred-weight of cleanly-dressed meat could be acquired at a considerable saving over the prices at which the foreigners were selling it in the rough—and many times they include meat of cattle which die in epidemics, as well as that of other animals. Several barrels of salted meat from Montevideo, which seemed very good, have been taken to Spain, but inasmuch as this project was so vast, it was abandoned by the administrator; it is a pity that it is not being undertaken by some company from this country or some other. I only fear that the flavor of the meat and the juice would be of short duration, and that much would be lost in the extended trip from Montevideo to Spain.

Many sheep, of the size of the Castilian merinos, are raised, in addition to the cattle, on the large farms in the western part of Paraná. Each is sold for 1½ reales. A quarter of a calf or a cow is bought for 2 reales, and sometimes less; 12 partridges sell for 1 real. All species of fish are in such abundance that servants go to the riverbanks to fish with as much confidence as if they were going to market to buy them.

It is a pleasing spectacle to see the gulls and other aquatic birds toss fish onto the land and pieces of meat into the water. This incredible abundance is of great detriment because it fosters such a multitude of rats that houses are undermined and threaten collapse; and in the midst of it, hens are sold for 6 reales each because, although there is much wheat at a very low price, no progress can be made in the raising of them since the rats, tired of fish and meat, eat the eggs and destroy the chicks, snatching them from beneath the wings of the hens without the latter being able to fend them off because of their large size and daring; for this reason hens are brought in from Buenos Aires and are worth the aforementioned price. As I said before, the result of this abundance is a multitude of idlers, who are fittingly called

Gauderios

These are youths born in Montevideo and the neighboring districts. With ragged underclothes and worse outer garments, they try to cover themselves with one or two ponchos, from which, along with the saddlecloth of their horses, they make a bed, with the saddle serving as a pillow. To the accompaniment of a guitar, which they learn to play very badly, they sing, out of tune, many ballads which they ruin, and many which they get out of their own heads, usually treating of love. They wander over the countryside at their will, and to the great pleasure of the semi-civilized settlers, they eat at the latter's expense and spend entire weeks stretched out on a hide, singing and playing. If they lose a horse or it is stolen from them, another is given to them, or they take one from the open country, lassoing it with a very long rope which they call a *rosario*. They also carry another, with two balls at its ends, the size of those with which pool is played, often made of stone covered with leather, so that the horse becomes entangled in them—just as it does in another which they call *ramales*, having three balls, with which the horses are frequently injured and of no further use; but they consider their usefulness very lightly, as do the owners.

Frequently four or five, and sometimes more, of these men get together under pretext of going to the country to amuse themselves, taking no provisions for their sustenance other than a lasso, bolas, and a knife. One day they will agree to eat the rump of a cow or a calf; they lasso it, throw it down, and with its four feet securely tied, they pull from it, almost alive, the entire rear quarter with its hide, and making a few punctures in the side of the meat, they roast it badly and devour it half raw without any condiment except a little salt, if by chance they are carrying some. Other times they kill a cow or a calf merely to eat the *matambre*, the meat between the ribs and the skin. Sometimes they kill only to eat the tongue which they roast in embers. Another time they may take a fancy to the *caracuces*, the bones containing the marrow, which they turn over and over with a small stick, and they feast upon that delightful substance; but the greatest monstrosity is to see them kill a cow, extract the tripe and all the fat which they pile together in the belly, and with merely a live coal or a piece of dry cow dung they set fire to that fat; as soon as it begins to burn and the fire spreads to the fat meat and bones, it produces an extraordinary illumination, and then they close up the belly again, allowing the animal to breath fire through its mouth and nostrils, leaving it all night or a considerable part of the day so that it will be well roasted. In the morning or in the afternoon, the *gauderios* gather around it, and with his knife each cuts off the piece which suits him and eats it unaccompanied by bread or any other seasoning; when their appetites are satisfied, they abandon the rest, with the exception of a few who take a piece back to their rustic paramours.

And now let the London newsvendor try to amaze us by recounting the size of the pieces of beef which are put on the tables of state in that capital. There the largest is 200 pounds, on which 200 milords dine, while here 500 pounds are served up for seven or eight *gauderios* who occasionally invite the owner of the cow or heifer, and consider themselves well served. So much for the *gauderios*, for I see that my travelers desire to leave for Buenos Aires.

Two routes present themselves. One is by land, as far as the army camp of San Carlos. This road is traversed with speed in dry weather, but in the rainy season small streams and dangerous, unfordable rivers are formed. In the camp of San Carlos is a King's cutter which continually comes from Buenos Aires with orders and provisions across the La Plata River, which is 10 leagues wide at this spot. But I inform my readers that the most common and regular route is down the river, disembarking in Riachuelo, a trip which is made in one of the many cutters which are almost always found in Montevideo. With favorable fresh winds the trip is made in 24 hours, the distance to Riachuelo being 40 leagues. The disembarkation occasions some annoyance since the cutters drop anchor at some distance, and the small boats proceed, for the most part, through the sand, by dint of the strong arms of the sailors who remove passengers and baggage and frequently deposit their cargoes in very muddy spots, since there is no wharf. Sometimes boys appear on their horses, bareback, and remove the passengers with comfort and less risk than that encountered in the small boats.

There are occasions when it takes a cutter a fortnight to reach Riachuelo, because with unfavorable winds the river becomes turbulent, and it is necessary to make numerous emergency stops on one bank or the other, sometimes in places where it is difficult to find supplies; therefore I advise you to take from Montevideo the provisions necessary for four or five days. Four leagues from the exit the water in the river is fresh and very good, for which reason it is not necessary to provide oneself with water on the trip going, but it is essential for the return trip to Montevideo, in case one does not reach the port and finds himself obliged to cast anchor in salty water. Outside Riachuelo are the buoys, which are huge stakes driven into the river bottom, by which means one determines whether or not there is sufficient water for entering the port. Passengers disembark near the fort, at its back; its main entrance is on the principal square facing the town hall of Buenos Aires.

CHAPTER II

THE city is situated west of the voluminous La Plata River, and it seems to me that it may be considered the fourth largest in the great realm of Peru, according first place to Lima, second to Cuzco, third to Santiago de Chile, and fourth to this city. The first two surpass the other two in elaborateness of churches and buildings. The one in question here has advanced greatly in size and in number of buildings since the year 1749, when I was there. At that time they did not know the word *quinta*, country house and plot, and they had no fruits other than the peach. Today there is not a man of average means who does not have his plot with a variety of fruits, vegetables, and flowers, which some European gardener has forwarded to him for the principal purpose of fostering peach orchards to supply firewood, since it is greatly lacking in this city. They generally utilize thistles, which abound in the fields, much to the annoyance of the cooks who must tolerate their thick smoke; but at present a great supply of wood chips is brought to the city by boat from the western regions of Paraná, and by carts which come from the mountains of Las Conchas. There are few tall houses, but some are spacious and many well-built with fine furniture of rich wood from Janeiro which they have brought in through the colony of Sacramento. Some have large and bushy grapevines in their patios and back yards, which the inhabitants, European as well as Creole, affirm produce abundant and savory grapes. This adornment is characteristic only of the houses in the country, and even there it has been abandoned by refined settlers because of the hordes of harmful small animals which breed in the vines and have access to the houses. In large cities and towns, in addition to the damage which overshadows the worth of the fruit, one may easily experience other worse consequences since well-cultivated grapevines produce a thick and twisted trunk with many knots, which facilitates ascent to the roof and offers good descent into the patio of the house itself, providing the servants a means for their misdemeanors.

The expanse of the city is 22 common blocks, both from north to south and east to west. The men and women dress like European Spaniards, as is the case, in varying degrees of refinement, between Montevideo and Jujuy. In my opinion the ladies of this city are the most refined of all the Spanish American women, comparable to those from Seville, inasmuch as, although they do not possess as much spark of wit, they do pronounce Castilian more purely. I have seen a soirée, attended by 80 women, robed and coiffed in the latest fashion, accomplished in French and Spanish dances; and, although not comparable in cost to that of Lima and the rest of Peru, their dress pleases with its cut and adornment. All the common people and the majority of the principal ladies do not patronize tailors since they cut, sew, and embellish their gowns and toilettes with perfection because they are clever and exquisite seamstresses; without any prejudice toward the other ladies of ability I have heard extolled in Buenos Aires, I observed for many days the great art, prudence, and talent of the beautiful and creative Spanish lady Doña Gracia Ana, in copying the finest needlework and embroidery brought to her from Spain and France.

Those ladies of middle class, and even the poor ones, whom I do not choose to call second and third class lest they become angered, not only make and adorn their own clothes, but those of their husbands, children, and brothers as well—particularly if they are from Tornay, they say—with extra profits realized from washing and starching done by some of their slaves. The men are circumspect and of considerable creative talent.

Inasmuch as there are no secular schools, some send their

children to Córdoba and others to Santiago de Chile, not desiring an ecclesiastical career for them in their own country, since it provides a very small income, sufficient only for a frugal life.

· · ·

The number of souls which comprise the city and its common land is clearly seen in the following chart:

Resumé of the Number of Souls, in the Year 1770, in the City of Santísima Trinidad and the Port of Santa María de Buenos Aires, with the Account of Those who were Born and Died in said Year, According to the Parochial Records and Information Given by the Religious Communities of both Sexes, and Others

Parish	No. of Souls	Born	Died
Cathedral	8,146	523	316
San Nicolás	5,176	344	185
La Concepción	3,529	318	158
Monserrat	2,468	184	96
La Piedad	1,746	151	91
	21,065	1,520	846

Regular clerics and nuns	77		
Santo Domingo	101		
San Francisco	164		
La Merced	86		
Recoleta de San Francisco	46		
Bethlehemites	88	Died, from this group	85
Capuchins	40		
Catalinas	72		
Orphans	99		
Criminals at hard labor	101		
Prisoners	68	Born	1,520
		Died	931
	942		
Total:	22,007	Increase:	589

Distribution of the Number of Souls in the Preceding Chart

3,639 Spanish men, including 1,854 Europeans, 1,398 peninsulars, 456
          foreigners and 1,785 Creoles
4,508 Spanish women
3,985 Children of both sexes
5,712 Officers and soldiers of the standing army, clerics, friars, nuns,
          and subordinates of one or the other, prisoners, Indians, free
          Negroes and mulattoes of both sexes and all ages
4,163 Negro and mulatto slaves of both sexes and all ages

—————
22,007

The militia of this city, composed of 3,639 men, is divided as follows:

24 Cavalry companies, made up of citizens, of 50 men each, not counting
        officers, sergeants and corporals
 9 Infantry companies, composed of foreigners, with 77 men each, not
        counting officers, etc.
 1 Artillery company, men from the provinces, with 100 men
 8 Companies of Indians and mestizos, of fifty men each, *idem*
 8 Companies of free mulattoes, also cavalry, *idem*
 3 Companies of free Negroes, infantry, *idem*

—
53 Companies, 40 cavalry and 13 infantry

Married Spaniards

Europeans   942, the remainder, 912, being single
Creoles   1,058, the remainder, 727, *idem*

          —————   —————
          2,000   1,639

In the city hospital, designated for the treatment of indigent
women, no count was made of the patients, and it is known only
that in the year 1770, seven had died, which were included in
the number of deceased.

Until the year 1747 there was no postal establishment in
Buenos Aires nor in all of Tucumán despite the heavy trade

which this city had with all three provinces, the kingdom of Chile, and a part of Peru. The merchants dispatched couriers at their own expense, according to their needs. Some residents availed themselves of this service, but most of them sent their correspondence with travelers, who usually made the trip in carts to Jujuy and Mendoza, returning very late, or never, with replies.

The first to promote an established post was Don Domingo de Basavilbaso at the end of 1747, or the beginning of 1748, the province then being governed by the Field Marshal Andonaegui, a native of the Canary Islands.

The proposal made by Don Domingo was forwarded to the house of the Count of Castillejo, who, arousing himself from his indolence, sent authorization to Don Domingo to take the office under lease himself or to award it to the highest bidder, which he did, but not in agreement with the terms proposed by the Count; and in the year 1748 began the epoch of postal service in Buenos Aires and the other provinces of Tucumán.

This city is well located and laid out in a modern fashion, divided into equal blocks and having streets of equal and regular width, but they become impassable on foot in the rainy season because the heavy carts that transport supplies and other materials make holes in which even horses become mired, and thus passage for those on foot is impeded, particularly in crossing from one block to another, obliging people to retreat and, many times, to miss Mass when they find it necessary to cross the street.

The residents who had not built homes in early times and who had plots or bought them later built houses with an elevation of more than 1 *vara* and surrounded them with a balustrade 1½ *varas* high, along which people pass with considerable ease, but the old houses are seriously damaged by the traffic of carts and horses heeling toward them, which often makes exit from them impossible; and if the rains are copious the houses are inundated, leaving most of the rooms uninhabitable, a situation almost without remedy.

The city square is not complete, and only the sidewalk of the town hall has arcades. On it are the jail and offices of the notaries; the high constable lives above. This town council has a special practice in that when they go to the fortress to get the Governor for the tournaments the honors of lieutenant general are accorded him within the fortress where the Governor's guard is. The entire fortress is surrounded by a very deep moat, and one enters it by means of a drawbridge. The building is large and solid, and in its main patio are the royal money chests. Its walls are of considerable elevation on the side by the river so as to be level with the top of the cliff, which overlooks the river. The present cathedral is a very small chapel. A large and substantial temple is being constructed, and even if they succeed in completing it, I do not believe the present generation will see it with fitting adornments because the bishopric is poor and prebends of the canons do not exceed 1,000 pesos, nor do those of most of the parish priests. The rest of the churches and monasteries are of very common and ordinary aspect. There is a great wealth of merchants, and even on the most remote streets one sees clothing shops. I believe there must be four times as many as there are in Lima, but all of them together are not as great as four of the largest in that city because the big merchants have stores from which they supply all of Tucumán and more.

I know only one large-scale farmer, Don Francisco de Alzáibar, who has an infinite number of cattle divided among several farms on the other side of the river, but even with all this it has been a long time since 4,000 pesos could be found in his house at one time. I have not heard of any family estates, nor do the residents think of anything other than their business, being content with a good home and a country plot which serves only for recreation. Meat is in such abundance that it is taken in quarters to the square by the cart load, and if by accident a whole quarter slips off, as I have seen happen, the driver does not dismount to recover it, even if he is aware of it, and if by chance a beggar passes, he does not take it home because it is not worth the trouble of carrying it. At the hour of the Angelus, meat is often given away gratis in the slaughter houses because each day many animals, more than are needed by the town, are killed, merely for the hide.

All the dogs, which are in great number without distinction as to master, are so fat that they can scarcely move, and the rats go out at night for fresh air, in efficient detachments, because in even the poorest home they have an overabundance of meat, and they feed on eggs and chickens which come in great quantities from the neighboring regions. Hens and capons both are sold for 2 reales each, very large turkeys for 4, partridges at 1 real for six or eight, and the best lamb for 2 reales.

The water of the river is muddy but, when allowed to settle in the large earthen jars commonly used, it becomes clear and is excellent even if it is kept for several days. The common people, and those not taking the necessary precautions, drink impure water from that which is left between the rocks when the river lowers, where clothes from the whole city are washed; there the Negroes draw it in order to avoid the bother of wading into the current of the river. When I saw such a crass maneuver, due to the indolence of all water-carriers, it caused me such annoyance that thereafter I drank only from the reservoir that Don Domingo de Basavilbaso has in his home, which can compete with the best in Europe in its precautions and cleanliness. They say there is another like it in the house which the defunct Don Manuel de Arco built for his dwelling. Perhaps other residents will strive for this cleanliness achieved at considerable expense, taking heed to collect water at the proper time and exercising other precautions utilized in the house of Basavilbaso.

The city and its common land are lacking in springs and surface streams, thus having no water for irrigation except that of the rains. Nevertheless, some diligent residents have made wells at their country homes for watering flowers and vegetables. Some have obtained fresh water, but the others found spring water which is saltpetrous and harmful to trees and plants. The river holds a variety of fish, and the atherines grow to a length of 3 palms and a proportionate thickness, but they are tasteless compared to those in Lima. Fishing is done in carts which the oxen pull into the water up to their chests; these pacific animals remain there two or three hours until the driver tires of fishing and returns to the square where he sells his catch from the cart at whatever price he can get, always very small.

In all the district of Buenos Aires and in a large part of Tucumán snow has never been seen. The city is accustomed to an occasional hoarfrost which some diligent persons collect for chilling mixed drinks, extraordinarily exquisite, which they serve.

One day as Don Manuel de Basavilbaso[1] was talking to me about the delicacy of these drinks and the lack of them in his city, I placated his desire by assuring him that the inhabitants of the city needed no other cool refreshment than that of bathing in the La Plata River and drinking its fresh, pure water, or that of the reservoirs; that snow was craved in hot countries; and that with its pleasure it caused three pains, not considering the high cost of the mixed drinks of exquisite sweetness from the bottle shops, which arouse the most prudish ladies and reduce the size of the most stingy purses. My friend laughed, and I think from then on he forgot about the frost, just as he did the dinners on masquerade nights which had been introduced into that city, as the buffet suppers had been, at great expense and with some cases of apoplexy.

I do not believe the number of carriages in the city exceeds 16. In former times, when there were fewer, residents brought mules from the country and tied them to a stake at their homes, leaving them without food until they were emaciated and could not work, whereupon they ordered that others be brought in.

[1] Undoubtedly Don Domingo de Basavilbaso, the postal administrator referred to above. This name is apparently an error of the author.

At the present time they have applied themselves to raising green barley, which they bring into the city with loads of hay for the riding horses which live very poorly, with the exception of those belonging to a few people who gather straw and barley from the nearby fields.

The comparison between the numbers who are born and those who die attests to the healthfulness of the area. In the months of June, July, August, and September many fogs rise from the river causing ailments of the chest. The *pamperos,* which are strong winds from the southwest to west-southwest, are quite disturbing because of their force, causing carts in the field, loaded with the weight of 200 *arrobas,* to shake. I shall describe these carts later for the benefit of curious readers. Now I am going to give some pertinent information to travelers, particularly those who came from Spain to work in this vast kingdom.

Those destined for the district of the *Audiencia* of La Plata will travel with me, choosing the mounts best suited to their constitution; but those headed for the district of the Royal *Audiencia* of Lima, and especially for Chile, will take the necessary measures in Buenos Aires to arrive at Mendoza at the time when the cordillera becomes passable, which is usually the beginning of November. This is the month for the courageous ones; December and January are normal and pleasant. February and March are months for those from the provinces who never wait until April or early May, so as not to expose themselves to a storm which might break out. The remaining five months are risky and difficult, and despite the small huts which have been placed along the way, the couriers are forced to take great risk, necessarily traveling a considerable part of the road on foot, since the animals would die of hunger because of the snow, and the little money which is paid would not suffice to take the animals half-loaded with straw and barley, although it is not impossible.

One may travel comfortably to Mendoza and Jujuy in a carriage, shay, or small cart, but it is necessary for one who desires this comfort without experiencing any delays to send ahead a lackey to ready the horses because, although there are many mules, few of them are tamed since they are not used for carting except by the muleteers from San Juan de la Frontera, with whom one may travel according to the custom of the country, carrying along good field tents for use in the numerous uninhabited areas and exposing oneself to attacks by the pampa Indians, who, since they maraud in groups of only 50, can be beaten off and held back by 12 good riflemen if they do not become confused by their formidable howling. It is advisable to take from El Pergamino two or more soldiers to reconnoiter the countryside morning and afternoon. These Indians and those of other nations have their spies, called *bomberos*, sent out on foot and unarmed in order that they, pretending to be ignorant, might inspect the armament and provisions of the travelers, the pack and riding mounts, as well as the carts and other equipment, so they can give a report to their companions. One must not trust them in the deserted areas but rather send them away arrogantly even though they may ask to be admitted to your camp to flee from their enemies.

These pampa Indians are highly inclined to the execrable unnatural sin. When they are not in battle, they always carry along, on the horse's rump, their concubines—or their common-law wives, which is more common among them—and for this reason they do not greatly increase their numbers. They are traitors, and although extremely adept at horsemanship and in the handling of the lance and bolas, they do not have the necessary stamina to keep up an extended battle. Whenever they have defeated the Spaniards, it was either by surprise or because they were fighting 50 against 1, which is very common with Indians against Spaniards or mestizos.

After Saladillo de Ruy Díaz, where the road for Chile turns aside, one rarely finds any bread and wine along the way until reaching San Luis de la Punta; these provisions should be taken on in Buenos Aires, as well as spices and other things which contribute to pleasure. In the vineyard regions and on the farms there are all kinds of meat, and in Mendoza sufficient provisions should be taken to reach the Valley of Aconcagua, where begins the abundant and charming kingdom of Chile.

It is time now to take our travelers out of Buenos Aires, and we shall proceed in carts since this is the customary and comfortable mode, along the following itinerary, which I shall divide into districts, beginning with that of Buenos Aires.

CHAPTER III

MIDWAY between Buenos Aires and Luján is another post established by the administrator Don Manuel de Basavilbaso.

To travel to Luján from Buenos Aires there are two routes, both suitable for carts; the most popular one is to the west, designated as the Merlo Chapel Route, and the other on the eastern side, called the Las Conchas Route, from a river of this name which waters much territory. This route is delightful and fertile for more than 8 leagues with farms and fruit trees, among which the peach abounds. There are also many fields of wheat and corn in which the cattle graze by day, but at night they are locked in corrals made of high stakes set at a distance the width of a bull's skin, with which the stockade is covered; these corrals are common in the entire district of Buenos Aires due to the scarcity of wood and the lack of stone. Having passed the river, which is never of great depth since it is so extended into the fields—causing great mudholes and marshes in time of high water which obstruct and delay travelers—one finds a forest of little density called Tala, which extends for 2 leagues. The owner has his house within the very forest, near the high-way, on a most agreeable cove, and I found him on his patio splitting firewood, clad only in some ragged breeches. He said he was 85 years old and his wife the same age, both Spaniards, with a number of sons and grandsons who supported them-selves with the proceeds from the firewood taken from that forest and bought by the cart drivers from Buenos Aires. The family is composed entirely of Creoles, and they told me that near their house (that is what they say when the distance is only 4 or 5 leagues), they told me, I repeat, there lived a man from Galicia who was 110 years old and had experienced no decline except in his sight.

Buenos Aires and its entire district are very salutary, and I believe two thirds of the deaths are caused by falls from horses and gorings by bulls which maim the victims; since there are no good surgeons nor medicines, these are the principal ailments from which they suffer and die.

The rest of the territory, as all that along the Merlo Chapel Road, is pasture country, with an endless number of thistles which serve as firewood and cause discomfort and considerable harm to the smaller cattle. It is 18 leagues to Luján on this road, which is used by the couriers in order to avoid the marshes of the detour on the Las Conchas route, which is 4 leagues longer. Luján is called a town, having 60 residents more or less, among which there are scarcely two capable of administering justice; thus they customarily select *alcaldes* from the residents of the region of Areco. Its jurisdiction covers 18 leagues, from the Conchas River to the Areco River. At the entrance to Luján is a rivulet by the same name which on occasion, in times of high water, covers the bridge.

The district of Areco, with a river of little volume by the same name, has many farmers and spacious fields in which all species of cattle are raised; but they apply themselves most to the raising of mules which they sell when young to the men having winter quarters in Cordoba. The horses they use are all fleshy geldings, and there is one resident who has 50 riding horses for himself, and for his family the same number, which they keep in small detachments of 13 or 14 with a lead mare called the *madrina,* from which they never stray. This same situation exists, with little difference, in all the countryside around Buenos Aires. The rivulet has good fords, and a bridge could easily be built to facilitate traversing a narrow valley.

Here Don José Florencio Moyano, who can provide 200 horses with dispatch, was named postmaster.

The district of Arrecife, so designated because of a river having this name, is similar to that of Areco. In this district there is a chapel around which are grouped 15 or 16 houses, and at a little distance five others, in all of which there are 20 families dedicated to the raising of mules and very little to farming. It should be understood that this chapel, and the others I shall mention in the future, is a small parish annexed to another, wherein Mass is said on feast days, and which is regularly served by friars who can better accustom themselves to a small stipend. The town named Baradero, where the priest presides, is 14 miles distant.

In the place called Pergamino there is a fortress having a very good moat with a wooden drawbridge capable of lodging within it the 40 residents of the town and as many militiamen with their corresponding officers. It is armed with four field-pieces and firearms appropriate to defending itself from a surprise attack by the pampa Indians on whose frontier the fortress is located; it is commanded by the dragoon lieutenant Don Francisco Bamphi, at whose persuasion the postmastership was accepted by Juan José de Toro, the only one suited for it in such an important place. In the fortress are four paid soldiers, and the King keeps horses at his own expense; as long as an official is maintained here by the Crown there will never be a lack of animals necessary for the mails and carriers. Of the 16 leagues to India Muerta, 3 are inhabited at intervals by poor mule breeders; the remaining 13 are cross-country, having water only in the rainy season. There are many ostriches, and piles of eggs are found, sometimes numbering 60, which convinces me that some females lay them in a specific place. The strongest males hatch them, defending well their eggs and chicks.

The 24 leagues from here to Esquina de la Guardia or to a place called Carcarañal—from a cacique of that name who had lived there—are inhabited only by a multitude of ostriches. In all this extensive plain there is no water in dry weather, but in the rainy season pools and small lagoons are formed, to which wild herds go to drink, and it happens sometimes that the travelers' mounts are lured away, leaving them on foot at great risk to their lives. Considering this, it was arranged that on this stretch the royal couriers should pay 8 additional reales, and private individuals 16, for a change of horses. In this place is an estate owned by Fernando Sueldo, who was named postmaster; another dragoon lieutenant with four paid soldiers, who was going to establish another fortress nearby, also cooperated in having Sueldo accept the postmastership. It is my observation that military men have a particular charm and method of persuasion for inducing one into the service of the Crown; it causes in me happy compassion to see a man of honor reduced to living within the confines of a cart. Inside, in considerable neatness, he had his bed; a small trunk served as table on which he had paper, ink, and some books, and a suitable chair. With a martial air he was host at a meal for the inspector who stopped there one day, and with the same mien he showed him his palace, offering its compactness as an excuse for not having offered him lodging within it.

Traveling from this spot to the eastern border, one sees the Tercero River and enters the district of Tucumán; the dividing line is considered by everyone to be in the small town a short distance to the west, named Cruz Alta, into which one need not enter. In all of these 84 leagues of highway, with the exception of the two cross-country stretches, you will find cows, lambs, and chickens in abundance and at a low price. The post houses are among the best, where travelers may rest at their will; when vexed by the slowness of the carts they may wish to proceed with a comfortable bed which can be carried on a horse. The road is flat, hard, and suitable for galloping at all times. The 24 leagues of this stretch may be traversed in 8 hours with only one change of horses, but care must be exercised against the mischievous tricks which some people effect in the country, concealing with grass the burrows which *quirquinchos, bolas* and other small animals make for their homes and into which horses fall; and with the speed at which they are running it often causes hazardous falls for the riders. The horses are so accustomed to making this crossing in a few hours that, without urging, they willingly gallop at half rein; but the traveler should take care to plan the hours so that he will not suffer much from the sun. The best time to begin this stretch, if there is no moon, is at two in the morning so that it will be finished by ten, even if he dismounts a while to take some breakfast and change horses, always carrying with him a supply of water and other provisions which he needs, according to his taste and constitution. With these remarks, which serve as a general rule, let us enter the province of greater expanse, Tucumán, which will be divided into districts according to the itinerary of the inspector.

CHAPTER IV

THE DISTRICT OF CÓRDOBA. THE CITY AND THE COUNTRYSIDE.
SANTIAGO DEL ESTERO AND ITS TERRITORY. THE SOLDIER
FROM SANTIAGO.

LEAVING Carcarañal, (or perhaps we should call it Esquina de la Guardia), one enters the province of Tucumán, following the royal postal highway through the district of Córdoba, traveling along the western bank of the Tercero River. This river is of great volume, of muddy and gentle waters, somewhat salty, with numerous fish which the youths catch for mere diversion, leaving them on the river banks, since the inhabitants do not take advantage of them in spite of the fact that meat is less abundant than in the region of Buenos Aires; not even the dogs choose to eat them. It is lined on both sides with willows, *chañares*, and Carob trees. The pasture lands are not as excellent as those of Buenos Aires, but they provide better aliment for the cattle. The horses and oxen are strong and hardworking. Some stretches of its banks are inhabited by small animal breeders who also raise wheat and barley. The most common fruit is the peach. Although they do not know how to swim, the men, women, and children cross the river on horses which are extremely adept. Strangers are carried from one bank to the other in the hide of a bull shaped like a rectangular basket for the small fee of 2 reales, without getting off course at all, because the horses are so adept that they always buck the current with their chests, and in each trip they take two men and their horses' trappings, saddle cloths, and gripsacks.

Just as India Muerta and Fraile Muerto are so named because some tiger killed an Indian woman or a friar there, so also Cabeza de Tigre derives its name from the fact that a man killed a wild tiger and impaled its head in that place. Saladillo de Ruy Díaz, and all *Saladillos*, are so called because the water is usually somewhat salty, becoming more so in times of high water when it remains dammed up in low spots in the salt-petrous sand, and although it flows away in the rainy season, it always preserves a sickening bitterness. *Esquinas* is a designation for those low places where the river is more extended and there is no perpendicular descent from which to ford it; such is the case in Castillo and Colman. It is the common belief that the word Colman was the name of an Englishman so brave that, having lost an arm in combat and after having been healed, he continued serving against the Indians with only one arm, brandishing the lance and cutlass with the same daring and terror as his colleagues and enemies.

Up to the aforementioned place named Saladillo de Ruy Díaz, the post offices of the two routes from Potosí and Chile are ordinary, an account of which I shall give at the conclusion of this first part so as not to interrupt my journey. The post situated in Fraile Muerto, at just 2 leagues distance, was established on the petition of the residents of the region and is a small place hardly convenient for travelers to stop to take on supplies or to rest. A post was placed more wisely in Paso de Ferreira where the river is usually forded; this may be done more safely with fresh horses. At Esquina de Castillo, the water had increased in volume whereupon the carts could not pass through it. The couriers and gentlemen traveling lightly can pass, in any season, at the spot which best suits them, but for maximum security they will heed the settlers of the immediate area.

Before passing to the eastern side of the river, those passengers traveling lightly should try to take a supply of water in case of sudden need, inasmuch as, even though the river is at hand, only in low places does it have easy access; and in spite of the fact that near the highway to the west are some lagoons formed by the rain, water cannot be taken from them because in the entire circumference (extended over 4 *varas*) there are great mudholes caused by the multitude of cattle which drink from them. All the houses, although they are near the river, have wells without any artifice other than an excavation and a low breastwork of clay. The buckets with which water is extracted are of crude leather, distasteful to behold, but the water is colder and more crystalline than that in the river.

The Puestos de Ferreira are so named because of a house and several ranches on a rather extensive plain, owned by a farmer of that name, Don Juan Ferreira, whose possession of them has been disputed. The place called Ampira, the farm and lands owned by the master sergeant Don Juan Antonio Fernández, has several perennial springs of fresh and crystalline water, with many small, dense forests which are pleasant to behold. His son, Juan José Fernández, is postmaster here, with the consent of his father. This spot has fine houses and invites weary travelers to rest and ease their discomforts.

From this place on, the Tercero River begins to be lost from sight and 5 leagues beyond the Río Segundo appears, of much volume and with the best and most crystalline water in all of Tucumán. One fords it near a chapel and a few houses where travelers and couriers can provide themselves with food and water for passage for Córdoba, which is 9 leagues distant, since the river veers to the west, far from the highway. This land is quite hot, and only in the rainy season are there pools of water which is muddy and not potable because of the many cattle that drink from them. At 3 leagues before entering Córdoba begins the dense forest which extends to the limits of the district. The city is supplied with dry firewood, brought from the surrounding area in small cart loads, each of which is worth 4 reales, and is sufficient for one month in a house exercising normal economy. From the interior of the forest logs are brought for roofing the houses and for making various pieces of furniture.

Córdoba

This capital city of the district, and residence of the bishop of the entire province of Tucumán, is situated on a narrow cove between the Primero River and the dense forest, on flat and sandy land. Immediately after a rain, its surface dries so that one can go into the street without inconvenience, but the vapor from the hot sand is noticeably felt on the soles of the feet. The city is almost square, with seven churches including the main plaza with the cathedral, which is of irregular perspective since the two towers which it has at the corners of the façade are no higher than the cupola. The size of the church is adequate. Its poor and scanty adornments, with a lack of many essentials, manifest the limited incomes of the bishop and capitulars who perhaps do not have sufficient to live in an honest and decent fashion.

It is worthy of note that in a province of such expanse in which the annual trade in mules and cows totals over 600,000 pesos, with great profit for merchants and owners of pasture lands, the churches should be so indecent that to enter them causes irreverence. This is especially curious considering, on the one hand, that the residents of Tucumán, particularly those from Córdoba and Salta, so liberal with their money that they are almost wasteful, see almost every year the Indian churches between Potosí and Cuzco, which are so highly ornamented. It gives pleasure to see the efforts made by these wretched souls to engrandize the Lord with their exterior acts, which are arousing to behold and give the Spaniards reason to give thanks and congratulate themselves on the felicitous conquest made by their ancestors. The seat of the bishop was moved to this city from Santiago del Estero for reasons which will be given in their proper place. At one side of the cathedral is the building of the secular town council which shows its antiquity in its humble construction.

In the remainder of the city are many fine, strong houses, and although few have upper stories, the roofs of the low ones are very high and the rooms of adequate size. The city has three monasteries of friars—Santo Domingo, San Francisco, and La Merced—as well as a hospital of the Bethlehemite fathers, the foundations of which are just begun. It also has two colleges where science and arts are taught. One is called the Royal College, its rector being a cleric; the other is Monserrat, directed by the Franciscan fathers, with the title of university, which provides degrees to the three provinces of Tucumán. There are also two convents of nuns: Santa Teresa and Santa Clara; and all five religious establishments are reputed for their respectful obedience. In few places of equal size in America does one find so much wealth, and it would be even greater if they did not waste so much on impertinent law suits, because the men, Europeans as well as Creoles, are of great industry and vigor. Their principal business is the purchase of young mules in the regions of Buenos Aires, Santa Fe, and Corrientes, which they take for the winter to Cordoban pasture grounds, where there is also some breeding; after the animals are strong and robust, they are taken to the environs of Salta, where they spend the second winter season which is of no less than six months and no more than one year. There they effect their business with those who come down from Peru to purchase the animals, the price of which has been, these last few years, 7½ or 8 pesos a head. Others send them, or take them at their expense, to be sold at the *tablada,* or market, in Peru, where the price is computed on the distance, their value regularly being 30 to 35 pesos a pair in the *tablada* at Coporaca, near Cuzco, where the greatest sales take place. I shall explain with clarity the contingencies and the risks in this business as soon as I come to Salta.

There was not a person who would give me even an estimate of the number of residents comprising this city, because neither the secular nor the ecclesiastical council has a register, and I know not how these colonists prove the ancient and distinguished nobility of which they boast; it may be that each family has its genealogical history in reserve. In my computation, there must be within the city and its limited common lands around 500 to 600 residents, but in the principal houses there is a very large number of slaves, most of them Creoles of all conceivable classes, because in this city and in all of Tucumán there is no leniency about granting freedom to any of them. They are easily supported since the principal aliment, meat, is of such moderate price, and there is a custom of dressing them only in ordinary cloth which is made at home by the slaves themselves, shoes being very rare. They aid their masters in many profitable ways and under this system do not think of freedom, thus exposing themselves to a sorrowful end, as is happening in Lima.

As I was passing through Córdoba, they were selling 2,000 Negroes, all Creoles from Temporalidades, from just the two farms of the colleges of this city. I have seen the lists, for each one has its own, and they proceed by families numbering from two to eleven, all pure Negroes and Creoles back to the fourth generation, because the priests used to sell all of those born with a mixture of Spanish, mulatto, or Indian blood. Among this multitude of Negroes were many musicians and many of other crafts; they proceeded with the sale by families. I was assured that the nuns of Santa Teresa alone had a group of 300 slaves of both sexes, to whom they give their just ration of meat and dress in the coarse cloth which they make, while these good nuns content themselves with what is left from other ministrations. The number attached to other religious establishments is much smaller, but there is a private home which has 30 or 40, the majority of whom are engaged in various gainful activities. The result is a large number of excellent washerwomen whose accomplishments are valued so highly that they never mend their outer skirts in order that the whiteness of their undergarments may be seen. They do the laundry in the river, in water up to the waist, saying vaingloriously that she who is not soaked cannot wash well. They make ponchos, rugs, sashes, and sundries, and especially decorated leather cases which the men sell for 8 reales each, because the hides have no outlet due to the great distance to the port; the same thing happens on the banks of the Tercero and Cuarto rivers, where they are sold at 2 reales and frequently for less.

The principal men of the city wear very expensive clothes, but this is not true of the women, who are an exception in both Americas and even in the entire world, because they dress decorously in clothing of little cost. They are very tenacious in preserving the customs of their ancestors. They do not permit slaves, or even freedmen who have a mixture of Negro blood, to wear any cloth other than that made in this country, which is quite coarse. I was told recently that a certain bedecked mulatto who appeared in Córdoba was sent word by the ladies of the city that she should dress according to her station, but since she paid no attention to this reproach, they endured her negligence until one of the ladies, summoning her to her home under some other pretext, had the servants undress her, whip her, burn her finery before her eyes, and dress her in the clothes befitting her class; despite the fact that the *mulata* was not lacking in persons to defend her, she disappeared lest the tragedy be repeated.

I relate the case only to show the character of the ladies of Córdoba, extraordinary in all of Tucumán. In general they stir up factions and are the cause of numerous law suits. This province has five cities, which all together are not as large as Buenos Aires, and all had recourse to the governor and the *Audiencia* of Chuquisaca over the annulment of the election of *alcaldes* in 1772. The one who was running the election, effected in Córdoba, in order to terrorize the opposing party, ordered that 400 men on horseback, whom he had gathered from the countryside, be cantoned in advance, causing a delay in the harvest of wheat in which they were engaged at the time. On the march he removed from office the master sergeant and the captain of the strangers, because they asked for written orders of what they were supposed to do on election day, and he named others in their place, giving no reason other than that he reserved this right for himself. Affairs are conducted in this despotic fashion in Tucumán, a province which by itself supports the lawyers, attorneys, and notaries of the city of La Plata.

Five rivers are formed by the waters which flow down from the elevations and forests of Córdoba, which, although they have other names, are commonly known as the Primero, Segundo, Tercero, Cuarto and Quinto—First, Second, Third, Fourth and Fifth—all of considerable volume. Only in the environs of the city does one see cliffs and loose rock in the Primero River, which offer no inconvenience, nor do they cause noise to be made by the water which is clear and without bitterness to the taste. The residents of Mendoza provide this city with flour a large part of the year, and always supply the wines, which are customarily sold at a lesser price than in Buenos Aires. The inhabitants of San Juan de la Frontera bring in much brandy in skin bags. The liquor they call *resacado,* or *de cabeza,* is so strong and fiery that mixing it with two parts of the ordinary brand, which is very weak, gives it as much fire as the common stock from Andalucía and Cataluña. Here one may take on all provisions except chickens for the journey to Santiago del Estero or San Miguel del Tucumán.

The carts, when they depart from this city, following the route which I am taking, do not usually leave the other side of the river; travelers should take a supply of fresh water for two days, not placing much confidence in the bottles provided in the carts, because on the highway only an occasional pool is found, muddied, in the rainy season, by the cattle. No water is to be found in 13 leagues of hot and dense forest until arriving at the farm named Caroya, belonging to the college of Monserrat in Córdoba, and between this and Sinsacate is the King's estate, named Jesús María, administered by Don Juan Jacinto de Figueroa, its owner, who is in charge of providing horses for the couriers of the King and private individuals.

From Sinsacate the couriers formerly took the route through San Antonio and San Pedro, but they persuaded the inspector that it was a better road through La Dormida because in those places there were only *maestres de campo*, master sergeants, and captains; therefore the postmastership could be abolished. The governors of Tucumán seem to make a profit from this multitude of officers, which exceeds, I believe, the number of soldiers whom they dismiss, enroll, and demote at their will; I have seen a young man of 30 years, very robust, demoted from master sergeant. Wherefore it was decided to follow the route through La Dormida which is 16 leagues from Sinsacate; although there are seven colonists in El Totoral and El Simbolar, which have perennial water, they are people of little account, the larger part being *gauderios* to whom the posts cannot be entrusted, wherefore it was necessary to place it at the distance of 16 leagues, as will always happen under similar circumstances.

All this territory, up to Cachi, where the district of Córdoba terminates, is dense forest, having coves at distant intervals where a few dispersed colonists have their houses and farms. Those who travel by cart are supplied with meat by the owner each day, or every two or three days, depending on the number of carts. At the farms and houses of other inhabitants they willingly sell fat, tender lambs and hens at 2 reales each, and pullets at 1 real, without distinction as to size. Squash and onions are also found here, but rarely bread. Much precaution must be observed with eggs, because in this hot temperature they spoil easily, since the inhabitants do not eat them, nor do the majority of the passers-by.

In addition to the five rivers which I said this district had, with the names of the numbers one to five, there are very many streams on all the coves which provide adequate water to several farmers and other colonists; but inasmuch as the land is flat and sandy, they are accustomed to finding themselves suddenly without water, which then springs up in a spot where it has never been seen before, only to reappear in the original place. On the highway to Las Peñas, veering a little to the northeast and entering the forest, one finds several cattle and horse paths leading to the aforementioned Las Peñas, where there was a town recognizable from the ruins of the houses standing on a pleasant and extensive field, protected at intervals by lofty and thick trees, which was abandoned because the water of a voluminous river that passed there suddenly disappeared underground as is indicated by the large river bed. We traveled along it for one-fourth of a league, always seeking the high ground, and at last we saw, with great astonishment, a rapid and abundant river of crystalline water, which filled the entire width of the bed, but with the length of only a gunshot. One league beyond is the parish of Turumba, in a town well equipped to provide assistance to travelers who need horses and food supplies. On our return, which was probably about five in the afternoon, we met groups of cattle coming and going from the aforementioned stream.

In the place named Los Sauces no water is found for a quarter of a league due to the sinking of a voluminous river which has its head in the town of Guayascate, 1 league to the northwest. In the spot called Los Cocos, the water is 2 leagues away; nevertheless there are huts with small plantations and cattle. Another 2 leagues beyond is the Los Tártaros River, the water of which also disappears in the multitude of loose sand, and one cannot draw from it unless he goes 2 leagues up the riverbed. Don Pedro del Pino, the *maestre de campo* and a man of wealth, lives 1 league farther into the interior. He has in his house an oratory where Mass is said on most of the feast days.

The fort named Río Seco is a delightful spot, with a few colonists, and at its edge a stretch of river appears suddenly, flows approximately one-half league and sinks again into the sand without making any noise or extraordinary movement. In the heights of the town, and in its plaza, there is a well-constructed draw-well with an abundance of crystalline water. One boy alone operates it and draws water in abundance, but these fine residents, numbering about 30, deem it more convenient to get their supply from the Ghost River, as they call it, than to defray the costs of the ropes which break on the aforementioned well. This town is the head of the district, where the priest resides, and has an excellent chapel of adequate size.

All the interior of the district is full of these meandering rivers along which one finds numerous wild wood-lice which diligent persons use to advantage for the extraction and production of cochineal, which, although it is not as fine as that from the Bishopric of Oaxaca in New Spain,[1] is much better than the *magno* from the province of Parinacocha and others in this kingdom. Perhaps in the interior of these extensive, dense forests other products of great utility could be found. Travelers should not enter far into them because of tigers and the danger of becoming lost in the labyrinth produced by the many paths.

Santiago del Estero

As soon as one leaves the post named El Cachi, he enters the district of Santiago del Estero, a territory exposed to floods and the least populated in all of Tucumán. The couriers always cross the 30 leagues from Ayuncha to Ambargasta, paying 8 reales for three fresh horses: one on which the courier is mounted, one for the pack, and one for the postilion who is to return the horses. Passengers and private couriers pay 2 pesos for the same change of horses, and a proportionate amount for other things they request for safety and greater dispatch. In time of high water there are numerous marshy spots which hinder the

---

[1] New Spain, the colonial viceroyalty which included the territory of present-day Mexico, Central America, and the West Indies.

speed of the trip, and on the cart roads, mudholes and ditches are formed which hamper progress, making reparations with tree trunks and heavy branches necessary. On this road one takes a detour of 7 or 8 leagues, but there is no lack of farms to provide lambs, pullets, eggs, squash, watermelons, and other products at the same price as in the district of Córdoba. The river which flows at the edge of this city, having the same name, is voluminous, and it forms three enormous lagoons in the lands of the Avipones, gentle Indians, around which are copious salt mines.

The episcopal seat was in the city of Santiago del Estero until 1690, when it was moved to Córdoba for fear of floods of the river which had already carried away many things. The cathedral is still maintained on the plaza, serving as a parochial church, which they call "mother church" in these parts; it is of far better construction than the one in Córdoba. The residents who may be classed as distinguished do not add up to 20. Some of them winter a group of mules to sell in Salta or to take to Peru at their own expense; the rest, scattered around in huts, are miserable souls, since meat is somewhat scarce. This country is saltpetrous. The women weave excellent carpets and coverlets, but since they have little retail market, inasmuch as they are produced all over Tucumán, they are made only on request; the best proof of their poverty and slight trade is the fact that the profits from their commerce of one year, in all the district, do not exceed 30 pesos. All the inhabitants of the city of Santiago and its communal lands could be lodged comfortably in the house belonging to the regular clerics since it has such an unusually large array of rooms, patios, and backyards which form a labyrinth.

Everyone in Tucumán asserts that the soldiers from Santiago are the best in the province and the terror of the Chaco Indians. In wartime they have hanging constantly, on their saddletree, a small pouch of toasted maize with their waterhorns—large ox horns in which they carry water—an article very much used in all this province. With only these provisions the early soldiers presented themselves for battle at the slightest provocation from the enemy. At the present time they are at peace with the Indians of the immediate vicinity. In the interior are many Indians who are valorous and favored by the location of their land; the present governor, Don Gerónimo Matorras, promised the Court that he would subject them shortly, proposing to populate four cities at his expense. This would be of extraordinary benefit if he could bring colonists from Flanders and Catholic regions.

Before leaving this district, let me pose a problem to the wisemen of Lima. A certain Spaniard, crossing these forests in times of war with the Chaco Indians, found himself obliged to rest his horse one night, tying it to a tree with a lengthy rope so that it could graze with ease. Not wishing to lose time, he lay down to sleep beneath a bushy tree, placing near his head a carbine loaded with two balls. A moment later he felt someone awaken him, lifting him by the arm, and he found himself facing a barbaric Indian, armed with a lance and with the carbine in his hand, who said to him serenely, "Mr. Spaniard, *haz tun*," which meant that he should shoot the gun so that the Indian might hear the noise at close range. The Spaniard, taking one step backward, raised the hammer and lodged the two balls between the chest and the back of the Indian, leaving him stretched out motionless.

I ask the disciples of Mars whether this act of the Spaniard sprang from courage or cowardice; and let the disciples of Minerva answer as to whether or not the decision of the Spaniard was just.

CHAPTER V

AT the edge of Vinará, which is about 20 leagues from Santiago, the district of San Miguel del Tucumán begins with its extensive forest, tall trees, and good pasture lands, and here one sees for the first time the *quebracho* tree which is so named because it is of such hardness that axes are frequently broken in cutting it. Its surface is white and smooth when cut; the center is colored, and serves for making columns and many other things of similar nature. They say it is indestructible, but I have seen columns which were worm-eaten. After the white exterior has been removed, it is put in water where it becomes as hard and heavy as the most solid rock.

When I entered this district, I observed along the royal highway many white threads of varying thicknesses, entwined among the branches of the *huisache* tree; others were as much as 8 *varas* in length, so thin and delicate that they could be seen only when the sun shone on them. They were all alike: smooth, free of any gummy substance, and as resplendent as the finest silver thread. I noticed that some little animals shaped and colored like small beetles were scurrying over these threads with great speed. I dismounted several times to watch their activity, and I observed that if by chance one of them was too slow in his pace, these skillful rope-walkers would pass him by swinging underneath without stopping him or making him change his course, just as sailors who want to get ahead of others in the work being done on the yardarms of a ship. I tried making noise to see if these little animals would be frightened and stop their movement; but I succeeded only in making them increase their speed. On the extended strands I saw several dead creatures, hanging by their legs, shaped like ordinary spiders and the color of boiled shrimp. I was unable to perceive whether the living ones exuded from their bodies any substance which would thicken the thread. I picked up some of the threads and discovered they were strong enough to be wrapped around a stick without breaking.

On this trip from Córdoba to Salta we were passengers in the cart of the Creole Don Luis de Aguilar, who was a citizen of San Miguel and a well-educated, observant Spaniard. He told me that these little insects were the silk-producing spiders, a fact which was confirmed by Don Juan Silvestre Helguero, a local resident, who was the proprietor of the Tapia estate and postmaster, a man of unusual strength and courage, accustomed to trips through the forest of Tucumán—who added that the silk threads found in this region were so imperceptible that their presence could be known only when one felt them strike him across the face and eyes. With this warning, I and those who accompanied me exercised more care, and sometimes when we were entering wooded areas, we saw, at a short distance, threads of great length, entangled in the trees. Other times we observed single branches embroidered with exquisite designs of fragile thread—objects worthy of being presented to a princess, were it not for the fact that the leaves would dry up and lose their delicate shape. We saw a large bird's nest embroidered with this delicate fabric, reminiscent of a coif or hairnet worn by the ladies of Madrid. In its hollow we saw a great number of creatures clustered around a skeleton which, judging from its size, was that of a pigeon or a house dove. It appeared that they were working in shifts, because many of them were coming to work from the place on the tree trunk where others were asleep. With the point of a scissors I picked up one of the latter which offered resistance, moving his legs and mouth with great speed, and cutting him in half, I discovered that he was filled with a solid, white substance resembling pork grease.

It seemed to me that those working on the long thread were attempting to make it thicker, since I found some strands which at one end were more delicate than a silken hair, but increased in size until they were similar, at the other end, to the twisted threads produced in Calabria. With these threads the people of the region make kerchiefs or ribbons for their hats, which shrink, when hanging loose, but may be stretched up to three times their length. Their natural color is that of a cocoon of the silk worm. On the fence of a pasture I saw many branches, cut from the *huisache* tree, bedecked with these fibers, without the presence of any animals, since they had perhaps abandoned

the branch for lack of flowers or because they found the leaves without juice. I did not see a nest of these creatures in any other tree, which convinced me that they thrive only on the flower and juice of the *huisache,* or on other flowers which they find on the ground, although I did not see them take provision from the latter, nor did I find any skeletons, except those in the shape of spiders which I said I saw hanging on the threads.

One league outside the city of San Miguel is a river named Sali. Its water is crystalline and more salty than that of the Tercero. Along its banks are wells where drinkable water seeps through the pores. On its edges are other small natural wells which hold good water, but they are useless since they are covered in times of high water. The river is formed by 12 small streams which have their source in springs in the interior of the district, and all of them feed the large Santiago del Estero River.

San Miguel del Tucumán

The capital city of this district, which today is a headquarters for postal service, occupies the best site in the province; it is on high, unobstructed terrain, surrounded by fertile fields. The city is reduced to five square blocks, but it is not populated accordingly. The parish church, or mother church, is adorned like a country house; the convents of San Francisco and Santo Domingo are much less elaborate. The principal residents, the *alcaldes* and *regidores*, who probably do not exceed 24 in number, are men of circumspect who defend their rights tenaciously. There are some wealthy inhabitants who live frugally; and others increase their wealth by raising and selling mules; but their main industry is that of raising oxen which they break and train for use on the carts traveling to Buenos Aires and Jujuy. The abundance of fine wood facilitates the construction of good carts. With the permission of the men from Mendoza, I shall describe these carts from Tucumán.

Description of a Cart

The two wheels are 2½ *varas*, more or less, in height, the center of which is a heavy hub, 2 or 3 spans wide. In the center of this is an axle of 15 spans' width on which rests the bed or box of the cart. This axle is made of a beam which is called the *pértigo,* 7 or 8 *varas* long, which is accompanied by two other beams 4½ *varas* in length, and these, when joined to the *pértigo* by four pins called *teleras,* form the box 1½ *varas* in width. To this structure six pointed stakes are added on each side, and between each pair is an arch made of a kind of willow wood, thus forming an arched or oval roof. The sides are covered with woven reeds, which are stronger than the cattails used by the inhabitants of Mendoza, and for protection from water and sun, the roof is covered with pieces of hide laced together. In order that the cart may be pulled, a yoke measuring 2½ *varas,* is attached to the end of the *pértigo* which is 7½ *varas* long, and to this yoke the oxen, which are usually called *pertigueros,* are harnessed.

On long trips, these carts normally carry a load of 150 *arrobas* and are pulled by four oxen, the forward pair of which are called *cuarteros.* They are hitched to the *pértigo* by means of a strap known as the *tirador* which is of a thickness appropriate to its function, made from the hide of a strong bull or older calf, folded four times. These oxen are likewise joined by a yoke, similar to that of the *pertigueros,* which is attached to the aforementioned strap. These *cuarteros* are placed at about 3 *varas* from the *pertigueros;* this being more or less the length of the goad, called a *cuarta,* which is usually a piece of very thick bamboo or other suitable wood. It is made of several pieces fastened together by the attendants and decorated with multicolored feathers.

This goad is suspended, in a balanced position, from a pole about 1½ to 2 *varas* in length, which projects from the roof of the cart in such a way that if it is in proper balance, the drivers may goad the *cuarteros* with one hand and with another smaller goad, called a *picanilla,* they may prod the *pertigueros,* since it is imperative that all four oxen be prodded at approximately the same time. Every cart must have one attendant who sits under the forward roof on a large box in which he carries his belongings, dismounting only for repair or adjustment of the harness straps or to guide the cart through rivers and other difficult passages.

Besides the 150 *arrobas*, they carry a large jug of water, firewood, and pieces of wood necessary for repairs on the cart, which, together with the weight of the attendant and his belongings, increase the weight to 200 *arrobas*. In the entire cart there is not a piece of iron or a nail because everything is made of wood. The axles and wheel naves are greased almost every day so that the hubs will not be worn away, since in these carts the axle is secured to the bed and it is only the wheel that revolves. The larger carts are no different, except that the body is made entirely of wood, like a cabin on a ship. The floor of the carts is 1½ *varas* above the ground; one mounts by means of a short ladder, and from the floor to the roof it measures 9 spans. The bed of the cart is covered with pampa grass or cowhide which is very smooth since it is well stretched.

The carts from Mendoza are wider than those from Tucumán and can carry 28 additional arrobas, since they do not encounter as many obstacles as the latter, which, traveling a route from Córdoba to Jujuy, pass through two thick forests which make the road narrow, while those from Mendoza cross the pampas experiencing no damage to their bodies. The men from Tucumán, although they cross many rivers, never unload their cargo, since the oxen seldom lose their footing, and if they do, it is in some small space from which they extract themselves with the aid of the thick goads, placed on the bottom for the support of their strong hoofs. The drivers from Mendoza unload their carts only during the season of high water in the deep gorges which they call *desaguaderos,* and to pass along the cargo they hastily construct little rafts out of the yokes tightly bound together with the harness straps and halters. These rafts are also made out of hides similar to those employed by people inhabiting the banks of the Tercero and other rivers.

This kind of beast of burden is considered the most useful all over the world. They have become more useful in Spain at the present time for the construction of the great highways. It is 407 road leagues from Buenos Aires to Jujuy, and the cost of shipping by oxcart is 8 reales per *arroba*, a price which seems incredible to anyone lacking in experience. The transporting of cargo from Córdoba to Jujuy by mules would be difficult and extremely expensive because the largest part of the road leads through thickly wooded areas in which mules would get lost and the harness, even though made of leather, would become entangled in the thorny branches and be torn apart, damaging both the cargo and the mules, which are constantly becoming incapacitated by straining their backs or injuring their hoofs. Add to this the great number of large rivers which mules would not be able to cross when they are loaded, due to their natural timidity and their inclination always to cross downstream. Since oxen are affected only by the heat of the sun, the caravans regularly stop at ten o'clock in the morning, and after a roundup has been made, depending on the number of carts, each driver hastily unhitches his four animals and the oxen-keeper puts them with the replacements so they may eat, drink, and rest until at least four o'clock in the afternoon. In these six hours, more or less, food is prepared for the people; the attendants are content with roasting, rather poorly, a sizeable piece of meat. They kill a bull if necessary and grease the wheel hubs, all of which is done with considerable speed. Some of the passengers sit in the shade of the high trees, others in the shadow cast by the carts which is extensive owing to their height. But the most sturdy and best ventilated arrangement is made when two carts are put side by side with space between large enough for another cart to fit. Two or three goads are placed across from roof to roof and upon them an awning is spread to ward off the rays of the sun, thus providing a country shelter capable of accommodating eight people with comfort. Some carry their own small double-sawbuck stools with seats of reed or canvas. I consider the latter to be better because even if it gets wet, it is quickly dried and it is not as stiff nor as apt to split as the reed, since the attendants always pack these stools on the side of the cart, outside the box, with the result that they get wet and are often torn by the branches which protrude into the road from the low trees; wherefore, a diligent person will take the trouble to pack them inside the cart, along with a folding table which is useful for eating, reading, and writing.

At four in the afternoon the trip is resumed, and a second stop is made for preparing supper, because if the night is clear and the road not hazardous, the caravan assembles again at eleven o'clock and travels until daybreak. Then, while the oxen are being changed, there is time to have breakfast of chocolate, maté, or some light fried tidbit for those who prefer to partake of more solid food, and in an hour they again take to the road until ten o'clock. The lazy passengers stay in the carts with the windows and doors open, reading or observing the condition of the road and other aspects presented to their view. The more energetic and curious persons ride horseback, going ahead or falling behind at their will, examining the farms and their rustic inhabitants, which are usually women, since the men go out to the fields before daybreak and do not return until they are exhausted by the heat of the sun or are ravished by hunger which they usually satisfy by eating exactly four pounds of fat and *descansada* meat, which is the name given to the meat of those animals which they bring in from the forests and kill on the march. As has always happened in the large slaughterings in sizeable cities such as Buenos Aires, they drive a large group of animals through the afternoon, lacerating them with whips, and then these wretched animals, stretched out during the night in the fields or on the beach, bellow until the following day when their throats are slit and they are divided into bloody pieces. This meat the inhabitants called *descansada*; I call it poisoned.

A regular day's journey from Tucumán for a caravan—which is what a group of carts traveling together is called here, as well as in other places—is 7 leagues, although since they cross many rivers, I have calculated that they do not average more than 5 leagues per day. These from Mendoza make longer trips per day, since their territory is less obstructed, with few rivers and many *travesías*, which is the name given to those extensive fields having no water. For these trips, especially for the one from Corocoro, they have several relays of skillful oxen which they call draft oxen. The rest of the herd walks along lightly, while the draft oxen pull the loaded carts without drinking sometimes for 48 hours, and if there is a little water in the drainage ditches, they do not drink it since they know it is bitter and polluted, whereas, in contrast the inexperienced animals, although they are driven on with great haste, always stop to drink, from which sickness and sometimes considerable mortality result. In crossing these extended fields stops are made only for the siesta, if the sun is very penetrating, wherefore it is imperative that the servants have the necessary food for the night, although the most satisfactory way is for them to go on ahead in the afternoon, taking along some sticks of firewood and whatever is necessary to prepare supper, bearing in mind that these draft oxen travel quickly and far in the course of an afternoon, night, and morning, and one must be informed about the place where these animals are to be changed so that there will be ample time to arrange the cooking equipment and other necessities without delaying the driver; but little trust should be put in the servants, since they are usually inexperienced Negroes who lose a great deal of the necessary equipment.

Some travelers have their own horses, which are usually bought for 2 pesos each. This is a great mistake, for during the night they break loose and return to the farms from which they were bought, or they are maimed by prowlers. It is best to make an arrangement with the owner or the overseer of the caravan, who seldom loses a horse and frequently increases his herd with the animals which are scattered through the field or with those brought in by the mule drivers by way of reprisal.

Those who may be surprised at the endurance of the draft oxen from Mendoza will be amazed at the valor of those from Tucumán, which can be seen crossing the treacherous rivers, bucking with their chests against the most rapid currents and making extraordinary resistance against the force of the waves as they drag along the carts loaded in the manner described earlier. When they first enter the river they show some timidity, but they do not withdraw nor become frightened when the water covers their entire bodies, including the eyes, as long as their ears remain above the surface. If they cannot pull the cart, they hold steadfast until the goads are thrown in for their rescue, an act in which they participate with spirit; they make the second, third, and fourth crossings with more assurance and daring, while the drivers urge them on calling them by their names. If they become entangled in the goads, they indicate it with their front and back legs so that the attendant may remove the obstruction from them; in short, this spectacle was one of the most pleasant ones I have ever experienced in my life. When I first saw those peaceful animals under the water for an hour with only the tips of their ears protruding, I thought they were undoubtedly drowning, but numerous experiences have made me see the endurance of such useful animals and the esteem which their important service merits.

When a passenger travels in one of the carts, the cargo is reduced by one third in order to accommodate him, his bed, his trunk, and other encumbrances. The carts which carry only cargo have no door in the rear, but they are open in the front to enable the driver to operate and to watch for downpours and other dangers.

It is advisable, almost imperative, that passengers inquire about the background of the cart drivers, since they are usually divided into three categories. The first consists of the most distinguished men from Mendoza, San Juan de la Frontera, Santiago del Estero, and San Miguel del Tucumán. These men established this enterprise in order to retail, in Buenos Aires, the excess products of their farms such as wines, liquors, flour, dried peaches, and other fruits, chartering the rest of their wagon to passengers and private individuals at a very reasonable rate. The money from these products is usually spent for goods from Europe for the operation of their homes and private businesses; but since one or two carts suffice to return the goods purchased with the money earned from the products which they took in 20 carts, the rest are chartered to the first carrier who comes along at a price contingent on the size of the load and the number of carts. The second group is made up of those having less means at their disposal, who are usually poorly equipped and experience delays in their trips. The third group consists of men of question. They always ask for the freight charges well in advance, and often when they are ready to

leave, a creditor appears to detain them and the shippers are obliged not only to pay the driver's debts, but also to supply the necessities of the trip and to suffer other disappointments; therefore, it is more advantageous and reliable to pay 10 pesos more per cart to the men of the first group.

. . .

The postal operation of San Miguel is leased by Don José Fermín Ruiz Poyo, and Don Francisco Norry, a local citizen, is the postmaster. Before arriving at the Tapia estate one encounters the delightful Nogales glen, so named because of the walnut trees growing wild in the forest. In the interior there are excellent woods such as the *quebracho* and the *lapacho* which are commonly used in making carts, since they are strong and sinewy. Another wood called *lanza* is excellent for cart axles and wagon poles, because it is strong, sinewy, and so flexible that it never splits even if the cart is loaded excessively. There is such a variety of wild fruits that it would be tedious to name them. From Nogales to the Tapia River, which is of great volume and contains numerous rocks, and from there to the banks of the Vipos River, the road is somewhat narrow and difficult so that heavy carts are able to travel only with the aid of lead-oxen. This is accomplished by adding two or four more oxen, exchanging them and taking them from the other carts; on a steep downgrade, the lead teams are put behind the cart to hold it back so that it will not upset or run over and injure the *pertigueros*.

The Vipos River is also stony and of great volume, and at 1 league beyond is the Chucha River, also rocky and of crystalline water. It is advisable that travelers have water taken from a clear stream which is encountered before reaching the Zárate River, since the waters of the latter are usually turbulent, and its flooding has caused great ditches one-eighth of a league in length to be formed in the road, which are an obstacle to people traveling on horseback.

Fourteen leagues from the Tapia River is the town of San Joaquín de las Trancas which consists of scarcely 20 houses and a stream with many fish. At the watering place by the same name, which is three-fourths of a league away, one finds the post office under the charge of José Joaquín de Reyna, the owner of the aforementioned site, which is very pleasant because it has several streams of clear water, and among them is a large spring which flows over into the countryside to form the Trancas rivulet.

The place in which the post is situated is usually called Pozo del Pescado, because formerly it contained many fish, although now only by chance is one found there. It is commonly said that they disappeared in a great flood and took up residence in the Trancas River where many are found today. It is a fact that the waters from this spring and others in the area are the source of the rivulet that passes through the town. Here ends the district of San Miguel del Tucumán, which is the smallest in the great province of the same name, but in my opinion it is the best territory of the province due to its large number of rivers providing water for irrigation, its expanse of coves for pasture lands and cultivated fields, and its more temperate climate.

CHAPTER VI

IMMEDIATELY beyond Pozo del Pescado, this district begins and at about one-eighth of a league's distance one
crosses the river Tala, of considerable volume, flowing over
very small stones, with marshy banks, making it necessary to
tread over it two or three times with the oxen and horses to
make the ground more firm so that the wheels of the carts do
not become mired. Having crossed the river, one travels along
an expansive stretch between two forests so dense that they
allow passage of only one cart at a time, until reaching a
spacious plain after about 5 leagues. Before arriving at the
Rosario estate, belonging to Don Francisco Arias, one passes
two places named El Arenal and Los Sauces, where there are
houses and some provisions such as lambs, hens, and pullets
which already begin to be sold at a price doubled over that of
the three districts left behind.

The first post of this district is situated in El Rosario, at 13
leagues from Pozo del Pescado, and the majordomo of the
estate will provide horses. There is a store there, and if one
detains himself for some time, bread will be kneaded and
baked, since it is not kept on hand continuously. At a distance
of 1 league is the voluminous river called Rosario, a name
used commonly by the natives, applying to it the name of the
immediate estate. This same river has different names depending on the place through which it flows, as do many others in
Tucumán, and although it is of great volume it is easy to ford
since it is so widely extended. In the center it forms some islets,

En la Jurisdicion de San Miguel del Tu cuman, que es la menor en extenfion de la Gran Provincia de efte nombre, pero en mi concepto, ès, el mejor Territorio de toda ella, por la multitud de Aguas útiles que tiene para los riegos, extenfion de Enfenadas, para paftos, y fembrados, y fu temperamento mas templado.

JURISDICION DE SALTA.

Del Pozo del Pefcado, al Rofario ... 13
A la Eftancia de Concha......... 10
Al Rio del Pafage. 15
Al Fuerte de Cobos 16
A Salta 09
A las 3 Cruces. 09

Son Lèguas 72

Nmediato al Pozo del Pefcado dà principio efta, y al medio quarto de lègua eftá el pafo del Rio nombrado Tala, de baftante caudal, fobre piedra menuda, pantanofo en fus orillas, por lo que es precifo
Ce

very delightful since they are graced, as are its banks, by lofty willows. Thus this estate, like the rest which follow on the route to Jujuy, has its pasture grounds with several streams of crystalline water. There are many having a circumference of more than 6 or 8 leagues, surrounded by rather lofty forests, with great ditches of water and, in many places, by large stakes and fagots, cut from the multitude of trees, which are adequate to confine young mules since they are very shy.

The Palata River follows, having passed the farm of Don Miguel Gayoso, which took the name of the river; it usually flows in two branches, easy to ford. Preceding and following this territory there are several coves to the east and to the west, with fields of *simbolar* and ichu grass. *Simbolar* is a species of pasture grass which greatly fattens cattle, similar to barley in its stem and leaves, but not so thick. Some stalks grow to 3 *varas* in height, and on the head have bunches of spikes called *cadillos*. Others do not grow so tall nor as thick, and their heads are similar to those of the hay in Galicia and Asturias. Carts are woven from this straw, which is very flexible and quite strong, in all the province of Tucumán.

. . .

Bordering Don Francisco Toledo's farm, and still on his land, across the river Mita, deep but with a stony bottom, lives Don Francisco Antonio Tejeyra y Maciel, of Portuguese birth, married to Doña María Dionisia Cabral y Ayala, a Spanish lady, native of Salta. The aforementioned nobleman and the ancestors of his wife were among the first inhabitants of this frontier. They have nine children, almost naked, very blond and fat because the good nobleman always keeps the pot on the fire filled with savory beef, mutton, bacon, and cabbage, which he picks in a nearby garden. He supplies travelers with good cheeses, meat, onions, and other things which he has in his well-cultivated garden, and we were assured that in his money chest 200 pesos could be found with more celerity than 50 could be located in that of Toledo. . . .

It is 10 leagues from El Rosario to the Concha estate, so named after its founder and first owner. Before arriving at the houses, one crosses a river of considerable volume which keeps the name of Concha; but the farm is now the possession of Don Juan Maurín, a Galician by birth. The larger part of his land, and especially the environs of the houses, has a perennial supply of water and is capable of raising everything which is planted; but they cultivate only what provides the scant necessities for the maintenance of the family, reserving the rest of the excellent farm for the raising of cattle and the wintering of mules. Here travelers may provide themselves with what is needed to reach Salta, because even though there are many small farms in the area, nothing is to be found on them but a few pieces of beef.

They should also be informed about the condition of the ford of the voluminous river Pasaje, so they may await, in the houses of Maurín, the time propitious for crossing, in order not to expose themselves to the inconveniences experienced on the detour turning off one-half league before reaching the Pasaje with its turbid waters and sandy bottom. At the eastern side of the detour, or to the right as one begins it, one should look for a pathway leading into the forest, and within a few steps a corral will be seen, constructed of logs, and about a rifle's shot beyond there is a beautiful spring of fresh and crystalline water with a design of combs formed by the water descending from a slight elevation; one may take a supply of this water sufficient for several days, reserving it only for himself, so that it will not be wasted by the attendants who adapt themselves well to the river water, which serves everyone for the purpose of cooking stews since it has no disagreeable quality other than its cloudy and somewhat muddy color. It is worthy of note that on both sides of this river mosquitoes are not to be seen, nor their annoyance felt, in the seasons of rain and high water since they appear only in the dry season.

Don Juan Maurín was obliged to place an inn at the ford of the river to supply food to the King's couriers and passengers, and to have fresh horses with which to cross it more safely; and for his kindness and bother I assigned him a gratuity of 2 extra pesos for every three horses, or every four in the case of the King, and doubled the rate for the private individuals. The same was granted under proper conditions and circumstances to Don José Fernández, who is to receive the horses on the other side and return them, crossing the river, to the inn of Maurín, and in the event that both conditions are not fulfilled, each person will pay for his mount at the price commonly charged.

Before reaching the fortress of Cobos, several streams are encountered descending from a moderate and stony declivity, with near-bloody waters which cause terror at first sight. Awaiting the arrival of the carts, I detained myself for a short time to contemplate these waters, and observing that all the attendants went down to drink, I learned that this was the best water in all the province of Tucumán for the healthy and the infirm. For all of this I resolved only to taste it, and I found no peculiarity until the owner of the carts told me that we would drink the water in crystalline form in Cobos, because that annoying color was taken from the earth through which the water flowed, of which I was convinced when I saw whence it came. With these remarks from the overseer of the fortress and his family, we all drank abundantly, and no one felt any effects, but I did observe that the entire family, with the exception of his wife, was indisposed.

The fortress of Cobos was erected 80 years ago as a safeguard against the Chaco Indians. It is at the foot of a declivity, 9 leagues from Salta. Today it is the house for the farm of Doña Rosalía Martínez, who has several parcels of land and a pasture plot within her boundaries. This lady from Salta is married to Don Francisco Xavier de Olivares, who was born in the city of Santiago de Chile. The house is in such a state of dilapidation that I was obliged to exercise great care in climbing the stairs leading to the upper story where they had their quarters, which the husband was unable to leave because he was half crippled, despite the excellent water which he drank. The lady displayed no robustness in her face and delicate body, which was of normal stature, but it caused me much astonishment to see her hair 2⅛ *varas* long, and she told me that a cousin of hers, living in Salta, had hair the same length. This woman had no other elegant qualities with which to be ostentatious, and even this one elegance amounted only to the length of her hair.

In the forests and pastures belonging to the farm, there are also black spiders, silk worms, and other products. This information was reported in good faith by Don Francisco de Olivares, who seemed, at least in other matters, to be a man inclined to exaggeration. The rode from Cobos to Salta is somewhat rough for carts and very difficult in the rainy season; thus only with care can it be traversed, as happened to us, when the cart driver executed the trip in the same time as if he had gone to Jujuy on the regular road. The traveler who has no need to enter this city should take post horses in Cobos for use up to Jujuy, near which no posts have been established, since this is not a courier's route; therefore it is necessary to proceed into

Salta

which has the name of San Felipe el Real. It is a city renowned for the numerous assemblies held there every year in the months of February and March, which I shall describe presently. It is situated in a marshy spot on the edge of the Lerma valley, being completely surrounded by a ditch filled with water. One enters it by a wretched causeway that does not quite span the ravine, which, although it is not of great expanse or profundity, makes impossible the passage of all kinds of beasts of burden in the rainy season, at which time the city cannot be traversed on horseback because the animals become mired in the thick clay in the streets, and thus in the afore-mentioned rainy season travelers find it more convenient, and even necessary, to go about the city on foot, remaining close to the houses which usually have balustrades, although not as wide and well-built as those in Buenos Aires; but it is an obstacle and a risk to cross from one block to the other. The valley, if I am not deceived, is 5 leagues long and half a league wide. It is covered with useful pasture lands and fields sown with wheat, all of which are watered through a plowed furrow. Its settlers are robust and tireless workers when riding horse-back, a skill at which they are extremely adroit, as are all the other inhabitants of this province.

The common people, or speaking with more propriety, the poor people of the city, experience a malady known as San Lázaro, which in reality is nothing more than a kind of itch. The principal men are robust, and are usually the owners of the neighboring pasture lands used for the last winterings of the mules. The remainder of the inhabitants are merchants, the largest or most illustrious part of which are Galicians. The wives of both groups, as well as their daughters, are the most spirited in all of Tucumán, and I believe that they surpass the women in all America in the beauty of their complexions and particularly in the abundance, beauty, and length of their hair. Rare is the woman whose hips are not covered with this esteemed adornment, and for this reason they usually let it hang loose or make elegant full-length braids; but to offset this charm, one rarely finds a woman who is not suffering, after the age of 20, a swelling in the throat, which in all the Spanish territories is called *coto* or goiter. At the beginning it enhances the throat, but as it increases in size it creates grotesque shapes, causing both astonishment and laughter, because of which the women try to conceal the imperfection with kerchiefs of fine cloth, covering their neck and serving as an adornment, just as the Jews wear the San Benito; although everyone classifies these women as goiterous, they prefer not to display it nor to divulge its shape and size, wherefore they conceal it in their bosom with great modesty.

Everyone, men and women alike, declares that this inflammation causes them no discomfort, that they have experienced no harm from it, and that life is no shorter for them than for those to whom nature has not dealt this damaging blow, which may be so considered only in the years of their splendor and luster. The entire city is built, like Mexico City, over water. Clear, drinkable water may be found by digging down 1 *vara*. There are some houses with upper stories, but I observed that the owners occupy the lower quarters and rent the uppers to strangers, which are numerous due to the mule trade. They would be more comfortable on the lower floor, thus avoiding the nuisance of the ascents and descents, but the owners, just as the Dutchmen, are not concerned about the dampness. In all the city and its common land there is only one parish church, with two priests and two assistants. It has two convents, San Francisco and Merced, and one college in which the members of the Company of Jesus hold their assemblies at the time of the fair.

The number of inhabitants of this city and its common land

could not be ascertained, but the rector priest, which is the title given to the oldest one, assured me, putting it in writing, that in the year 1771, 278 infants had been baptized—97 Spaniards and 181 Indians, Negroes, and mulattoes; in the same year, 186 from all four races had died, which results in an increase of 92 in the population of the city and its common land. From this computation one must not draw conclusions about the healthfulness and the favorable climate of the city. I consider it morbifical, and I have no reason other than that of not having seen old people of either sex in numbers proportionate to the population. The governor usually resides here with the title of Captain General, whence he issues his dispositions and remains within sight of the movements of the barbaric Indians occupying the lands, known as the Chaco, about whom he receives reports from the captains garrisoned at the frontier. The post is administered, with general approbation, by Don Cayetano Viniegra, who is from Galicia and married to a young lady distinguished in her birth and her personal qualities.

The principal business of this city and its district consists in obtaining profits from the wintering of mules, which concerns the owners of breeding farms and the traders, in the private sales which each makes, and in the preparations for their departure for Peru for the great fair which opens in the month of February and lasts through March; this is the largest assemblage of mules in the entire world, because in the valley of Lerma, contiguous to the city, 60,000 are congregated along with more than 4,000 horses, for uses which I shall explain later. If the fair could be held in the dry season it would be a most agreeable diversion for those possessing a warlike spirit; but since said fair is held precisely at the height of the rainy season, in a small and humid spot, it is annoying even to the very people interested in buying and selling, because the weather, plus a continual coming and going of 64,000 animals in a limited area, on land which is humid by nature, render it uncomfortable and disagreeable. Those who must of necessity remain in the fields—usually the buyers—scarcely find land upon which to erect their tents and field-beds.

For the purpose of enclosing the mules at night and keeping them in check for part of the day, extensive corrals are made, utilizing logs and cut branches from the neighboring forests, which are common to the area; but in just one night and part of one day these animals make such holes that they render said corrals unfit for further use without serious detriment to the owner, and thus every two or three days they move the mules so they will not become incapable of making the extended trip to the center of Peru. Almost all the muleteers (by whom I mean the drivers and the owners of the herds) used to think erroneously that the mules suffered from an epidemic of *mal de vaso*, hoof disease, which rendered them useless, causing death in considerable numbers. Others who had no experience understood it to be *mal de bazo*, a disorder of the spleen.[1] Both were incorrect, because experience has taught that the hoofs became very soft on those mules which had spent the winter in marshy pastures since these animals, so inclined to eating in the wet places in their search for green grass, become accustomed to living in them.

The opposite happened in the dry and stony pastures where they drank the water which flowed through and sought grass in the high hills and dry fields. These are the pasture lands best suited for the winterings since the mules become accustomed to somewhat arduous exercise, their hoofs harden, and they are robust and capable of making the trip into the innermost parts of Peru. The reason that some muleteers thought the hoof disease was contagious came from their experience that on the first day's journeys 20 or 30 mules would be incapacitated, and on succeeding days they suffered similar losses, without it coming to their minds that the resistance of the animals was related to the elements of nature and to the state of damp-

[1] An obvious confusion between the two diseases resulting from the similarity of pronunciation of the sounds *b* and *v*.

ness of the pasture. Thus they attributed it to a contagious disease, not noticing that other mules in the same herd did not suffer similar damage although they walked in the same footsteps, traveling side by side, eating the same grass and drinking identical water.

Now that the principal reason is known why so many mules are lost because of bruised feet in the arduous drive from Salta to the narrow hills of Peru, it is proper to warn those who deal in mules that not only those wintered in humid pastures suffer from hoof damage, but also those born within the district, which animals also usually become exhausted, since they have not been exercised by working. For this reason those raised in Buenos Aires and Chile, which have been taken to Córdoba and then to the pastures in Salta, are called "harassed animals," which is a way of saying that they have been trained in difficult work, and it is these that best endure the last days of a drive. Care should also be taken that the foreman and his helper be thoroughly acquainted with the kinds of pasture, so the animals do not eat *garbancillo* and other bad grasses. In the environs of Mojo grows much of this species which the mules crave and eat greedily, but they soon become swollen and fall dead, bloated, no remedy for this malady having been found.

This grass called *garbancillo* and other worse varieties are not a possession of some particular regions, since they crop up suddenly in others, always in protected spots of little extension. Some unknowing persons believe the mortality of the mules arises from, and is increased by, the close proximity in which they travel, that they contaminate each other, because they see 20 die one day, for example, 10 the next, and more the following days, until all have died which ate *garbancillo* in any quantity, without reflecting on their degree of hardiness or their size. The truth is that it arouses pity to see numbers of dead mules in the field and ravines, and I have observed that the greater part of them spew blood from the nostrils, either due to the effect of the bad grass or to the blow which they suffer in their fall. Some of them recover, when the herds stop a few days to rest in a spot with good pasture or in stubble fields, but these are the ones which were only threatened with the sickness, having eaten very little of the grass or being so hearty that they could resist its malignant effect. I was going to conclude the subject of mules here, but my intimate friend, Don Francisco Gómez de Santibáñez, who has been a dealer in this species for many years, told me it would be useful for me to continue, discussing the matter from the beginning, including the cost and expense of the drives, winterings, and the markets where sales are held. It seemed to me that any information, even if it is not extremely useful, cannot displease the public in general. The opinion of said friend and others removed all doubt in my mind and strengthened me in the observations I had made out of curiosity. It did not seem proper to delete what had been written or postpone its conclusion; therefore, I am continuing the subject in a retrogressive manner, imitating the pattern of epic poems.

There are many people concerned with the great Salta fair. The larger part is comprised of people from Córdoba, both Europeans and Americans, and the rest, from all the provinces, with some private individuals who make their purchases in the fields of Buenos Aires, Santa Fe, Corrientes, and a part of the Cuyo province; so it may be said that the mules are born and raised in the fields of Buenos Aires until they reach two years, or a little more, at which age they are taken from the feet of their mothers, as is commonly said; they are fed and strengthened in the pastures of Tucumán; they work and die in Peru. I do not mean to say that there no native-born mules raised in Tucumán, but they are few compared to the large number coming from the pampas of Buenos Aires. The owners of the pasture lands in Tucumán are men of good judgment, knowing well that their land is more propitious for strengthening the animals than for breeding and raising them, and those farmers from the pampas have proper motives for selling animals at a young age, since they do not have land suitable for keeping them after they have left their mother's side.

Those purchased on the aforementioned pampas, from one and one-half to two years old, cost 12 to 16 reales each, with the following prices having been affixed for several years in this area: 12 reales for the inferior animals, 14 for the average, and 16 for the superior; there was a time when they were sold at 5 reales or less per head while still at their mother's side. I will doubtless find the same regulation in effect for those sold in Córdoba and Salta since they are the two most common places for winterings. The herds taken from the fields of Buenos Aires comprise only 600 to 700 mules, due to the scarcity of watering places in which many animals may drink together, to which is added the lack of forests for making corrals and enclosing the animals at night. To supply these needs they carry stakes, and with leather thongs they make an enclosure to contain the mules, a task which takes the diligent efforts of 12 men, guarding in turns, and 40 horses costing from 8 to 10 reales each. If the purchaser uses a larger number of horses, not only will he not lose anything—although a few may die and be lost—but rather he will reap some gain because in Córdoba they are worth 2 pesos each and are bought by the residents and pasture owners, who fatten them at their own risk and expense in order to sell them at a profit in the adjoining areas.

The purchaser who is going to winter the horses may also turn them over, at his expense, to the ranchers, but I do not consider this wise because the attendants who round up and guard the mules maim the horses for their own purposes and those of the owner, an act in which they have few scruples. The aforementioned 12 men necessary for the drive of every herd of 600 to 700 mules, earn, or rather they are paid, from 12 to 16 silver pesos, depending on the distance, and in addition they are provided with meat to their satisfaction and some Paraguay maté. In this drive no taming of mules is necessary because the horses do all the work. The charge for each mule, from the fields of Buenos Aires to Córdoba and its immediate pastures, is set at 4 reales, independent of its original price and the expense contracted by the owner.

Those young mules, which they calculate to be two years old, are kept in their pastures for 14 months, more or less, and the owner of the ranch is paid from 5 to 6 reales apiece and 6 mules per hundred as a bonus for upkeep, making the cost for wintering come out to 8 reales each, with the rancher being obliged simply to hand over the number of animals having the brand or mark of the owner, even if they are emaciated or suffering from some other affliction; but those that are missing must be replaced to the satisfaction of said owner. In this city outsiders pay excise of 1 real for each mule which they take from the districts for the pastures of Salta. The local residents pay nothing; therefore, taking the average price and expenses, it may be wisely computed that every mule taken from Córdoba, from among those brought from the fields of Buenos Aires, costs 26 reales more or less. In Córdoba they are valued at approximately 36 reales, wherefore each herd estimated at 600 mules, taking into account the reduction by 6 per cent, brings in 750 pesos; but from this one must deduct the expenses of the buyers and his helpers over the space of more than two years spent in the trip down, the stay through the winter season, and the return; these expenses are very different, depending on the frugality, or lack of it, in the owners, the number in his employ, his industry, and often his own personal labor, which is very crude, considering also the sudden flights and the legal frauds, which is the attendants' name for open robberies from which the owners should try to protect themselves and prevent by unceasing efforts.

Now we have the herd capable of making a second trip, to Salta, where the general assembly is held, leaving Córdoba in the end of April or the first of May so as to arrive in Salta in early June, making allowance for accidental and often necessary stops for the animals to rest in fertile fields with abundant water. In this second journey the herds are usually composed of from 1,300 to 1,400 mules, with the charge for each being 5 reales. Accompanying each of these herds are 20 men and 70 horses which cost from 16 to 18 reales each. The foreman earns from 70 to 80 pesos, his aide 30, and the attendants 20, in stamped silver, and in addition to this stipend, they are provided a cow or a heifer every two days, so that the 20 men, including the foreman and his aide, consume half a beef daily; they are likewise given Paraguay maté, smoking tobacco and paper for cigarettes, all of which, costing more or less 12 pesos, is handed to the foreman for daily distribution.

Although I said the charge for mules taken from Córdoba to Salta was 5 reales, they are computed on a very scant figure, not including those that die, are lost, or stolen. Those who do not wish to be exposed to this risk, and desire to undertake a task of great effort, may avail themselves of a carrier who will take them at his expense and risk for 7 reales a head, but it is imperative that this person be trustworthy; and, for maximum security he should carry in his herd 200 or 300 mules at his own expense, so he may fill in and hand over in Santa Fe the exact number which left Córdoba, obtaining a receipt from the rancher designated by the owner of the herd, delivering to him all those mules which had his mark or brand and making up the shortages with other animals, which is called "delivering and being receipted" after the fashion of commercial enterprises.

These herds rest in the pastures of Salta around eight months, and in selecting this locale one should observe what I said at the outset about the dampness and the illegal acts of the owners, who, although in general they are honorable men, can perpetrate many frauds, listing as dead, stolen, or runaways, many of the best mules of the herd, which they replace with local-born animals, which, as I said, are not suited for the hard trip to Peru. For their feed and keeping the rancher is paid 8 reales per animal, which are realized when the animals, with the mark

and brand of the owner, are delivered to the pastures of Córdoba, as I said before. For exporting animals from Salta, the
purchaser or owner, if he is an outsider, pays 6 reales excise
per head, a tax destined for the maintenance of the fortresses
on the Chaco frontier and for the annual campaign for recon-
naissance of that frontier.

. . . For every herd, two droves of horses are necessary; one to
separate and round up the animals, and 4 reales a day per man
must be paid to the owners, even if each one rides 20 horses,
crippling them or killing them. The other group of horses is
hired for use until reaching Abra de Queta, 60 leagues from
Salta. This drove serves to head off and hold back the mules
which leave the winter pastures of Salta with vigor and spirit.
The owner of these horses is paid 4½ pesos for the three horses
which each man rides: one in the morning, one at midday, and
one at night; so for the services of three horses for 60 leagues
the owner is paid the aforementioned 4½ pesos, and he has the
obligation of sending two young men, at his expense, to return
the horses still fit for use, of which there usually are few and
often none, because the trips are long and the animals are kept
at half rein, so as not to permit the mules to disperse and return
to the wild haunt. Every day 50 horses are ridden up to the said
ravine, wherefore at least 150 accompany each herd. On the remainder of the trip horses are not needed because in addition
to the fact that the mules have lost their first impetuousness,
they now walk along as if enclosed between the towering hills,
and beyond Salta no corrals are made to enclose them at night
because they would die of hunger due to the bad quality of the
little grass on the royal highway in most of Peru; therefore it is
imperative that they rest and eat at night on coves and hills.
Beyond the aforementioned gorge of Queta it becomes useful
to tame mules for service.

Each herd leaving Salta is comprised of 1,700 or 1,800 mules.
Each needs from 70 to 80 tamed mules, provided they are good
and serviceable, with which great care should be exercised be-

cause these animals not only serve for the drive, but also for the transporting of cargo, and the people alone on the trip need 6 or 7 for carrying biscuit, flour, meat, valises, lassoes, and other trinkets, besides the trunks of the foreman. These tamed mules, being very common, cost 1 additional peso, but for those called *rocinas,* that is, tamed and adept at carrying both saddle and cargo, one pays 3 extra pesos each. They are well worth the 12 pesos paid for them when they leave Salta, but scarcely that much is given for them in Peru because they arrive overworked, thin, half dead, and with as many bad habits as if they were animals for hire.

Only 16 men accompany each herd from Salta to Peru, including the foreman and his aide. The former earns 300 pesos for the trip to Oruro, 500 to Cuzco or the market in Coporaca, and 850 to Jauja or the market in Tucle. His aide receives 160 to 170 for the first portion of the trip, 225 for the second, and 360 for the third, give or take 10 pesos. The attendants earn 65, 120, and 175 pesos for the trip to the last market at Tucle; and if they go beyond, such as to the market in Pachacama or Travesías, an agreement is made, either with the owner of the herd or the purchaser, without considering the proportionate distances. The owner allows the foreman to include in the herd 20 or 30 of his mules; the aide, 10 to 12, and each attendant 2 to 4 which are considered to be used for their return trip in which there is inevitable trickery. The fact is that the attendants leave the last market with a mule in lamentable condition, maimed, limping, and one-eyed, and by means of devotion to their rosaries, they arrive in Salta with 3 or 4 good, healthy mules, although some meet owners just as clever with whom they amiably come to terms, giving up the booty without resistance; but the fine residents of Tucumán are as skillful as gypsies, and they turn the hills upside down and make as many changes as the Genoese do with their drafts. Much could be said on this matter if it were only directed toward diversion. The pay of the foreman, aide, and attendants of each herd probably seems exorbitant to those who, like me, are accustomed to observe and experience how poorly personal effort is appraised in Peru, a matter which I shall explain in detail later; now it is only fitting to explain the way in which these salaries are spent in Salta, and the profits which remain in that city due to the fitting-out done b ythe merchants for the benefit of the mule buyers, who regularly use all their wealth in this, for their own convenience. The merchants or shopkeepers of Salta take it upon themselves to supply the men of the herd with silver and effects.

A tent is assigned to the people, that is, to the attendants, which they fit out with effects for use of their families and themselves. These are provided by the merchant on credit, if he chooses, the merchant trying to make an agreement with the owner of the herd and attempting, on his part, to give as little as possible in stamped silver, in order to assure an outlet for his goods. The owner of the herd or herds should try to limit this aid as much as possible, because if the attendants find themselves very much in debt and without the means necessary for the return trip, they usually flee, and the foreman is obliged to hire others, with grave detriment to the owner of the herd who rarely collects from these public usurpations.

The supplies of silver and goods are considered by all herdsmen as deserving of being paid first, and thus most attendants settle accounts with the money from the first mules they sell for cash, as is proper, and this business is considered the most effective and useful to the merchants of Salta. They place no limit on the foreman, since he is usually an honorable man, and the same applies to his aide, with very little difference. About the settlement which I mentioned earlier, when it is a question of cash silver, the owner deducts from the foreman 25 per cent, from the aide 50 per cent, and from the attendants 75 per cent, instead of 100 per cent, which used to be the rate before by reciprocal agreement, in which there is no usury, as some unknowing people believe; what many herdsmen have told me is true, that is, that the majority used to do damage to the ignorant people with the demand of 25, 50, and 75 per cent, since they are unfamiliar with the rule of three, which they popularly call a reduction; therefore I think it advisable to correct their thinking on this matter which is perhaps imagined, or, as I shall prove, impossible in some cases.

If the foreman, for example, who earns 500 pesos for the drive to the market of Coporaca, has a deduction of 25 per cent of this amount, he is reduced only 25 pesos. This amount is almost imperceptible, because it is being demanded of men unversed in accounts, much less in calculations which require more sagacity. The aide, much less enlightened, would be more aware of the trick, and even more so, the attendant who is more barbarous and gross; but the clearest and most evident proof of the fact that they have never made a calculation, according to what they have told us, at least among the aides and attendants, is that formerly these were reduced 100 per cent, and those guilty of the first error in thinking must confess that these men were paid nothing for their hard toil. The amount of 100 per cent opens the eyes of the blindest man, because he should have received nothing, or he should have been paid half of the fantastic amount in silver and goods at the regular price on credit, as if it were for cash silver. For example, the attendant who earned 120 pesos between Salta and Coporaca, was given 60 at the 100 per cent reduction, and at the present time, with the reduction lowered to 75 per cent, they must give him 68 pesos and 5 reales, half in stamped silver and half in supplies which he chooses at the current price at which they are sold for cash. This is the pay really accorded to an attendant, and not 30 pesos, as some people think, deducting the 75 per cent of the 120 pesos.

The calculation is, in reality, a rule of three, as all schoolboys know, although they do not understand its application in these cases; take, for example, the 500 pesos earned by a foreman on a run to Coporaca, which, with the increase of 25 per cent which makes 125, totals 625, and so I say: if I have 625 pesos and they include a profit, it amounts to the same thing: 500 pesos. How much will I have of the 500, or what profits will they give me? The 500 are multiplied by 500, and dividing then by 625, it comes out that the foreman gets 400 pesos, not the 375 resulting from the first calculation. This is the method which should be used in all calculations with a reduction of higher percentage, according to the distances and what each one earns.

I have not been able to ascertain the exact time that this method of calculation was established in Salta, when in Córdoba, in the same province, and in the province of Buenos Aires, workers are paid in stamped silver, as I said, without a deduction. I believe that when this commerce was first established, the people were paid for their work in goods, and thus they bargained for certain things at a high price, as is the case in Chiloé and other provinces of this kingdom, when the minted money was not so common. I have some information and experience in the province of Sonora, in New Spain, where every article has had a value fixed since the days of the conquest, but since an intrinsic value was given to silver, when the exchange of goods for silver is transacted, the articles are distinguished by three prices: inferior, average, superior, according to the quality of the product; thus anyone buying with silver, in leaf or stamped, asks the merchant the price at which it is sold, and in a word he tells him all the prices of his articles which he has that are subject to tariff, as well as those of the native products. If it is tit for tat, which means the same for one article as for another, he sells according to the standards of each one; he exercises precaution at certain times due to the abundance or scarcity of certain items, or their quality, and each man tries to gain the advantage.

It would be very easy to fix definite amounts which should be rigorously paid in stamped silver to the foreman, aide, and attendants, according to the three markets of Oruro, Coporaca, and Tucle, which are almost equidistant, but since there is a variation in the calculation, such a figure would be only a vain display of authority. If the people were paid for their work entirely in stamped silver, one would not find in Salta anyone who would make loans for provisions, and the mule dealers would find themselves obliged to keep a portion of their funds for expenses, payments of tariffs, and would use mules less for these purposes. The attendants would spend their money on illicit diversions injurious to their families, and thus the way to control them is to assign them a tent where they gather with their wife and family, and each one takes what he needs in linen, wool, or silk, receiving a small part of his pay in silver, to pay the seamstress and to "chase the rooster"—which is their way of saying to eat, drink, dance, and to sing to the accompaniment of their untuned lyres. The rest is reserved to hand them in silver upon their return, or to take care of needs arising on the trip—or to put it better, to force them to make the round trip, as I said elsewhere.

.   .   .

The contractor—or carrier, if he acts as foreman, which rarely happens—may engage in some inevitable trickery. The foremen, to stay on good terms with the owners of herds, are in the habit of performing an act which seems incredible to those not familiar with this business. Finding themselves with a herd weakened because of the thinness of the animals, which herd they call spiritless, the foremen try to overtake the herd which is one or two days ahead of them, or with more success, to wait for that one which is behind them, if they consider it robust; and on a dark night they intermingle their weakened herd with the other, and in the morning around 4,000 mules are found together in the same pasture, with the foremen, aides, and attendants having no other recourse than to hem in the two herds and divide them into platoons or units, and each foreman removes, at a distance, those which belong to him until his herd is complete. The one who mixed his emaciated or languid animals with those spirited ones of good flesh can never be deceived or fail to improve himself, and although this rarely happens, one does not realize the serious damage done to one party, because besides the emaciated animals being worthless, they become very much maimed on the march, since they cannot keep abreast with the healthy animals without serious hardships.

The damages which foremen, aides, and attendants can do to a carrier or an owner of a herd are innumerable, in spite of every imaginable precaution. Stealing is inevitable in some countries where this crime is considered a craft, causing great horror among the other nations of the world. For a herd of mules of 1,800 to 2,000 to eat well a pasture of more than 1 league in length is needed. This league is not always found at the market places, wherefore it is often necessary to stop among hills, and when they are cleaned of grass along the skirts, the animals go to the heights to search, making the work of the people in these pastures extremely difficult. They remain on horseback almost all night, especially if it is gloomy, but during the hail storms it is doubly hard work to restrain animals that are not accustomed to this kind of storm which destroys much. Wherefore it is advisable to advance as far as possible from Salta, especially for those doing business in the market at Tucle and its environs, in order to escape the snowstorms in the Guanzo cordillera.

Mule dealers are divided in their opinions as to whether on this trip it is better to take animals through the heights, with the craggy road and scarcity of grass, or over the highway along the slopes, called the Mercury Road, along which there is poisonous grass. Of course, the carriers elect the first, because they fulfill their mission by handing over the exact number of mules, even if they arrive lank and languid, which is the same as emaciated, crippled, and lame. The owners who become carriers—which means taking the animals at their own expense— if they have a set contract for a specific number of mules, in whatever condition they arrive, will follow the carriers' route; but those who are going to sell their animals at the market at Tucle to buyers coming from several provinces, think only of delivering them in healthy condition and rested, so that their spirit can be recognized and they are able to travel longer distances.

.   .   .

This trade or *trajín*, as it is called, is more stable than any other which has great losses and in which the profits are not in proportion to the work. Robust and courageous youth, particularly those who crossed Tucumán, undertake it with happy calculations which delight their fantasy, and with their spirit and fickleness they conform to the practice of not remaining long in any town. Variety affords their entire pleasure, the greatest of which consists in relating their adverse adventures. They compensate for three or four unfortunate days and nights with four hours of sleep, a good meal with their friends and two hours of gambling, during which they continue to talk about the condition of their herd and others; but since one deal leads to another of the same kind, either because it had a prosperous, or bad, conclusion, they usually grow to old age in this business with great detriment to their health on the extended and difficult trips. There is no merchant in the entire world who has such hard physical labor because, besides coming and going, these men are forced into continual movement for their sales and much more for their collections of money. The latter are usually done through the *corregidores*. Those who have procured credit, or have their own means, usually pay a quantity in cash, but they contract somewhat extended credit for the completion of the payment. Other men of their word, who have no other means than the success of the collections, and who usually come out badly from the risk involved in spite of their great activity and diligence, are considered to be useless men by some fools, who merely hold friendly intercourse with these men of sound judgment and rate them as second class.

The members of the third group, truly worthless because of their little skill, will deny the muleteers punctual payments on the credit, which they cannot pay off because, the first year, they are scarcely able to amass an amount equal to the taxes paid by the Indians, and thereafter they have to satisfy likewise the excise tax and the payment of other supplements for their transportation, carrying charges, clothes, and infinite other expenses which they must pay first; the third year they begin to pay the price of the mules and the effects of the allotment. The muleteer can thank God for the fact that after four years he collects the money for his herd, which, with another year spent in the round trip to Salta, makes five years, during which he is supposed to eat and buy clothes and shoes from the earnings, which on a herd of 2,000 mules does not amount to 10,000 pesos at the present time, if all works successfully. The muleteers, or rather the courageous and dusty merchants, know very well that I consider the profits from mules as more than an ordinary reward, and although I go on and on talking about the time delays in collecting, I have more examples in favor than against; and finally, the old merchants understand well that I am merely urging the young men to exercise a little economy in playing at cards and dice, and much more in their diversion with the ladies, which is the only nourishment and entertainment in the sierra.

CHAPTER VII

ORIGIN OF THE MULES. METHODS OF TAMING USED BY THE
RESIDENTS OF TUCUMÁN. METHOD THE INDIANS HAVE FOR
BREAKING MULES. THE MULE TRADE.

TO conclude the subject of such great interest to dealers, whom I esteem most among the carriers, I shall provide an account for the public unfamiliar with these matters of origin and propagation of the vast multitude of mules born to mares on the pampas of Buenos Aires. The latter naturally mingle with horses, being an animal of its species, just as female donkeys do with asses, which may really be considered two distinct species created by God and taken into Noah's ark. Men, considering that the product of the accidental union of an ass and a mare was an infertile monster, but at the same time useful for work because of its strength, tried to increase its number; but observing some resistance of the mare at receiving the male ass, and even more in raising and feeding the young mule, they decided to enclose the mare, before delivery, in a dark stable, and as soon as she had given birth, they skinned the colt and put the skin on a newly-born ass which they gave to the mare for her to raise without rejecting it. The little ass, needing food, took his place at the side of the mare, who, thinking it was her own offspring due to the exhalations of the skin, nursed him in the darkness until a few days later the skin was taken from the little ass so as not to cause him more damage, light was allowed to enter the stable, and the mare accepted the creature, who considered her his mother, from whom he never separated himself even if he were fondled by the animal to which he was really born.

Thus they increased the males of the species until there was sufficient for the number of mares. In Spain contrivances are used, which it is not fitting to explain, in order that the males may fecundate the mares, but this arises from the fact that there are many breeders having a small number of mares, and each one tries to keep his rate of births from lagging behind. On the pampas of Buenos Aires there are few breeders who have many mares, and for this reason they lose many ass colts due to the lack of midwives and other assistance. The male asses, called *hechores,* are so jealous that they guard their flock and do not permit, under penalty of death, the entry of any male horse capable of begetting, allowing quarters only to eunuchs, as the Great Turk and others do in their harems. Tigers are the animals most feared by horses and mules, but the male ass comes forth bravely, and not being able to defend himself with his strong weapon, his teeth, because of his awkwardness and lack of agility, he allows the tiger to jump on his back and after feeling him well-secured by his claws, the mule throws himself to the ground, rolling over and over until he breaks the tiger's delicate spine, and afterward he tears it to pieces with his strong teeth, without being frightened and paying no heed to the wounds he has received. And finally, the ass, which appears on the pampas to be a stupid animal with no activity other than that of procreating, defends his herd or his number of mares better than the most spirited horse. He rejects the females of his species, considering them inferior to the mares. The latter like him for all the qualities which contribute to his brutality.

From an early age the young mules, male and female, adapt themselves to the ways of the foster mother, wherefore they tag along behind a horse, mare, or colt, scorning their parents; and thus at two years of age they leave the pampas, following the drove of horses like sheep, showing fright only at some ridiculous object but easily brought under control by the attendants until they reach the pastures of Córdoba. Here they are turned loose, and each platoon or group joins with one or two geldings, or perhaps mares, since it makes no difference to them, forming a kind of ranch herd which eats and drinks together. When they leave this wintering they are robust and spirited and begin the second lap, to Salta, between two dense forests which have only narrow pathways departing from the road in a straight line, or others that cross it, leading to waterholes. To keep them from straying, the attendants must proceed with great diligence, without any guide lights other than their opaque footprints.

These young animals are very curious, and they wish to investigate, with notable attention and candor, everything they perceive. A cart which has stopped, a tent in the country, a mule, or a horse, are for them, it seems, objects of great pleasure; but this is true only of the fattest and most spirited ones which travel ahead of the others, and often, if they were not frightened away, they would stand bewitched for hours; but it is best to try to lure them away, passing a hand over their mane or back, at which they leap and frisk back to the rear guard of the herd, only to advance again to a place where they can make new investigations. The vanguard and the remainder of the herd always travel at a fast trot, and since they go along in close union and driven by attendants, they have no occasion to be distracted. The first ones may be compared to the army scouts who open the way; but unfortunately, if they see a tiger, which is the object of most horror to them, they always retreat and take with them the rest of the army which, at full speed, splits into platoons along the road and paths until they recover from the sudden fright, which usually is not until they are exhausted.

· · ·

Method of Taming Used by the Residents of Tucumán

Before beginning this subject, it seems opportune to say that the garment of hide given by Nature to these mules in question has not been touched, even by a hand, until they reach the

market at Queta. When the sellers present them in the corrals
of the valley of Lerma, adjacent to the city of Salta, they consider as *desechos*—a word used to designate animals which are
defective in general—all white or grayish mules, the males
which, due to oversight, were not castrated, and all those mules
which were lassoed of necessity, because these animals throw
themselves violently to the ground and are considered maimed.
This happens when the foremen or the buyers express doubt as
to whether or not a male has been castrated, and the lasso
thrown at the animal by the attendant to separate him, or some
mule which they label as defective, frequently falls on one of
the best mules; therefore it is considered *desecho*.

As soon as they arrive at the aforementioned Queta gorge,
the horses are dismissed and the tame mules are pressed into
service, but since there is not a sufficient number for all tasks,
they begin to lasso mules most spirited as shown by their
corpulence and strength, and the attendant is obliged to mount,
without objection, the animals lassoed and presented by the
foreman or his aide. This mule puts forth extraordinary resistance, but they subject it by throwing another lasso around
its feet, and at the moment when it tries to leap, they clip it in
the air and throw it violently to the ground; before the furious
animal regains its composure, they tie its four feet, and clasp-
ing its head with a strong rope, they place on it a barnacle
halter and a saddle, with the cinch around its belly making a
kind of strap which almost cuts off the respiration. In the mean-
time the poor animal strikes its head on the ground several
times, injuring its eyes and teeth, until blood streams out. In
this position it bellows like a bull, and upon removing the
bindings from its four feet they leave another rope on one rear
leg, equal in length to the rope attached to the headstall. As
soon as the animal finds itself unfettered, it gets up from the
ground vehemently, and since it is held by the two ropes and
cannot escape, it gives some formidable leaps, and when it
least expects it, they throw it down again without letting its

feet touch, repeating this inhumane act until they consider it exhausted. They then remove the rope from its foot, cover its eyes, and an attendant mounts it, grasping its ears, while another restrains its first impulses with the rope which remains fastened to the iron ring hanging from the headstall; but in spite of the torment suffered by this animal, it begins to buck and bellow like a wounded bull pursued by dogs of prey.

If the poor animal tries to flee in order to relieve itself and to shake off its impertinent cargo, the attendant stops it with the halter, twisting its head and neck, an act which they, with much propriety, call breaking them. Some mules in this condition attack the attendant who is holding them, much as a brave bull would do. The rider, besides clutching its ears, secures himself with his spurs, which is a martyrdom in itself; they say that everyone defends himself with his fingernails. When the poor animal finally becomes stunned, all bloody and covered with sweat and dust, the rider removes the spurs. He then leaves hold of the ears, and taking the reins of the headstall with the longer halter rope free, he allows the mule to walk at will. Sometimes it jumps around and around, sometimes it rushes for a cliff or attempts a high and rocky hill; but the attendant continues giving sharp tugs on the right and on the left, and from time to time he sinks in the *nazarenas*, which are the monstrous spurs, until the mule, following the royal highway, overtakes the herd which is traveling from Queta at a slow pace. The foreman and aide examine the mule to see if it is *sobada* or well-beaten. This word *soba* in this kingdom commonly means an extraordinary punishment. If it is found that the mule still has some spirit, the attendant is ordered to take it to the first cove and to make it skirmish. The tormented animal knows nothing but to run and jump, and to turn it to the left they pull heavily on the rein on the halter and with the right hand give it strong blows on the jaw until it turns its nose which they fasten to the saddletree; in this position they make it do a dozen turns to the left, executing the same procedure, so it will weaken, on the right side. The mule bellows, and as soon as they let loose of the false rein, it runs blindly through the hills and gullies, often throwing itself on the ground furiously, and if the strong rider does not exercise great care, his leg will be broken or his foot maimed, but this rarely happens. They relate and show their injuries with great glory, just as soldiers display the scars from stabs and bullets received on the battlefields in defense of their country.

I have painted a crude picture of the first punishment administered to a young and innocent mule. This act is performed daily with more than 20 mules because, as I said, every attendant has to mount the animals lassoed by the foreman or aide, who always elect the best ones, which are those most spirited and corpulent. This crude, barbaric, and inhumane method of breaking the animals could not be accepted by an intelligent man, because, quite aside from the many mules which are crippled and injured in many parts of their bodies, the owners of the troops and carriers accomplish nothing more than weakening the best animals, protecting themselves from a stampede, and saving a number of tame mules. I believe it would be more suitable for mule dealers to spend 2,300 or 2,400 pesos more in each herd to increase the number of mules already tamed, and thus free themselves from this rigorous work, or I should say punishment, on innocent mules incapable of learning anything by such violent means. Merely the hardship of extended drives would suffice to break the spirit which they derive from the Salta pastures, and at least they would arrive at the market without sauciness or physical defects other than those contracted by their nature.

The *corregidores,* whom we should consider as principal buyers, although not the only ones, do not apportion more than ten mules to the best muleteer, and only one or two to the others. They introduce these undisciplined animals into their herds little by little, and they unconsciously tame and control the animals with the example of the conduct of the veteran mules. Certain travelers observe which of the animals are best suited for pack and which for the saddle. They train the former by placing on them a light load, called *atapinga* or *carta-cuenta*, consisting of their small valises and other trifles of little weight. On those considered suitable for the saddle they place a simple saddle pad, without stirrups or crupper, so they will not be frightened; but on others they place, at the outset, a *mamacona*, which is really a halter made of twisted raw leather, so that the animal's head becomes accustomed to this kind of control, and it will not cause any vexation when it is necessary to ride or lead the animal. They later proceed to attach stirrups to the saddle, so the animal becomes accustomed to their rattling and movement, and on the cargo animals they put the harness. This method of breaking animals is in conformity with the thinking and practice observed in wise Europe. It is not at all tedious and certainly not costly. After a few days' trip the mules destined to the saddle let themselves be mounted by a youth, who rides among the herd slowly, sometimes going ahead or falling behind, so that the animal gets the practice. Those assigned to cargo need less attention, because as they become accustomed to walking at the slow pace of the herd, they gradually accept the increase in the load proportionate to their strength, and are tamed unconsciously, with the desire that the burden be taken from them in the resting places.

Method or Plan Used by the Indians to Tame their Mules

To each Indian the *corregidor* allots one or two mules, but to many he gives none, either because they have no need for them or are unable to pay for them. All of them desire this apportionment, some to utilize the animals for transporting their effects, and others to sell them at an inferior price, using the small amount for debaucheries and other excesses. The first-mentioned tame their mules in a method quite different from that used by the residents of Tucumán, and both of them are wrong to my way of thinking. The Indians, cowards and weak in strength, cheerfully receive one or, at most, two mules, and leading them to their houses they tie them securely to a strong tree trunk, called a *bramadero* in all America, in the patio or corral. There they leave the animal at least 24 hours without giving it food or drink, after which they examine it to see if it is broken or not, and if they see that it still has spirit and strength to resist the cargo or the saddle, they leave it another 24 hours, to rest, as they say, but more properly, to wear it down, after which they put on its back, without harness, a sack of wheat or flour containing 6 or 7 *arrobas*, well lashed to its belly so it cannot throw it off. The poor animal, weakened first by hunger and thirst and next by the load, follows at a slow pace the one who leads him, resisting only in order to stop and drink from a stream or eat grass which appears along the road. The patience of the Indians is long-lasting, and thus they gradually break their mules, in accordance with their pacific nature and manner of thinking; but the animals which they raise are always lean and lacking in strength because they work them before the proper time and without the necessary food, keeping them always in continual movement.

The result of this inconsiderate principle is the death of an infinite number of mules in the sierra, particularly among the Indians, because these fine countrymen of mine think that the duration of a mule's life and service is only from one apportionment to another. My fine fellowmen do not determine whether the mule is better suited for the saddle or for cargo, because since the *corregidor* allots them only one, they apply both the saddle and load to it by its third day in their possession, but if some Spaniard hires it from them, it gives him a couple of kicks, or bites him when he is off-guard, and if it succeeds in knocking him down, he may bid farewell to the bridle, saddle, saddle cloth, bags, and all the rest, because this good mule, that showed himself so slow in making the trip, returns at great speed to the pasture or his wild haunt. The fine Indian makes the equipment disappear, hiding it beneath a boulder in a deep ravine, and the Spaniard is left with his blow, kick, or bite, and without his equipment, unless he redeems it with money paid in advance, because the Indian never respects promises since he himself never fulfills them.

. . .

For more than fifteen years, (but let us say only ten so that no one will doubt it), 50,000 mules have been coming from the pastures of Salta and the rest of Tucumán; these are divided and sold between Los Chichas and Los Guarochiríes. Besides the opinion of the best herders, we have proof of this, which although it is not conclusive according to law, is convincing to natural reason. They all agree that the excise tax on this trade amounts to 32,000 pesos annually, with 6 reales being paid per animal. To make this amount, it is necessary that around 43,000 mules be recorded, which falls short of my calculation by only 7,000. Such a number makes a group of considerable size, but they are scarcely perceivable when distributed among many herds, just as in an army of 50,000 men, 7,000 are not missed, nor would such a number increase the size considerably. The royal officials allow some flexibility. The guards follow their example in this moderation, and the muleteers take advantage of the indulgence of some, availing themselves of the cunning of their foremen, aides, and attendants, to which is added the fact that groups of mules go astray on the side roads. There is much filching in this business, as in all others in which the King collects excise.

. . .

The mules in the valleys, like that of Cochabamba, and on all the coast, from Arica to Lima, work four times more and live four times longer due to the large amounts of alfalfa they have for food and to the mildness of the climate. The larger part of the sierra is very cold land where little pasture grows, and at the time when cattle are to be pastured on the stubbles, snow falls and destroys it. The cattle take advantage of the grass near the royal highway, which can serve the continual coming and going of the mule drivers, because their tired and debilitated animals cannot go in search of pasture in the hills and ravines which are 3½ leagues away. There are some moderately temperate areas which maintain adequate pastures, but these have private owners who defend them and reserve them for their own cattle. The members of the Company of Jesus were those most jealous in this matter, and I wish to conclude with a joke told me by the inspector. He says he heard that Don Fernando Cosio, who once was driving a herd of mules, was forced to stop in the pastures of a farm belonging to the priests. After the animals had grazed a short while, the administrator came out, with a group of servants, to frighten them away. Men from Tucumán waste few words, and they never resolve anything for themselves without giving an account to the master—which is what they call the owner of the herd because, being Spaniards, they follow European formality, not considering ignominious the term which in Peru is used only by slaves.

Well, the aide arrived at the tent in which Cosio was lodged, and addressing him, with hat in hand, he reported that a Theatin had come out with 25 men on horseback to frighten away his animals, and that the foreman, with his men, was restraining him, awaiting orders. Cosio, who, as a mountaineer, would permit no one to tread on his toes, took down the blunderbuss which was loaded with powder and balls, and confronting the Theatin said, "Hold on there, Father, if you do not want to be the fourth I've sent to Eternity." The monk, a very formal man, beheld through his thick spectacles the corpulence of Cosio, and at the same time sensing that this was a man capable of undertaking anything whatsoever, had no choice but to ask him if they had been priests that he killed. The arrogant Cosio replied that they had all been *lecheros*, winners at gambling, but that he would have no scruples about killing anyone who tried to insult him or trample over him. The good father, seeing this resoluteness, ordered his people to retreat, dismounted from his spirited horse, embraced Cosio and gave him free access not only to the pastures, but also to all his larder, with which the men from Tucumán were very pleased, and they dispersed their animals so they might graze to their satisfaction. There is another joke, of a different nature, but still it reveals the character of the men from Tucumán. A group of them caught a mestizo who had stolen two mules and were tying him to a tree when the foreman arrived, asking them what sacrifice they were going to exact, to which the attendants replied that they were going to give him four dozen lashes. The foreman, who is considered sovereign ruler among them, ordered that they should not commit such an inhuman act on the poor fellow, that they should turn him loose without paying anything—but first cutting off his balls. The wretched victim appealed the sentence and accepted the first punishment, since he feared the results of the second there in an area where there was no surgeon or apothecary. I must confess that if I found myself in such a dilemma I would have great doubt about which of the two choices it would be best to elect, because I have seen a man from Tucumán knock a haughty and robust Negro to the ground with one lash, leaving him almost lifeless. I trust the lashes would not be of this caliber because I must say that at just four, not four dozen, there would be no skin, flesh, or bone left that was not flying out of sight. Besides their great strength, they are so adept in the use of the whip that with the ends of the reins they give a blow to a mule that makes it sail more than a block without being able to straighten out its body. And with that we are going to leave such a lengthy subject, which I think even my friend Santibáñez will consider dull, in favor of discussing a city that is annoying in the rainy season.

I already said that the cart drivers who enter this city complete their trip as if they were going to Jujuy, cutting across from Cobos, and thus the traveler who has business in it may continue to Jujuy from said post, avoiding many bad stretches, particularly in the rainy season. In Salta there are lesser drivers who will take a small baggage train with loads of little weight to Jujuy. The man with a heavy load should solicit one of the drivers from Escara, from the province of Chichas, who regularly go down to Jujuy, and some as far as Salta, soliciting loads of wax and other products of Tucumán, with "something more" which will be well understood by the reader familiar with business matters. The exit from this city, memorable because it has the greatest gathering of mules in all the world for a city its size, is as difficult as the entry since it is necessary to cross a deep ditch by means of a small bridge, so frail that it serves only people on foot. A large stretch of the countryside, just as the city, is full of pools of water, called *tagaretes*, which serve as a hindrance and obstruct the progress.

The first 3 leagues are on flat country, without stones, and the rest is forest, through the largest part of which one travels along the stony beds of the rivers Vaqueros, Ubierna, Caldera, and Los Sauces, all of which are crossed more than 40 times in one day, due to the windings of their course. In the place named Tres Cruces this district ends and that of Jujuy begins.

CHAPTER VIII

THE DISTRICT OF JUJUY. THE POSTAL SYSTEM. SHORT
DESCRIPTION OF THE PROVINCE OF TUCUMÁN. THE
CUSTOMS OF THE *GAUDERIOS*.

THE place called Tres Cruces not being propitious for the erection of a post office, it was deemed advisable to establish it on the estate named La Cabaña, which is 3 leagues beyond and appertains to the district of Jujuy, as I said before. The spot designated La Cabaña has an abundance of water which descends from the adjoining mountain range. Its present master is an honorable Frenchman, Juan Boyzar, who accepted the mastership of the post under the same conditions as did the other men from Tucumán. This post is one of the most useful on all the route, both for mail and passengers because, being situated on the banks of the perilous river Perico, its horses are so adept in crossing the stream that, thrusting their chests against the rapid current, they look to see if any rocks disengage themselves from the nearby mountain, and either halting, retreating, or advancing to avoid the danger, they proceed straightway to the narrow strip where they are to exit. It also serves profitably in providing a rest stop for mules and horses which arrive exhausted from Potosí or from the province of Los Chichas, since it has a well-secured pasture land which is closed off by the gate from the patio of the house; to eat and drink, the horses need walk scarcely one block. However, I observed that this pasture, being situated on low terrain, would be very humid because of the copiousness of the waters descending from the mountain, as well as the height of the grasses that in some parts cover the animals, which probably serves to prevent them from detaining themselves too long in one location providing nourishment for the bodies but damaging their hoofs by softening them to excess.

Jujuy is the last city on our course, or vice versa, it is the first of the five within the province of Tucumán. Its area and population are comparable to those of San Miguel. Its inhabitants were, in former times, more numerous and highly esteemed for their wealth and the tenacity with which they upheld their rights. They did not allow the members of the Company of Jesus more than one institution, to which the latter assigned the name *residencia;* but the most singular fact is that they, being as much disposed to litigation as the rest of the inhabitants of the province, would not admit a notary in their midst. Their principal industry is the raising of cattle, which they sell to the ranchers in Yavi and Mojos and to the provinces of Los Chichas and Porco, where great slaughterings take place to provide the meat, tallow, and grease for the persons engaged in the many silver mines on the banks of the river Potosí. They also derive profit from the purchase, from small farmers, of mules which arrived late for the Salta Fair or of other feeble, emaciated animals which they then winter in their pastures for one year. Judging by their small number, I have sufficient reason to believe that these animals are apropos for Peru, a matter about which those who deal in these animals would be better informed. The city is surrounded by a voluminous river, formed by the convergence of two large streams, of which one is of crystalline water, the other muddy, resulting in a mixture like that of a Spaniard and an Indian woman. One enters or leaves this city by means of a beautiful tableland, one-half league long and half as wide, then winds down through a short ravine, traveling 10 leagues among the forests and arid plains of Guájara, which is the second post in this district.

Facing this place is a volcano in which it seems that Eolus has locked the winds of the district. They burst forth in the mornings with such impetus, whipping up so many whirlwinds and dust storms, that they cause fright in the inexperienced and detain the mules in their course. These winds, although their force gradually diminishes, are troublesome until one passes beyond Quiaca. From the site named La Cueva to Yavi, all the land is in the possession of the Marqués del Valle de Tojo, who was in charge of locating posts on his estates in Yavi, Cangrejos Grandes, and La Cueva. He who wishes to take on provisions will go from Cangrejos Grandes to Yavi, whence he will proceed to Mojo, but he should be advised that there is a very high and perilous cliff, and if the marquis has not made reparation on it, as he promised, it would be safer to proceed directly to Quiaca, which is the first post in the district within the province of Los Chichas.

The river by this name, flowing through a deep ravine, separates the provinces of Jujuy and Los Chichas. An estate which took the name of the river is located at a stone's throw from it, in this district. Before undertaking a description of it, it seems of some utility to give a general idea of the province which, considering the territory which it occupies, is the largest that our Monarch holds in his domain.

A Concise Description of the Province of Tucumán as Seen along the Postal Route

The distance along the route from Esquiva de la Guardia to the Quiaca River is 380 leagues, in the judgment of the best pilots, with posts situated as demanded by the expanse of the territory. Three hundred and fourteen leagues of the route traverse fertile ground suitable for carts of the size already described, the remaining 66 for horses galloping or at a fast trot. A barren country, it has a benign climate until one reaches Salta or Jujuy, although it is inclined more to be hot and somewhat humid. With some precautions, as I said before, one may travel in comfort, there being an abundance of eggs, hens, and cocks, cheap and very palatable. The most common game is the *pava*, which is in the crow family, although of larger size. It does not provide a very delectable dish, yet it serves in the absence of chickens. There is likewise, in the district of San Miguel and part of Salta, a species of hare or rabbit, the meat of which is as tasty as that of the fattest pullet, but it is essential that before it is skinned, it be subjected to the fire until its fur is consumed, and in this manner it is roasted in a shorter time; they are especially tender if eaten immediately after being killed. All other game, as far as the hunt is concerned, serve only for pleasurable entertainment of the travelers. As I said before, the rivers encountered contain some fish, but the traveler never takes advantage of them, either for recreation or to supply his necessities. The *bolas, quirquinchos, mulitas*, and other testaceous animals are a pleasure to behold and to observe for the precautions which they take to protect themselves and to survive; but only in the case of exigency, does one make use of their flesh, which is, in reality, very tasty.

We have seen no ostriches, as in the countryside around Buenos Aires; neither were they encountered by the hunters in the retinue who traversed the forests through the narrow paths, or in the coves. Likewise they saw not a single viper, the abundance of which is very exaggerated. Partridges are as rare here as they are common on the pampas. The inspector informed us that three times he had crossed the pampas and once the forests of Tucumán, and that neither he nor those of his entourage had observed a tiger, but that there could be no doubt that there were a great many despite the lack of fecundity of this species, a fact attested to by the many skins that are sold in these provinces, taken to Spain or transported, although in less abundance, into Peru; therefore, one cannot doubt what cannot be seen, when there exists such lucid proof. The inspector does not believe that the large, stupid snake, called *ampalaba*, of which there are many in the forests of the island of Puerto Rico and in many other parts, attracts the animals on which it is reputed to feed. This snake, of monstrous proportions, is found only in the thickest forests, and being so sluggish in its movements, would experience great difficulty in catching rabbits and even more in attracting deer, all of which convinces me that it sustains itself on certain insects and principally on the juice of the trees in which it has been seen hanging, supporting itself on the ground with its tail coiled in the manner of a snail or an augur. As it advances or pauses to swallow some animal of a size permitted by its strength, this snake proceeds noiselessly, and enveloping its victim with its body and holding it fast with a section of its tail which is concealed, it suffocates it and sucks it down as a common snake does a toad, until it is completely devoured without being dismembered. As to whether or not it possesses the power of attraction or some kind of bewitchment, there is no one who can confirm, and one may conjecture that some small animals such as the hare, rabbit, deer, and perchance calf, stop short, motionless with fright, before its stare and are thus snared, but one may also ascertain that this game is not its principal source of aliment, inasmuch as it is a very torpid creature and will permit itself to be dragged away alive behind a horse, as if it were a log, and to be killed, without resistance, by anyone who may accost it. In Tucumán, at least, they tell of no tragedies occasioned by this monstrous snake, which I believe to be more rare than tigers.

In the entire world there is scarcely another region where everything is more propitious for the plentiful production of whatever is planted. Twelve species of bees have been counted, all of which produce honey of a different flavor. The major part of these useful creatures make their nests in the trunks of trees, commonly in the interior of the forests, and it is a regular occurrence for a tree to be lost each time honey and wax are harvested, because the fine people who are engaged in this business, to avoid the least tedium, make incisions with their hatchets which destroy the tree. There are some bees which establish their dwellings beneath the earth, and sometimes near to houses, the fruits of which are gathered by the boys and servants of travelers, and we have observed that the bees do not defend their honey and wax with the vehemence of those from Europe. No means whatsoever is employed to preserve such a beneficial species, nor have we encountered any hives or other artifice to make them home-loving and domesticated. This abandon and indolence arise from the scarcity of large cities whose inhabitants would consume these and other infinite products such as cochineal, indigo, and the silk produced by worms and spiders, as well as the endless number of other

products. Thus the scant number of colonists are content to live in a rustic manner, sustaining themselves with a piece of meat and drinking their *aloja,* which is frequently made within the forests in the shade of the tufted trees producing the carob beans. There they hold their bacchanals, with *gauderios* spinning tales among themselves, as in their country festivals, where, to the accompaniment of their badly-strung and untuned guitars, they sing or bandy their ballads, which are more in the manner of obscene verses. If propriety permitted, I would repeat here some of the more extravagant ditties treating of love, all revealing the individual genius of the composer after warming himself with a draught of *aloja* and then increasing his glow with a second round, although this dessert is not the practice among the younger group.

The beginnings of their songs are usually of good harmony, considering their gross and barbaric manner, since they utilize ballads dreamed up and composed in the head of some merry wag. On a certain afternoon, when the inspector chose to mount horseback, he, in company with a guide, conducted us to one of those dense forests where there was gathered a sizeable troop of *gauderios* and their women, and he admonished us that we should partake of the laughter resulting from their nonsense without taking sides. The inspector, being a most skilled guide, approached first the assemblage, who greeted him in their particular mode, and asked license of them for him and his companions, who were weary from the excessive sun, to rest for a time in the shade of those bushy trees. They received us cordially, extending in their hands a cup of *aloja.* The inspector downed the concoction and we all followed suit, trusting in his good judgment. Four bumpkins vacated a log upon which they were seated and gallantly offered it to us. Two buxom damsels were swinging on ropes secured tightly to two thick trees. The others, numbering about twelve, were busily engaged in squeezing juice for their drinks, preparing maté, or slicing watermelons. Two or three men applied themselves to roasting, in the coals, pieces of half-dried meat, in company with some marrow bones, and finally, others were attempting to ready their guitars by splicing together strings made of scraped hide. An old man, who appeared to be 60 years old, but in reality enjoyed 104, was leaning against the foot of a bushy beech tree, whence he issued his commands, and, as he was of the opinion that time was nigh for lunch, he sat down and made inquiry of the women as to what detained them from serving their guests; the damsels replied that they were awaiting some cheese and honey to be brought from their houses for dessert. With this the old man was satisfied.

The inspector, unaccustomed as he was to warming his seat at any length, quickly advised the oldster that his entreaty had been badly put, "and so, Señor Gorgonio, may it please you to instruct the lads and lasses to sing some entertaining verses to the accompaniment of their harmonious instruments." "So be it," replied the venerable old man. "Let Cenobia and Saturnina be the first to sing, with Espiridión and Horno de Babilonia." They came forth gallantly, asking the aged one whether they should sing verses they had entoned during the day or compose others in their heads. Here the inspector spoke up, "It is the latter which would please me most, since they will be more witty." They sang 20 stanzas, which the old man labeled wretched, when in sallied Mother Nazaria with her daughters, Capracia and Clotilde, much to the pleasure of Pantaleón and Torcuato, who were scurrying about with some scorched meat. The inspector had already pulled out his watch two times, by which we all knew that it was his desire to leave, but the old man, realizing this, instructed Rudesinda and Nemesio to sing three or four of the ballads composed by the friar who had passed through the previous week. The inspector advised us to pay heed and that each of us memorize the stanza of most appeal to us. The first they sang contained, in reality, nothing worthy of repetition. The last four seemed to me deserving of print, as they were full of folly, and thus I shall reproduce them here, destining them to perpetual memory:

> *Lady:*   I'm familiar with your conduct
> And your many vile habits;
> You eat the choicest melons
> While you slip us cats for rabbits.

> *Gallant:*   Leave off the over-politeness;
> No one will oblige me with that!
> My belly's already stripped of its hair
> From going on all fours like a cat.

> *Lady:*   You are a big, boring dullard,
> Moved only to action by drink;
> At swallow number sixty-nine,
> You begin to raise a big stink!

> *Gallant:*   Let the whole tribe here clear the way,
> Including that elegant male;
> Let all of them leave who wish to,
> So I can clean my t——!

"The storm has broken," said the inspector, "and before the bolas begin to pelt down, there being no stones, it is best we return to our company." Whereupon we took our leave with considerable reluctance, as we younger members wished to witness the conclusion of the fiesta even if we had to stay up the entire night, but the inspector did not deem it wise, since he feared the results of the sixty-ninth drink! The joke about the cat for the rabbit seemed to us an invention of the friar, but the inspector advised us that although it was not much used in Tucumán, it was a popular phrase in Paraguay and on the pampas of Buenos Aires, and that those verses of original composition matched in excellence those sung by the old shepherds

of Arcadia despite the labors of Garcilaso and Lope de Vega.[1]
We expressed great wonder at the extravagant names of the
men and women, but the good old man informed us that these
were names of new saints which Don Cosme Bueno had introduced into his calendar, and that customarily the newly canon-
ized effected more miracles than the old ones who were weary
of pleading to God on behalf of men and women, a bit of folly
at which we all laughed, but made no attempt to rectify because
the inspector, placing his index finger across his mouth, made
a perfect cross. It gave us no surprise that the young men address each other as *macho* [male] as they do with any passer-by,
but it seemed improper that the young women be called
machas, whereupon the inspector informed us that in this manner of expression they were imitating the illustrious Quevedo[2]
who, with wit and propriety, spoke of the *pobres* and *pobras*
[poor], wherefore they say *machos* and *machas,* but applying
these terms only to young men and women.

These inhabitants, who comprise the greater part of Tucumán, would be the happiest in the world if only their customs
were more in accord with evangelical precepts, because the
country is delightful in its climate and the land thus produces,
with very little work, all the fruits which are planted in it. Wood
for the construction of dwellings is so plentiful that the inhabitants of the two largest kingdoms of Europe could be
housed, with fertile land to provide sustenance. The only lack
is that of stone for heavy structures, and seas and ports for
commerce, regularly spaced in order to facilitate the exchange
of their products; but the greatest need is for colonists, since
this fertile and expansive province has scarcely 100,000 in-

[1] Garcilaso de la Vega (1501?-1536), author of pastoral eclogues. Lope
Félix de Vega Carpio (1562-1635), best known as a dramatist, also composed pastoral verse and a pastoral novel, *La Galatea* (1585).

[2] Francisco de Quevedo y Villegas (1580-1645), writer of both prose
and poetry, is considered Spain's greatest satirist. Among his best-known
works are *Vida del buscón* (1626), a picaresque novel, and his vitriolic
Sueños (1606-1635), satirico-moral pieces describing his visions of hell.

habitants, according to the computation of those who have traversed the expanse. The two largest towns are Córdoba and Salta. The three encountered on the route, Santiago del Estero, San Miguel del Tucumán and Jujuy, together would scarcely comprise a town equal in size to Córdoba or Salta, and all five of them, each called a city, could not total a population equal to that of Buenos Aires. On fertile land, 100,000 inhabitants could make 20,000 units of five people each, from which there could be formed 200 towns of 100 units or 500 persons in each, and in a few years a multitude of small towns could be established along the abundant rivers found between Carcarañal and Jujuy.

There is no lack of water in this area, and although it is customarily absorbed into the ground, water wheels could be made with great facility, since the abundance of wood could provide trusses for the excavation of sizeable wells. The multitude of hides which are wasted could furnish plentiful buckets and cables, and the infinite number of livestock of all varieties could be employed in extracting the water with no other effort than that of changing them at certain times. The only expense of labor required would be in constructing reservoirs since there is a dearth of stone, lime, and brick, but in such a case, thick tree trunks could well be utilized, squaring them with hatchets or at least using them for foundations, as is the practice in Ica and other parts. There is no need for these wells to be of greater depth than one *vara*, provided their circumference be of sufficient size to accommodate the rancher or the group of settlers, and when this enterprise is considered of excessive difficulty and cost, an excavation may be made much like those formed naturally, which provide adequate pools from which cattle may drink, as has happened in the vicinity of the Tercero River and in numerous other parts of the realm. As I said before, it is certain that this kind of pool becomes inaccessible to all kinds of livestock except cattle, because with regular use by many animals, great mudholes are created on the edges in dry weather, something which would not take place in the reservoirs, since they do not depend on rain for their source of supply.

If one-hundredth of the small and wretched peasants of Spain, Portugal, and France had full knowledge of this country, they would abandon their own and transport themselves here: the Spanish Cantabrian, *de buena gana*, the Portuguese, *en boahora*, and Frenchman, *très voluntiers*—provided that our great monarch Charles would finance their trip with their tools for working the land and would extract from the royal treasury financial aid, which would be very slight, in order that each family might buy two yokes of oxen, a pair of cows, and two asses, designating certain land for their use for crops or pasture land, and keeping them within the limits determined by the size of the family. Thus the land could be well worked, not as is happening at the present, when one landowner has a parcel of 12 leagues' circumference, with his family capable of working only two of them, which results, as I have actually seen, in one or two meager families, taking up residence on the very edge of his ranch, settling in skimpy thatched huts which they build between dawn and dusk, with a scant shed to protect them from the rigors of the sun; and when asked why they did not construct more spacious and commodious dwellings, considering the abundance of wood, they replied that they built so to avoid being ejected from the place, or being forced to pay a high rent of 4 to 6 pesos each year. For these people such moneys are not obtainable, for even if they sell some chickens, eggs, or lambs to passers-by, this payment is not sufficient to provide the clothes which cannot be made by the women, the shoes, and a little Paraguay tea which they esteem as a real delicacy when consumed boiling hot and without sugar.

These wretched people, in a land of such plenty, know no other pleasure than Paraguay tea, tobacco, sugar, and liquor; therefore, they beg for them as for alms, as if succoring the sick, gladly giving their chickens and calves in exchange for

them rather than for coined money. For their meals they have
no set hour, and every one of these country rustics, if he is not
married, roasts his own meat which suffices for apéritif, entrée,
and dessert. On the banks of the river Cuarto there lives a man
who, not having the wherewithal to buy leggings or breeches,
daily kills a cow or a heifer to provide sustenance for seven or
eight persons, especially in the rainy season.

I shall explain how this meat is consumed. Two or three
young men go out to the fields to round up their cattle, and,
upon their return, bring one of the fattest of the cows or heifers,
which they then lock in the corral, kill with a knife, after having
bound its feet, and skin it wretchedly, exercising care only with
the four quarters and perhaps the skin and tongue; they then
hang these on the four corner posts of the corral, which are customarily made of strong trunks of the immortal *guarango* tree.
From these each individual cuts the portion necessary for his
repast, leaving the remainder hanging exposed to the elements,
vultures, and the multitude of flies. By four o'clock in the afternoon that fine family finds the meat already picked away and
filled with worms, because of which it is necessary that they
trim it away in order to utilize the meat next to the bones which
in turn are thrust into great fires and the marrow extracted; the
following day the same wasteful slaughter is executed, from
January to January. All this extravagance, which perchance will
astound all of Europe, is reduced to an intrinsic value of 8 reales,
considering the location of this country and its abundance.

Persons of little reflection will, of course, regard this wasteful
act as one to be coveted, particularly those poor people who
never eat, in an entire year, meat in a quantity sufficient for
their satisfaction. If they lived for six months in these regions,
they would be highly desirous of returning to their slender repast of a thin slice of bacon and some small chunks of salted
meat, pigs' feet, and ears, which they enjoy daily, like the
crumbs and salads of La Mancha and Andalucía, the difference
being that the colonists in this area, because of their laziness, do

not enjoy the fruits of their land, which could be produced with such little effort, while the above-mentioned poor people, for whom cattle raising is so dear, reserve their livestock to pay off their debts and taxes. In Europe, the slaughter, at Christmastide, of a cow or an old ox fattened through the winter, and two or three fat pigs, is the principal sustenance of a rural family of seven or eight members, to embellish their dried green and red beans, chick-peas and turnips from which they make abundant and sumptuous stews, in addition to the salads, cooked and raw alike, which are plentiful because of the family's industrious-ness, as well as chestnuts and porridges, all of which contribute to a diet of low cost and agreeable taste, to which are added, to excite the palate, spices such as garlic, onions, and some pepper, which the local barbarians lack, because of their indolence, in a country most propitious for the production of these spices. These local people are content thus, but they are useless to the state, since they do not increase their numbers through mar-riage, nor do they set foot in one spot with determination to establish towns capable of resisting invasions by the barbaric Indians.

The latter will never be vanquished with annual campaigns because a volant army of 2,000 or 3,000 men will do no more than drive the natives a short distance from the Chaco, and if they leave behind detachments—which will assuredly be small in number—they are exposed to the risk of being victims of the Indian multitudes, which will outnumber them 50 to 1. For the subjection of the latter, there is no other means than to enlarge our towns through marriage, confining the nomads within limited territories capable of abundantly supporting them and their cattle, obliging the proprietors of large estates to admit settlers for life up to a certain number, who will pay a small pension the first ten years and thereafter something more, in proportion to the return they realize from the quality of the land and their industriousness, though I believe it would be more satisfactory to do as is done in some European provinces, where the settlers pay their taxes with the fruits of the land itself such as wheat, corn, barley, for the farmers, while the shepherds and cattle raisers give cows and heifers, sheep, chickens, etc.; thus some of them make efforts to increase their productivity, eat better, and buy clothes with what remains.

If travelers but knew that these farmers waste bread, they would often save themselves the task of loading a supply for more than 30 days, as has happened to us several times, resulting in its being eaten green as alfalfa and so full of mold that it was necessary to destroy seven parts out of eight; and I say the same about other provisions essential for comfort and a life without misery. One who travels lightly, feeling the necessity of eating, is obliged to detain himself four or five hours while a lamb is brought from a great distance and a piece roasted; if he wishes it parboiled, in many areas scarcely any salt is to be found, and frequently not even a jar of water to drink, because farmers here have no provisions, living like the Isrealites in the desert, who could do nothing one day for the next, except Friday for Saturday, on which day all manner of work was prohibited by the ancient law. These farmers, rather *gauderios*, have no provisions other than a large slab of meat under their roofs or frequently exposed to the inclemencies of the weather, on which provisions depend all the pleasures of their lives. Their furniture is reduced to a miserable bed, a worse roof, a cooking jar, a roasting fork, a saddle, bridle, saddle cloth, rope, and bolas, essential only to riding horses and taking part in violent races and impertinent visits. These people, who constitute the largest part of the population of the vast and fertile province of Tucumán, should be subjected to a tax contrary to that so extravagantly imposed by the emperors of Mexico and Peru. These despotic rulers kept the vassals in continual movement and subject to an annual tax, but they employed the fantastic and barbaric scheme of certain disgusting and crude nations of collecting these taxes in lice, which in truth, increased the number of this species, because it was natural that these

subjects should attempt to foster their production. If Moctezuma and the last Inca had ordered that their loathsome vassals
pay one turkey or guinea pig for every louse found on their
bodies, they would have attempted to increase this useful and
tasty species and to wipe out the loathsome, dirty, and bother-
some one. I do not know whether these barbarians consider it a
delicacy to eat lice, but I am certain that at the present time they
are consumed by some Indian, mestizo, and Spanish mountain
women, although the latter conceal this ugly vice—just as those
pregnant women who have a mania for eating sweet-smelling
clay and pieces of adobe, the results of which are pitiful to behold. Finally, the inhabitants of Tucumán, in general, may be
compared to Pharaoh's cows which were skinny while living on
fertile pastures. The principal inhabitants of the province live
in a fashion sufficiently decent, especially in Córdoba and Salta,
rearing their children accordingly, sending them to school at
the appropriate time; thus they are outstanding subjects. The
remainder of the inhabitants there could live in a more civilized
manner. The majority of the women know the Quechua language in order to conduct affairs with their servants, but they
speak Castilian without the slightest difficulty, a fact which I
did not experience among the people of New Spain, and much
less of Peru, as I shall explain when I get to those countries,
through which I shall pass hastily. And while we are resting a
few hours in Quiaca, where the vast province of Tucumán ends,
awaiting the arrival of Mosteiro, a member of the commission
to Yavi, we shall make an imaginary trip through the pampas
to the capital of the kingdom of Chile.

CHAPTER IX

THE ROUTE FROM BUENOS AIRES TO SANTIAGO DE CHILE. THE
POSTS IN MENDOZA. THE INHABITANTS OF THE AREA AND
THEIR CUSTOMS. THE GAMES OF *CHUECA* AND
PATO. THE INCA'S BRIDGE.

ON the route from Buenos Aires to Saladillo de Ruy
Díaz the posts are as frequent as on the roads from
Potosí and Chile. Formerly the routes separated in the
town of La Cruz Alta, and some couriers crossed from El Pergamino to the point of El Sauce, taking their own horses, but
the inspector, under the advisement of experienced men,
ordered that they should be divided in Saladillo de Ruy Díaz,
for reasons of greater ease and security, up to the fortress
named El Sauce. Since it was imperative that the inspector assume charge of the general route to Lima through Potosí, he
commissioned Don Juan Moreno, a very active man, to establish
posts between the aforementioned Saladillo and Mendoza and,
in case of necessity, between Saladillo and the port of Valparaíso, charging him to follow instructions and observe the precautions he had suggested.

The couriers from Buenos Aires, who go to Chile, as well as
the passengers who travel with the post, can proceed from
Cabeza de Tigre to the pass of Saladillo with the same horses,
since it is a distance of only 7 leagues, and they may save themselves the delay of changing mounts at a short distance of 2
leagues, although it is always advisable to inquire of the
postilion about the place where the best and fastest horses may
be acquired.

The leagues from Saladillo to Mendoza perhaps may not be
well calculated because on this stretch there live few people of

keen observation, but it suffices to say that they are standard leagues, or at least so considered among the inhabitants. The great disparity in the posts is observed in the deserted areas, and those which it appears could have been omitted, due to the small number of leagues between, were established because of the colonists' continual moving from one place to another, and in order that there should be a subject whose duty it would be to provide horses to couriers and passengers. In the cross-country stretches to the frontier from the point of El Sauce, San Luis de Loyola, Corocorto, and from the turn-off for Ciénaga, it is advantageous, even essential, to provide oneself with a change of horses, taking measures to proceed as far as possible, and to travel the greatest distance between four o'clock in the afternoon and eight or ten of the following morning, due to the lack of water during the dry season.

The inhabitants between Buenos Aires and Mendoza occupy a vast, flat territory of generally firm surface. Their diversions, outside their homes, consist of playing the game of *chueca*[1] in a wild fashion and without order, inasmuch as, although they have a kind of net, there is only one ball which the numerous players hit in competition. Some players rush forward to lay hold of it, and since the ball, due to the disorder, does not always go in a straight line, there result cracked heads and, very often, injured legs and arms. They also play *pato*[2] in competent squads. One of the latter, between Luján and Buenos Aires, came up to the royal route around the hour of prayer, at the very time when Juan Antonio Casau was passing with some mules loaded with a considerable wealth, and after the animals had

[1] *Chueca.* A game, similar to hockey, played by two teams. The object was to drive a ball, struck with a club, across the opponent's goal line.

[2] *Pato.* A game in which two teams, on horseback, were aligned facing each other. A large ball, equipped with two handles and having a dead fowl inside, was tossed into the air. The riders scrambled to get the ball. The rider who succeeded held it by one handle, offering the other to the opposite team, while his own team tried to protect him and keep possession of the ball. The victor was entitled to keep the fowl for his meal.

been frightened and dispersed in various directions, it was discovered that a pouch of doubloons was missing, amounting to 3,200 pesos. After some assiduous efforts, he proceeded with the remainder of his cargo to Buenos Aires where, by good fortune, he found Don Cristóbal Francisco Rodríguez, to whom he recounted his misadventure, proclaiming the pouch a loss; but Don Cristóbal, without becoming perturbed, went to see the governor, who assigned him a convoy of dragoons to accompany him, along with the high constable. The rascal *gauderios* had broken open the pouch and divided among themselves the 2,000 coins which, in the darkness, they mistook for *pesos dobles*, this being the coinage normally circulated between Lima, Potosí, and Buenos Aires, where doubloons are seen only occasionally.

In the morning they were surprised to see that the white color had been converted into red, and believing that God, as a punishment for their crime, had reduced the pesos to copper medallions, they handed them over to their wives and sisters, with the exception of some youths, sons of an honorable man, who disappeared with a little more than 2,000 pesos. Without losing a moment, Don Cristóbal surrounded the district with his squadron and recovered all the doubloons except the 2,000 odd pesos which the clever young men had carried off, but their father, in a short time, made restitution, along with the corresponding costs. The other delinquents, who willingly allowed themselves to be apprehended, either because it seemed to them they were fulfilling their duty by handing over the loot, or because it seemed of little value, went off to labor for some years at construction work in Montevideo. It is certain that if Casau had not met with the ardor and keen dispatch of Rodríguez, he would surely have lost the larger part of the 3,200 pesos, since the former did not allow time for the *gauderios* to reflect on the matter and make inquiry of someone as to the worth of the medallions. In truth these rustic people, like those of Tucumán, are not inclined to steal, nor in all of Peru have any formal attempts been made on the numerous mule trains carrying silver or bars such as gold which are continually traveling throughout the kingdom with so little protection that a single man could put them to flight or do away with them, since it happens many times that two muleteers alone traverse large distances with ten loads of silver. Nothing more needs be said about this matter, but I advise the drivers of the money caravans which pass from Potosí to Buenos Aires that they exercise more precaution when they traverse the dense and extensive forests of Tucumán.

Along the route, as I said before, there is no lack of beef, mutton, and chickens, although they are found at extended distances, as may be seen on the itinerary; thus every passenger should carry provisions in accordance with the size of his family and the slowness of the journey, taking into account that there is a paucity of firewood in many parts, and it is often necessary to steal the large stakes from corrals, since the owners, who are not disposed to sell them, guard them tenaciously and with just cause in those regions distant from the willow groves which provide the only wood for constructing houses and corrals in those areas far from the river banks, for although an occasional forest is encountered, it is of peach trees, with short and twisted trunks, and other small trees of the same size. It is quite the opposite in Tucumán, from the Tercero River to beyond Jujuy, where whole trees may be burned for the sole purpose of the diversion of its inhabitants with their illumination, particularly between the entrance to Córdoba and that of Salta; but I wish to say in passing, since I forgot to note it in its proper place, that the passengers ought to spare from the fire those beautiful, bounteous, and lofty trees which Nature seems to have placed in the resting places for the relief and delight of travelers. I say this because many senseless persons derive simple pleasure from burning the best tree at night, after having delighted in its shade during the afternoon, all of which results from a lack of the slightest reflection.

The distance from Mendoza to Santiago de Chile measures 100 leagues, and although there is a postmaster in that city, he is reputed to be a common muleteer from among those in Chile, who are the best in both Americas, and by merely paying him for a change of mount, one can make the trip with light cargo in four days, in spite of the perilous and difficult slopes. In Mendoza one may take on provisions essential for the trip to the valley of Aconcagua, as was said before.

On this route there is nothing more noteworthy than the hazards and precipices, and a bridge called the Inca's bridge which consists of a huge boulder spanning the bed of the river, capable of detaining the waters which descend copiously from the mountain; it may be that one of the Incas ordered that boulder pierced or that the waters themselves made the excavation in their normal course. The vault of the boulder is very flat on the top and may be easily traversed to reach the skirt of the opposite hill, which is made up of stone slabs, and at the end of it, in a space the size of a bed sheet, there are a number of water holes, the water of which ranges from very cold to so hot that one cannot endure putting his fingers in it.

I deem it very wise that travelers determined to make their trips with muleteers request, from the owner of the herd, an attendant experienced on the route. He provides much relief for passengers who wish to journey in moderate comfort from Mendoza to the valley of Aconcagua. The servants, usually Negro slaves, taken by the passengers, are useless and almost harmful good-for-nothings, because in addition to their natural torpidity and lack of experience on the roads, they are so sensitive to the cold that frequently they stand fixed and frozen, and it is necessary to put them into motion with a crack of a whip, to saddle their horses and drag them from bed so that they may get dressed, just as happens occasionally to some Spaniard who must be provoked by some insult to arouse his ire and circulate his blood. The Chilean muleteers arise early in the morning in order to conclude their day's journey at four o'clock in the afternoon, when the sun has sufficient heat to warm and dry the sweat of their mules. At this stop, until the setting of the sun, they work at pitching the tents of the cargo owners. They make fires and bring water with great haste. The attendant conducts the passenger or passengers two hours ahead of the departure of the drove, taking supplies of food and necessities for feeding them at noon, and often earlier, in a comfortable spot situated at a distance of one-fourth of a day's journey and provided with water and firewood. The remaining three-fourths on rugged terrain is executed in five hours by one who travels lightly, so that if he departs at five o'clock in the morning, he arrives at ten o'clock, rests four or five hours and leaves for the completion of the jaunt at three or four in the afternoon, arriving at an hour when everything is all arranged for preparing supper and parboiling meat, which has already been dressed for the following noon. This attendant, in my time, earned only 5 pesos in the aforementioned 100 leagues, providing his own mule, and he made the trip with pleasure because he ate well and had less work than if traveling with the drove. He who can accustom himself to traveling behind the drove and eating cold food in order to save 5 pesos in 100 leagues, and to other discomforts, let him reject my advice and consider it useless at the expense of his inconveniences. Farewell, sir, I am returning to Quiaca without resting, after having traversed 728 leagues, round trip, in a few minutes, for it is as many more from Buenos Aires to Santiago which, according to my itinerary, is the capital of the fertile kingdom of Chile.

The general route from Buenos Aires to Lima, through Tucumán, proceeds in the following way, divided into provinces. Outside Quiaca begins the province of Los Chichas.

CHAPTER X

THIS province suffers from arid pasture lands and a paucity of provisions. Meat and other products are procured
from Tucumán and from some narrow valleys which
produce wine and brandy along with some dried vegetables;
but here, in its silver mines, begin the riches of Peru. Its silver
cones provide one of the principal sources for smeltings in the
great Potosí mint. This province has three names, which are
Santiago de Cotagaita, Tarija, and Chichas, the latter being the
name of the Indians who used to and still do occupy it. The
place called Mojo, belonging to Señora Doña Josefa Yribarre, is
situated on an elevation beaten by the winds, which form sizeable banks of sand in the streets and especially around her
house. There is a commodious inn, with no scarcity of chickens,
eggs, and some other meat products, which this lady keeps in a
store adjacent to the inn.

She liberally offers her house to any respectable person, and
in case of need she provides medicines and assistance. At the
entrance of her estate there is a river which gives no indication
of having much water, but is capable of supplying several mills
by means of a well-constructed and costly canal which this lady
has in order to supply the abundant waters necessary for the
operation of the mills, thus providing flour to the entire territory. . . .

In the town called Santiago de Cotagaita, of considerable
population, passengers may rest and take on necessary provisions, because in Escara, which is 4 leagues distant through a

ravine of very extended ascent and descent, on a somewhat stony road, but with good paths suitable for galloping, one finds only chickens and goats, which are not distasteful succor for those who carry the necessary condiments, along with bread and wine. Here one finds the first muleteers who carry cargo from Salta to Jujuy for these provinces and for Potosí as has been said. Between Escara and Quirve, a distance of 6 leagues, there is no water, and at the latter place begins the

Province of Porco

This province has many silver mines, the bullion of which, like that from Los Chichas, is sent to Potosí.

Through the Quirve ravine runs a stream of somewhat salty water, but wells of fresh water are not lacking. The road has two rather high hills, but is of good track. The remainder of the route is of loose stone suitable for traveling at a trot or a gallop. Between Quirve and Soropalca one crosses a river, having the name Grande, which waters the valley of Sinti. This valley produces some wine similar in color, taste, and strength to the common wine of Rivadavia, and also some brandy, part of which is bought by passers-by, while the rest is sent to Potosí and Chuquisaca. In a distance of one-half league the Grande River is crossed more than six times, due to the serpentine course of its bed; it is then joined by another river of half its volume, containing turbulent and somewhat salty water, named Torcocha. Here the Grande veers to the left and flows through the nearby town of Toropalca. Beyond there is another river called Pancoche, of fresh and frosty water, which is crossed more than 20 times, due to its windings and the fact that the royal highways traverse its bed. Heavy boots are of great utility in crossing these troublesome rivers, since otherwise the passengers become irritated at constantly raising their feet, considering it less bother to get wet, as happened to all of us with exception of the inspector who had, in addition to heavy English boots, some stirrups made in Asturias of strong wood, with iron bands, in which he thrust his foot up to the heel, protecting himself from all wetness; with these on his saddle, providing a hard seat, having no saddle cover or other protection, he went from Buenos Aires to Lima. On the journey he used neither poncho, cape, cloak, gloves, or sunshade, but always traveled well-protected by undergarments. He used to say that all other means of protection were a hindrance.

Two leagues before arriving in Caiza, there appear several large pools of hot water which would astonish anyone who was not forewarned, since each one makes as much noise as an ironsmith's forge, emitting water and smoke with the same force as the forge ejects smoke and sparks. At a short distance they had begun to construct a bathhouse in order to reap profits, but the owners, considering it folly, abandoned the undertaking since the residents of the only two towns, Potosí and Chuquisaca, have this resource nearer and more convenient, as I shall relate later. The town named Caiza is 12 leagues from Potosí, but rarely do the muleteers make this trip in one day. At 6 leagues along the regular highway is a place called Lajatambo, where passengers take lodging and are sold food at a very high price, with barley for the mules being the most highly valued, because the place is on a bleak tableland, and if the animals were turned loose in the field, they would foresake it and seek food in the distant ravine. Therefore no post has been established in this place which could be of the greatest importance, both for refreshing the mules and for lightening the day's trip, which in reality is very tiresome, because 4 leagues before arriving at Potosí there is so much loose stone that one cannot proceed at a trot without fatally injuring the mules of the wretched coal-mining Indians, who supply that great town with emaciated, crippled, and lame animals which are those commonly used for the mail route between the town and Caiza. It is fortunate that the couriers require only three mules, one saddled, one with the mail pouches, which are of little weight, and one for the postilion, which the poor fellow frequently spares by making the journey on foot so that his mule may rest.

After having rested two days in Potosí, the inspector asked for this diary, which he compared with his memoirs, finding it correct with regard to the posts and the distances, and although the treatise on mules seemed to him diffuse, he permitted that it stand because everyone does not understand the existing conditions. I preferred to delete the verses of the *gauderios,* but he would not allow it because that would deprive the public of the understanding and concept of the character of the *gauderios,* who cannot be appraised without their music and poetry. He merely made me replace the fourth stanza, since it had a double meaning, which could be applied to certain persons very distant from the *gauderios;* this I did quickly, just as I omitted many remarks, so as not to make prolix this first part of my diary, reserving them for the second part, which will begin in the great city of Potosí and conclude in Lima, the capital.

Part Two

CHAPTER XI

N OW, Señor Concolorcorvo," the inspector said to me, "you are in your own lands; I mean, in those frequented by your ancestors. From Los Chichas to Los Guarochiríes, where my commission ends, all the hills are bursting with gold and silver, of more or less fine quality, from which your forefathers benefited very little because, not having trade with other nations, they were able to fabricate great idols of gold in temples of silver, as well as the furniture of their Incas and chieftains, wherefore I say that the great riches which they are reputed to have buried or thrown into the lagoon, with the entry of the Spaniards, were either a ruse of the Indians or a dream of the Spaniards, or at least it was a misunderstanding. The Spaniards extracted more silver and gold from the entrails of this land in ten years than your countrymen did in the more than 2,000 in which they were established here, according to calculations of the most judicious men. Do not plan to make prolix your description of these areas, because even though they are more populated than those which we left behind, they are also much better known and traversed by the Spaniards who live between Lima and

Potosí

Nimborum patriam loca feta furentibus austris.

This imperial city was founded by the Spaniards at the beginning of the conquest, on a moderate hillock where the highland is divided by a ravine through which the waters descend and form a large stream of sufficient water to supply the buddles of all the estates which are on the edge of the hill, and these copious ditches facilitate transit from the town to the hill and the properties. The citizenry of the town and its bank is comprised of transient foreigners of all classes of people. The coldness of the territory is occasioned by its elevation and proximity to the snow-covered hills which surround it and cause discomfort on windy days, but the houses of the Spaniards and mestizos are adequately protected with their small rooms and the screens which divide them, to which they add the comfort of repeated steam baths and matés of hot water, drunk continuously by the women, and offered as a treat to the men at all hours. It is said that after the discovery of the wealth in that great hill, 15,000 Indians were assigned to work on it and the estates in which silver is exploited.

The decline in the fineness of the metals, or some other causes, reduced this number to 3,500, which is the current number, the majority of them with their wives and children, making a total of over 12,000 souls, counting those staying voluntarily and engaging in the honorable exercises of Chalcas,[1] who are robbers that raid the mines at night and, since they are experienced, extract the most precious metals, which they process and take to the bank that the King maintains for purposes of redemption; to be sure, these pirates extract much more of the silver than the owners of the mining property. Although the hill of Potosí is in great decline today, due to the lack of fineness of the metals, the foresight or diligence of men inclined to search for riches in the heart of the earth has discovered in the provinces of Los Chichas, Porco, and others nearby, minerals of higher quality which contribute to the royal treasury of Potosí.

In spite of such great wealth, there is not a sumptuous building in this town, except for the present mint, financed by the Crown, which is truly magnificent, being a model of the one in

[1] *Chalcas.* A Greek soothsayer who had the Trojan horse built and assisted in the siege of Troy.

Lima in the lower floors and some upper chambers, but the remainder, including the quarters of the superintendent, is composed of small rooms. The present superintendent adorned the façade with balconies of great projection, in imitation of the prows of old warships. These are supported by figures too ugly to be angels and not horrible enough to be devils, but they facilitate access to the superintendent's rooms which open into the rest of the building, thus making possible a robbery of considerable proportion. This fine city has always been governed by distinguished persons, what with the superintendency of the mint and the bank. It has its secular council, composed of *alcaldes* and several councilmen, for which honorable posts they engage any outsider whatsoever, possessing no qualifications other than a white face and sufficient means to support himself with propriety.

The post is administered by Pedro de la Revilla, a clever young man, fertile with ideas. It was divulged in Potosí that he had been a puppeteer in Spain, because they saw him doing some feats of legerdemain. "For just as much," said the inspector, "Don Pedro Sánchez Villalba, a man of more renown in this kingdom than Revilla, was denounced in Popayán and called before the Inquisition; but the difference in the two cases is that the people of Potosí did it with malice, while those in Popayán out of ignorance. A certain buffoon in Arequipa proved that Don José Gorosabel was descended from Jews, because he read in the book of lineage of the greatest man who ever was, or will be, in the world, the following words: *Sabathiel, autem genuit Zorobabel.* The fact is, Señor Concolorcorvo, that in 100 men you will scarcely find one who is not a puppeteer; and therefore, laugh at the residents of Potosí and Popayán with their two Pedros, applaud four P's as memorable as those in Lima, congratulate Gorosabel that Matorras has related him to the *Romaníes,* and then continue your discourse without giving attention to bagatelles."

Because of the large number of Spaniards who live in this

town, it is always well stocked with food supplies which come from the extensive valleys. The dried eels brought from the coast of Arica may be considered the best fresh fish, and they are sold at a moderate price, as are other delicacies brought in because of the heavy consumption, it being certain that they will not spoil because at a short distance from the coast or valley they cross a tableland so bleak that tainting is impossible. The cold becomes penetrating with the slightest wind because the town is surrounded by snow-capped hills, as I said before, and although the rains are copious, the streets do not become impassable, owing to the unevenness of the terrain which causes the water to run off on the regular pavements.

The distich at the head of this chapter expresses in large part the discord forever existing among the principal residents. This is converted into silver (*plata*) which goes to the tribunals of the city of the same name, La Plata. The principal luxury of this city, as is the case in all other large cities in the kingdom, is composed of magnificent clothing; there is a common lady here who has more dresses adorned with gold and silver than the Princess of Asturias.

No town on the highway has as great a need of a post as Potosí, because in its outskirts and surrounding area there are no muleteers, due to the scarcity of pasture. Those drivers who come with products from distant provinces arrive with their mules so maimed that they can scarcely support the harness. The animals of the Indians who supply coal daily are in worse condition. The Indians from Yocalla, who used to return their mules in the time of the Count of Castillejo, have withdrawn because the stop now made in Potosí is so short that they do not have time to go to their town, which is 10 leagues distant over a bad road, to bring back four times the number of mules to carry out the commissions of gold and silver, wherefore the postal administrator of that town finds himself obliged to seek mules from the magistrate, which is carried out through his servants and petty officers in a tyrannical fashion against the muleteers and coal carriers who deserve the greatest compassion. The inspector had cut short this notable mischief when the bakers of the town, who usually have fat and refreshed mules in their corrals, were obliged to provide them at the regular price, with the one condition that they be exempt from a contribution that they made annually to a profane festival, which would be a better service to God if it were eliminated; but his efforts were frustrated because they were opposed by a certain minister with a negative spirit.[2] These first steps taken by the inspector for the establishment of the mails in Potosí, although they did not dishearten him, did make him regard the success of his visit with suspicion, but as soon as he finished with matters relative to the operation of that post, he resolved to proceed to Chuquisaca to establish the one there which had been leased, since the time of the Count of Castillejo, for the sum of 200 pesos per year. This trip is 25 leagues . . . .

This cross-country stretch has 8 or 9 leagues of running road, that is, suitable for trotting or galloping. The remainder is of loose rock, flat stones, and hills, with the road demanding constant attention. Four leagues out of Potosí there is a very good inn, little used at the present time, because a short distance away, in a very delightful spot, is a house called Los Baños. The latter is, in reality, more than adequate and very well built, with good rooms, an arrangement of corrals for the horses, and a supply of straw. The bath is in a rectangular room, with an arched ceiling, and has a depth of 1 pike at the first ladder by which one descends. The water comes up over 1½ *varas*, and is brought in through a canal of the same height. It is naturally warm, and although it is said to be healthful and medicinal for certain infirmities, the inspector thinks it is very harmful,

2 The minister referred to could well be José Antonio de Pando, the Administrator of Mails in the Viceroyalty of Peru and Alonso Carrió's superior. The two men were in constant conflict over matters pertaining to the administration of the postal system.

morally and physically as well. Morally because men and women bathe together promiscuously, without notice or heed on the part of the administrator, as we have observed, the result of which is extremely disorderly conduct, even among persons who are not acquainted. Physically, because healthy and sick persons bathe in the same water for three or four days without its being changed or evaporated, because the room is so well enclosed that scarcely the necessary amount of air can enter lest it snuff out the artificial lights which remain gloomy or almost dying among the multitude of vapors exuded by the hot, nitrous waters and the sick and healthy bodies.

This barbaric innovation is what attracts the multitudes, although there are a few distinguished families who take the precaution of bathing in pure water, with the foresight to wash and sweep the room, and to open the doors and windows so the vapors may escape; but these families are rare, and even rarer are the cases in which they go to enjoy its benefits, considering it only as pleasure and not as a remedy for their ailments. . . .

Tambo Nuevo, New Inn, is really new, inasmuch as it was completed a few days before we passed the spot. It has two rooms for travelers, capable of lodging 20 persons comfortably, with corrals for the animals, a kitchen and a store stocked with articles most needed by common people, but often bought also by respectable and wealthy men. This is the only place on the stretch which can provide mules plentifully for the couriers and private individuals, but since the former promise little profit, the owner cannot pay heed to them, and so he applies himself only to storing barley for the passers-by and to the sale of some foodstuffs and brandy; the result of the first-mentioned provision is that the owner of the inn, with his excess supply of straw and barley, maintains three or four mules for his own use and for fitting out couriers.

In this short stretch, in which the inspector did not deem it wise to establish more than the two aforementioned posts, there are more than ten small inns, equipped with rustic rooms and common supplies for men and animals. In the Honda ravine is an inn which is usually the best stocked on this entire road. It has a good main room, with two sleeping alcoves and four good beds, but this room is available only to people of royal or apparent distinction, because ordinary and common men usually exhibit such crudeness in speech that it offends the ears and sight of a noble subject accustomed to a dissolute life, wherefore the owner forbids this room to men of low class or those who show the same by their manners. Besides the indecencies which they write on the walls with charcoal, there is not a table or a bench in which these fools have not carved their first and last names with blows of iron instruments. This practice is very old, having been used among the pilgrims from distant countries to give notice of their route to those who might be searching for them along the royal road, by putting dates on the walls of the hostelries; it has become so common in America that there is not an inn or cave which is not adorned with names and obscene words.

In the public inns of the posts this abuse ought to be stopped by a pecuniary penalty, proportionate to the degree of insolence, making certain the *mitayos* warn the travelers of the penalty they will incur with such inscriptions and other indecencies which they do in the rooms, which disgust people of good breeding and result in their abandonment of the public inns. The *corregidores* and *alcaldes* should be vigilant of such a policy, as useful in the moral as in the political sphere, formulating tariffs for its observation, with corresponding penalties, which should be put into effect in every town or inn situated in a deserted spot, not fining the offenders or concealing the fines from them until the penalty imposed by a competent judge has been satisfied. This justifiable means would be very useful to society as would that rule forbidding anyone to convert the rooms into a kitchen, or to put horses in them; in this way they would not be ruined so senselessly because of the acquiescence of the *mitayos*, but instead each traveler would use the common corrals and assign to one servant or paid *mitayo* the care of the horses of his personal use or esteem.

From Tambo Nuevo travelers usually go to the banks of the great river Pilcomayo to eat and to nap. One descends to it by means of a perpendicular slope one-fourth league long although without great risk because it has good footing. The ravine is hot and pleasant. On the Potosí side are several farms with small fields of maize and barley. If a flood occurs, even if it is not copious, the river will carry away houses, effects, and inhabitants. These fine people, in addition to reaping the scanty fruits of their small farms, engage in the service of river pilots, because those who go through Potosí to Chuquisaca—which is the greater number—commonly cross the river at this ford; but the settlers try to ruin it by digging several wells so that those travelers who are avaricious or overly audacious will fall into the trap, often at the risk of drowning, and the devil will take away their resolution, or as the old Spaniards used to say, "their nag and apples." These settlers, who consider themselves Spaniards, although they have a mixture greater than chocolate, reserve a canal or winding path with which they alone are acquainted, as experienced pilots; this occurs on all the rivers in this extensive realm. If someone traveling lightly finds himself obliged to cross the river alone where there are no pilots, and has a mule or track horse, he should let himself be guided by the animal's instincts or experience, because otherwise, if he tries to be governed by his natural reason, he exposes himself to losing his life, since the animal, frightened by the bit and spur, will leap headlong. One-eighth of a league from the ford, traveling on the opposite shore, one sees very clearly the famous river bridge used in going to Chuquisaca. I do not believe there has ever been a work made which is more sumptuous and impertinent; that famous bridge is used only by the muleteers who cross from Escara to Chuquisaca, avoiding Potosí.

The bridge is magnificent, strong and adorned on its edges by stone tablets with inscriptions bearing the names of the ministers whom the royal *Audiencia* of Chuquisaca assigned to its completion. The water tends toward the bank of the hill belonging to Potosí. In the direction of Chuquisaca there are several canals or branches off the main stream of the river. The bridge ends at the banks of the main channel, perhaps for lack of materials. The maestro knew very well that his work was not complete, as did the last minister who was superintendent of it, and to mitigate the disease which is difficult to cure—that is, the lack of money—he threw in some barricades so that the water, when striking them, would direct its course to the opposite hill, passing through the main channel covered by the only complete arch of the superbly elevated bridge, which is of little use in normal weather since the river has a ford. It is useful in times of floods because it is surrounded on the Chuquisaca side by some branches into which the river overflows because its waters are not accommodated in the main channel. In spite of the fact that the bridge is incomplete, the inspector said it could be very useful in many cases of extraordinarily high water, when it would facilitate the fording of two or three canals better than crossing the entire river along an extended beach full of wells and excavations made in the sand by the water. The inspector said that the road which the architect made over the hill of Chuquisaca was not as superfluous as the commoners had thought, because in case the canals turned their flow to the ravine, that road would then provide the means to protect and free oneself from the water holes and dangers by taking a short detour. The idea of this bridge is very good, but it could not be finished in this kingdom and province abundant in silver, but lacking in settlers and products.

After the great Pilcomayo comes the Cachimayo, which passes through an extensive ravine, most delightful and populated; this is the Aranjuez of Chuquisaca. It is populated on both banks; towards Potosí are several poor settlers who sustain themselves with small crops. The Chuquisaca side has some scattered houses with tile roofs and an expanse of land, much

like the ancestral mansions of Cantabria. They are inhabited
by families who come down from Chuquisaca to amuse themselves on the banks of the Cachi River, which has nothing artificial because no one chose any portion of that place for pleasure
or magnification. This river is very voluminous, and when we
crossed it in the dry season, we found in its ford as much water
as in the neighboring Pilcomayo, the only difference being that
the Cachi has a more solid bed and channels where one crosses;
but in time of high water, couriers and passengers are detained
several days because it does not even have the half-bridge of
Pilco. At neither river did we see fishing equipment in the
houses of the inhabitants, which may be the result of their
abandon and scorn for such a useful industry, or perhaps it is
because of the rapid current of the two rivers on the beaches of
these inhabitants who have too little industry and an area too
small to form channels and fish weir for providing the delicacy
of fish to two places of such large population as the town of
Potosí and the city of La Plata.

CHAPTER XII

LA PLATA. DESCRIPTION OF THE CITY. THE GOLD IN
THE HILLS.

LA PLATA is the name of the capital of the extensive district of the royal *Audiencia* of Chuquisaca, which is composed of several robed ministers and a cape-and-sword president, it being commonly said that these men make themselves so respected that they give orders to the ordinary *alcaldes* and the regiment of their servants and ministers—and when one of them goes walking, the merchants close their shops in order to accompany him and festoon him until he is restored to his home. Because of this it is said that a certain pious and devout matron designated in her last testament an amount appropriate for the acquisition of a robe for the Holy Sacrament in the Court, reproaching the residents because they went out to accompany the judges, but were satisfied to make only a bow when passing the Sacred Host which was being carried to a sick person. I believe this satire was unwarranted. Recognizing the seriousness of the public ministry is natural, as is also showing respect, although it is violent among some subjects. There is something of artifice in all of them, the only difference being that the ministers believe such obsequiousness is due them, and the public, seeing that it is artificial, vituperates what is done for their convenience and particular interest, and exaggerates the vanity and arrogance of some men who never thought of such submissiveness. I do not know what has happened in years past, but at the present time we submit that these ministers, while maintaining their stern mien, are very considerate and courteous in the street, and in their homes they are very polite and acquiescent in everything which is not contrary to good manners and civility.

The city of La Plata is situated on a bubble or swelling of the earth surrounded by a ravine of little depth, which is narrow, barren, and encompassed by a chain of hills, perfect in its orbicular form, thus seeming like a work of art. Its climate is mild; its streets, wide. The palace in which the president lives is a large house, falling apart in many places—which shows its great antiquity—as is likewise the house of the council or secular government. There are many large houses which may be considered palaces, and the inspector believes it is the best-planned city of all he has seen; with respect to the fairer sex, it has as many polished ladies as can be found in Potosí, Oruro, Paz, Cuzco, and Guamanga. It is true that the climate is beneficial to the complexion. The communication with men of letters makes the ladies well informed, and the gatherings of litigants and rich priests bring the best statues and engravings from the surrounding areas, and frequently from great distances. We did not go into the archbishop's palace because the abodes of the ecclesiastics are not as manifest as those of the seculars. The former, being more somber, instill a sacred fear; the latter invite mortals with their gaiety.

The cathedral is on the main square. The building is ordinary, and it is obvious that it was built before the bishopric was so opulent. Its interior adornment had one special feature which none of us observed, nor have we seen anyone else take note of it, except the inspector, who tried to find out from us what the special attraction was in that church. One said that it was the many mirrors with silver corner-bands which adorned the main altar. Another suggested the beautiful silver candlesticks, and thus everyone gave his opinion, but the inspector told us we were all blind since we had not observed an evident marvel and peculiarity which would not be seen in any church in the Spanish dominions.

The marvel is that although the candlesticks are made of

a metal as heavy as silver and are 2 *varas* in height, with a proportionate thickness, an acolyte no larger than my arm from
the hand to the elbow handles them and hangs them without
any artifice. In this there is a great mystery; but leaving aside
this wonder, the explanation of which is of little importance to
me, I am going to expound on the peculiarity of this church by
asking you if you have ever seen one in all your travels which
did not have something hanging from the vault, the ceiling, or
some transverse beam. The poorest church in Spain has one
hanging lamp, although it may be of bronze or copper, but the
greater part of the churches in large cities are filled with lamps
and chandeliers suspended from hemp ropes, subject to fire or
some other accident, which, if they break, may cause death to
some devout person occupying a place directly beneath the
lamp, chandelier, or lantern, not to mention the stains caused
by the oil, wax, or hot embers which fall from the candles.

Let no one think that what I am saying is a satire. I declare
that if I lived in Chuquisaca, I would not go to worship in any
church except the cathedral—to save myself the necessity of
searching for a spot free from danger—which greatly arouses
my imagination. Let us suppose that this is exaggerated, and
that there is little risk of losing one's life or receiving a blow
causing great pain and a prolonged recovery. But how can we
protect ourselves from the staining drops of wax which fall
from the lighted candles in the chandeliers, the hot embers and
other discomforts caused by the servants of the church at the
time the Divine Office begins, which is when the fantastic illumination is in effect and just when people are settled in the
places they selected? Some of superficial intellect will say that
the illumination is directed toward the grandeur of the sanctuary for the magnification of the Lord. I do not doubt that in
certain cases these outward acts move the people to the sub-
mission and respect due the divinity; but it seems to me that
these acts should be proportionate to the seriousness with
which cathedrals are usually governed. In them is observed a

pomp which breathes grandeur. The circumspection of the ministers, the seriousness and silence transcend all coincidentals.

An elaborate illumination scattered throughout the church offers only smoke instead of incense. The multitude of figures of angels and saints, richly adorned, do no more than occupy half the church and distract the people, so that they do not apply themselves to what they should and what is best for them, being attracted merely by means of curiosities consisting of artifice, theater, music, or pastoral dance.

In conclusion, the city of La Plata, as I have said, is the most beautiful and the best planned in all of this viceroyalty. Its climate is mild; the manner of the people is pleasant. Everything necessary for spending a life of comfort abounds; and although everyone generally agrees that water is scarce, due to the small spring which provides it, we have observed that in most of the principal houses there is in the patio a fountain, or *pila* as they say here, with one water spout, or at least a trough, which they make available to the common people without becoming irritated at their disturbances and crudeness, so that ministers and distinguished persons enjoy the privilege of getting together only at the expense of continuous noise and inexcusable quarrels. If the shortage of water were as great as some people think, they would have invented cisterns or reservoirs, collecting water which the heavens send annually in great abundance to this hardy territory where they could be built at little expense. All the roofs are of tile or brick, with the necessary slope so that in the rainy season the waters will descend with force, after the roofs have been washed by the first downpour, by means of one or two pipes, with the reservoirs being covered so that snow, hail, and the sand and dirt raised by storms will not penetrate them. All naturalists agree that the best water is that which comes from the sky, falling in rain on a calm day, and thus it is necessary that they also agree on the construction of reservoirs or cisterns for storing it; wherefore,

if the proprietors of the principal houses of Chuquisaca which have no water would choose to have a reservoir built, at little expense, the inhabitants would drink the best water which comes down to earth.

I suppose that those who are privileged to have water, or a *pila*, would not think of contracting this expense, but I caution them that the water from the fountains is less salutary than rain water, and even that of rivers which run through the territories free of saltpeter. The fountains in the large cities, besides the impurities which they bring from their sources, pass through suspicious conduits that are very filthy in some parts. The water which descends from serene clouds, and is caught in clean cisterns at the opportune time from the clean roofs, is the finest and conforms most to Nature, or else all the experimental philosophers have been deceived. I confess that this collection of water could not serve other purposes except at great expense. The watering of gardens and potted plants, the cleaning of the house, the kitchenware, the bedrooms, and particularly the watering place for horses and mules, all use a considerable amount of water, and if ditches do not run through the public and private streets, it would be necessary, in all those towns which Nature did not favor with rivers or springs sufficient for their needs, to seek it in distant deposits. This same reflection makes manifest the utility of reservoirs or cisterns, and the preservation of rain water in a territory like Chuquisaca and others of equal size and need of expedients.

The post of this city was being leased by a local resident with the sole obligation of paying 200 pesos annually for the income of the commissions and the correspondence by land; the inspector, reflecting that the royal treasury was being gravely injured, and at the same time that it was necessary to determine the legitimate income in order to formulate a regulation founded on good reason, named Don Juan Antonio Ruiz de Tagle, an intelligent, very formal man, as administrator of that post, temporarily assigning to him 15 per cent of the liquid proceeds of that office. With this matter concluded, the inspector asked for pack animals so he could continue his ministration. But before leaving, it seems proper for me to inform the public, and even the general directors, of the income from the postal system, of the differences existing between the ministers of good character and learning and the other inferior judges, generally without education or an iota of meditative power.

The inspector presented himself to the president and the royal *Audiencia* residing in this capital in order that the back carrying-charges of the official correspondence might be paid out of the fines forfeited to the royal treasury, and that a clear and sound method might be established for the future. These men, unjustly accused of being haughty and vain, are slow in their deliberation, and they decreed in the morning that this matter should be discussed, in the presence of the inspector, by Señor Lisperguer, the senior judge of said royal *Audiencia*, and Señor Alvarez de Acevedo, the treasurer. The same day it was arranged with the inspector that he should come, on the afternoon of the following day, to the house of Lisperguer, where he found Acevedo, and in less than a quarter of an hour, all doubts and difficulties were resolved; on the third day a writ was dispatched ordering that the legitimate official correspondence should be paid from the registered fines; and, in view of the lack of formality with which the lessee had kept records on the maritime correspondence, it was ordered that, in order to remove any doubt whatsoever for the new administrator, a royal notary should appear with the arrival of all couriers, whether by land or sea, and leave a formal receipt for all official parcels, designating their weight and value; other matters were clarified in the said decree, and a duplicate testament was given to the inspector, one of which was left for the administrator of the post of Chuquisaca, for his direction.

With considerable sadness on the part of us all, we left this city, so pleasant in all its aspects, and the inspector advised us that we should again join him in familiarizing ourselves with the cross-country stretch, which we found similar to the observations we had made on the trip to Potosí. Just as we departed from Chuquisaca, or I should say, from the city of La Plata, with reluctance, so we had left Potosí with pleasure, not so much because of its harsh climate as for the discord of the inhabitants. Rare are the men who maintain perfect, friendly relations for a whole week. One whom they applaud in the morning, they vituperate in the afternoon, over the same matter; they are consistent only in their amorous passions, because of which it has been the experience of real coquettes to make favorable progress, and more than four of them, after being in these parts only a few years, have been seen to retire from illicit business with a comfortable living, forcing their last lover to marry them, or seeking a husband from those who adjust to anything and have a good head, or one who is of the opinion that what he does not know, cannot hurt him.

Upon leaving this memorable town, the commissioner advised us to observe the labyrinth formed by the Indian cabins with their many paths, and the facility with which a load of silver could be embezzled on a dark night, or even on a clear one, because the Indians, upon leaving Potosí, drunk on *chicha* and brandy, turn the mules loose, and each one takes a separate path; for this reason it was decided that the couriers should leave Potosí at twelve o'clock noon, or within two hours either way. From this town one proceeds to Oruro by way of the following posts.

CHAPTER XIII

THE PROVINCES OF PORCO, POOPO, AND ORURO. THE
LEASING OF THE POST. INFRACTIONS OF THE PRIVILEGE.
THE CITY AND ITS CUSTOMS.

THE exit from Potosí and the San Bartolomé ravine are
at the present time passable at a trot because of the
road's having been restored, although in parts it is so
poorly repaired that with the first inundation it will be as it was
before. On this trip, up to Yocalla, there are two hills in the
form of an S, very difficult to traverse because the greatest part
is of flat stone slabs; but at the last descent to the town is a
very sturdy and beautiful stonework bridge, the second of this
kind, which will last forever if there is not some extraordinary
disturbance of the land and if the *corregidores* and other
officers do not fail to repair it after an irruption of the water
and the continual traffic of the pack trains. In all this distance
there is no danger of a sudden fall. The town of Yocalla is the
vice-parish of the curacy of Tinquipaya. There is no inn for
lodging travelers. The Indians have quarters which seem like
caves or ovens, in which one may, with difficulty, put a small
bed-sack to make a narrow bed, with all the baggage remaining
piled up in the narrow and small patio, and in spite of this
misery—to which Indians adjust themselves better than any
other race—they built a large house with numerous rooms,
patios, inner patios, and corrals to lodge, just six days out of a
year, their priest and lieutenant who come to celebrate their
festival days and to collect the taxes; therefore the inspector
advises couriers and travelers to take possession of one or two
of the many rooms in this house, to secure their loads and to
rest, utilizing the corrals and the kitchen, so that the household

gods may be nourished by the smoke. The Indians of this town
are industrious and quite intelligent. Formerly the couriers of
the King paid for only 9 leagues from here to Potosí, and the
inspector, considering how much these wretched persons' mules
toiled in the ascent, ordered it was 10 leagues both ways for
computing the charge, which was the same as adding 2 leagues,
although on the itinerary it is not more than 1.

The remainder of the road, as far as Oruro, is suitable for a
fast trot and without danger. The inns have no doors. The mules
are thin because the country is barren, and the smaller animals
and the freezing snow destroy what little pasture exists. The
trip from Las Peñas to Oruro was 9 leagues in length, which the
weakened mules of the poor Indians could not make without
rest, wherefore the inspector divided the one from Yruma in
two at the intermediate Venta, putting the latter in charge of a
governor, an Indian chief, who is perhaps one of the most
privileged in the kingdom. The latter immediately ordered that
sufficient materials be brought to construct a comfortable
dwelling, independent of his house which he regularly opens to
any honorable man; but the present *corregidor*, whom I do not
choose to name to save him ridicule, and much less to expose
him to punishment, opposed a benefit which had been done at
the petition of the Indians of his province, under pretexts so
frivolous and ridiculous that it causes one shame to relate them.
At 5 leagues from the intermediate Venta, and 4 from Oruro,
is a town named Sorafora, where the inspector intended to
divide the other post; but since the Indians are engaged only
in the transportation of metals to supply the great smelter of
Don Diego Flores, they use only llamas, having no mules because they do not need them for other purposes; thus the trip
remained at 9 leagues to

Oruro

This town follows Potosí in size, because in it is the royal
treasury in which they melt annually over 600 bars of 200

marks of silver, of a fineness of 1,100 pennyweights and 22 grams, which is worth 1.2 million pesos, more or less. The greater part is a product of the mines of the nearby river banks because the large hill, contiguous to the end of the same town and so convenient for reaping the benefits of its metals, has diminished in quality, considering what is needed to finance the labor due to the lack of water for its buddles. This fine town is situated in the middle of a pampa of almost 9 leagues' extension, the greater part of which is nitrous and marshy. The principal foodstuffs are supplied by the fertile valley of Cochabamba, as well as Potosí. Sugar, wine, and other beverages, as well as olives, dried fruits, and almonds, are brought from a great distance; nevertheless, these products are sold at a moderate price because the large consumption attracts an abundant supply, whence the low price most of the year.

The post was leased to a good old man who said he was a relative of the Counts of Castillejo. He had four *mitayos*, who were for no advantage or utility other than that of acquiring mules, that is, stealing them from the poor drivers for the dispatch of mail and passengers and locking them in a large corral guarded by servants of the *corregidor* and *alcaldes*, who comprised among themselves a competent band of robbers, collecting four times the mules that they needed; and the owners found themselves obliged to redeem the animals with silver, which those inhuman subordinates divided among themselves, leaving locked up, for the service of the couriers, the mules of the poorest drivers, which are consequently the thinnest and most maimed. There are really no words to describe this tyranny. The drivers were often forced to undersell some mules in order to feed those locked in a corral which had scarcely any manure for the journey of 8 or 9 leagues at a fast trot with double load that awaits them; as a result some mules did not arrive at the other post because they fell exhausted, while others arrived with broken backs and almost incapable of bearing the harness long enough to restore themselves in the pasture. The news of this cruelty spread to the drivers who profited from the business of supplying this town, and if they judged that the couriers were about to enter or leave, they stopped at a few leagues' distance so as not to exhaust their tired and thin mules, wherefore the town was frequently lacking in some provisions. A general and well-grounded complaint from the residents and from outsiders obliged the inspector to solicit an honest resident to accept the postmastership, to provide horses for riding and pack in that town, to the couriers of His Majesty and to travelers.

The idea of the inspector turned out so felicitously that he could have found no subject more suited than the person of Don Manuel de Campo Verde y Choquetilla, a Spaniard, descended through maternal lineage from the legitimate chiefs and governor of the Indians. It is true that this idea was suggested to him and corroborated by his intimate friends Don Joaquín Rubín de Zelis and Don Manuel de Aurrecoechea, in whose house Don Alonso was lodged. The *mitayos* of the former lessee of the post had made a strong complaint in writing against the latter, because he did not pay them for their work, nor for the service of their wives in the maintenance of his household. The inspector gave the title of postmaster to Governor Choquetilla with an attestation of the royal ordinances, so that he might be presented to the secular council, and the privileges accorded to him as postmaster by His Majesty might be made clear; but when the inspector expected the *corregidor* and the council to offer him their thanks for such an important service, he was met with the opposition which the *corregidor* had built up. The latter was a captain of more than 70 years of age, whose name Don Alonso ordered me not to reveal in my itinerary so as not to expose him to the scorn of everyone; I shall follow this policy with all the others who reject royal ordinances, and I shall not give the motives of this *corregidor* and others for such transgressions, because it gives me shame to relate them; but in order not to involve the magistrate and officer of justice in Oruro in this matter, I should say that at the next council meeting they received the aforementioned postmaster, in spite of the objection of the *corregidor*.

The inspector had already given an account to the superior government about the results of the first council, and in the next mail he received an express mandate from His Excellency, ordering that the subject named by the commissioner be received as postmaster. We were all astounded to see the opposition of these inferior judges to royal ordinances, and when the inspector perceived our criticism, he told us we were novices, little acquainted with the maxims and arrogance of the greater part of these petty *corregidores* of so little learning, adding that a few days earlier the one in La Paz had incarcerated the lessee of the post because he did not hand over to him his franked letters, which he took without paying anything, turning over the rest of the mail to plunder. It is known by everyone that the lessees of any branch whatever of the royal exchequer enjoy the same privileges as the administrators. The administrator in Cuzco, named by the superior government, was arrested by the *corregidor* because he resisted the latter in not obeying his orders concerning economic regulations about the arrival and departure of couriers, and was held prisoner in the council house, leaving abandoned a royal office in which there were interests not only of the King but of the public in the form of retarded correspondence and other confidential papers.

"I do not wish to give more examples, but rather that you should reflect on the gravity of these excesses and other more serious ones to which private individuals, who enjoy no special privileges, will be exposed, particularly the people of lower station; and in conclusion, I can assure you that, with the exception of a small number of intelligent *corregidores* with whom I have communicated in my more than 20 years in these provinces, all the rest have seemed to me to be fools, wherefore I believe any folly that is told about them." "On what is this change in men founded?" I asked the inspector. "That is, what makes docile men of gentle manner become harsh and arrogant?" "There is no such change," he replied. "Most men are a herd of madmen. Some are violent and one flees from them; others are funny and one amuses himself with them. And the rest are cunning and restrain their fury out of cowardice or the fear of meeting greater strength and losing a couple of ribs from some blow; this group, when they find themselves in authority, are worse than the raging lunatics, because the latter may be restrained either with force or with art, while for the others only a criminal decision or an insufferable tolerance serves, because refuge is not always afforded." I shall not speak here of the injustices which they commit, because this point is very long, or I should say, this ennumeration, or this paragraph, which, as far as everyone is concerned, are all the same, like the two olive trees, the *olivo* and the *aceituna*.[1]

In this great town, as in the imperial Potosí, one finds no building commensurate with the immense wealth spent in these parts for 200 years on excesses of ostentation, outings, diversions, and banquets. If the miners' guild deposited 1 real for every mark it melted—and the same applies to private individuals who buy virgin silver and in great need take it to a crucible—they would have 15,000 pesos every year without feeling its loss, and after ten years they would find themselves with 150,000 pesos to undertake a work which could be of great benefit to them, or at least they could succeed in bringing adequate water to the whole town and perhaps supply it with sufficient for washing metals, which do not pay for themselves when they are handled at the river banks; or they could undertake some other work useful to the republic. Potosí and Oruro will not cease to be leading towns as long as mines which are inexhaustible are maintained near their river banks, with metal of average fineness; either way, it alleviates some people and obliges others. Cisterns or reservoirs would also be very useful

[1] The *olivo* and *aceituno* are one in the same tree. The idea here is "six of one, half dozen of the other."

in this town. Since the soil is nitrous, very little pasture grows in the fields; the smaller animals which are grazing continuously crave it. Their meat is tasty, but somewhat tough. All their fat and substance accumulates between the ends of the tail and the kidneys, creating such monstrosities that we at first suspected it was an artifice of the butchers, because the loins of lamb seem no more than thin parchments.

In this town, as in Potosí, coquettes have been happy because some of them have retired in a state of matrimony, introducing themselves into the matrons' circles, where they are not judged on their past life. We have observed that the residents of this town, and even the outsiders who live in it under contract for supplying provisions, hold no rancor for each other for an extended time, and are docile to reconciliation, wherefore the inspector was very pleased—in spite of the badly-founded opposition of the *corregidor* whom he generously scorned for the same. And although we all thought he had concluded his visit in this town, considering that the commissioner and general administrator, who had arrived in Lima, had reformed and instructed the administrators along this highway, in the end he abandoned the route planned to Tacna, considering it of little use to the public and as a source of income, wherefore we took the route to La Paz by way of the following posts.

CHAPTER XIV

PROVINCES OF POOPO AND SICAFICA. PAZ DE CHUQUIAPO.
BUDDLES FOR GOLD. THE PRODUCTION OF COCA.

ONE departs from Oruro across a nitrous pampa of
more than 4 leagues' extension which is traversed at
a trot in two and one-half hours in dry weather, but
in the rainy season dangerous mudholes and ponds are formed
in the deep holes which it contains. In the latter season prudent
people direct themselves along the skirt of the nearby hills, a
detour of more than 2 leagues, with much delay occasioned by
the irregularity of the road in its ascents and descents. In dry
weather, at a regular trot or an even pace, one may proceed from
Oruro to Caracollo, a distance of 8 leagues, in five hours; in
the rainy season, following the low hills, eight hours will be
spent, and if the pampa is undertaken, especially at night, the
travelers are exposed to the risk of remaining in it until Judgment Day. The remainder of the road has no hazards except
those caused by the ardor and haste of the travelers. The entire
road, up to the entrance to La Paz, is suitable for the trot or
the gallop, with the exception of some small mountains formed
at the entrance and exit of the towns, which seem to be dividing
lines or boundaries prepared by Nature to avoid lawsuits and
disputes. In all of this country, in all seasons, my beloved
travelers will find: inns without doors, lank mules with many
bad habits, skinny lambs and chickens, and eggs that are frozen
or contain unborn chicks, because the fine Indians always sell
the rancid ones. Nevertheless, with some precautions and expense one may proceed comfortably, as was the case with us,
aided by the experience and foresight of the inspector.

Paz de Chuquiapo

This city is located half way between Potosí and Cuzco, in a deep ravine having a very good climate, the antipode of that of Toledo, since the latter is on an elevation while this city is located on low land. Both occupy irregular terrain, but the streets of La Paz are very much more orderly. If much gold was found long ago in the sands of the Tagus, a considerable amount is now being gathered from the streams interwoven about the city of Chuquiapo. The Indians have their buddles at a distance from these narrow ravines, where they find some grains with which they support themselves, in great hope of making a good haul, as happens to those who fish for shells in which pearls are raised. This does not provide a considerable source of income.

. . .

Coca is the only product of the very hot mountain lands, and it is a leaf which when dry is mistaken for that of the olive or laurel; it is raised on small trees of little height. Rare are the Spaniards, mestizos, or Negroes who use it, but its consumption among the Indians is great, particularly when they are working silver and gold mines. Some merely chew it, like sailors chew tobacco leaves; what we have been able to observe is that it causes the same effect of drawing much saliva and puckering the gums of those who are novices in its use. Many Indians, whose gums are already cut away and do not feel its natural effect, make use of a most extraordinary condiment comprised of ground salt and I know not what other piquant ingredient, which they carry in a small, dried gourd hung around the neck, whence they take out powders to sprinkle on the leaves, thus giving them an extraordinary effect. In conclusion, the Indians depend on their coca just as those addicted to tobacco, since it is equivalent to it as maté is to tea and coffee.

The city is one of the richest in the kingdom, but it has no outstanding building. Its entrance and exit, in spite of passing through two perpendicular hills, are at the present time in very good repair, presenting no danger of sudden falls. The cathedral, situated on the main plaza, has no special feature other than that of celebrating the Holy Offices seriously. Private houses are so cluttered with furniture, mirrors, and pictures that they confound one's sight. Exquisite furnishings are mixed with the most ridiculous. There is no house of moderate respectability which does not have trays and other objects of solid gold. Garments which are not made of silk interwoven with gold and silver, or of velvet and other cloth embroidered in relief with the same metal, are considered ordinary and commonplace, but in the midst of such ostentatious luxury, one sees no decadence among the families, as in other parts of America, for example, in Potosí and Oruro, where the wealth is transitory, since they have no other than that provided by the silver extracted from their mines. In conclusion, the opulence of this city is in accord with its name; but the greatest asset which it can count at the present time is its having as prelate and preacher the illustrious Señor Don Gregorio del Campo, an outstanding person about whom it may be said, without flattery, that in his face one may read his virtues, particularly that of charity.

When the term of the contract for the lease of the post of this city had expired, Don Jacinto Antonio López Inclán came to administer it on behalf of His Majesty, being a man of good judgment, with an exactness and punctuality which border on excess. The inspector gave him his instructions in writing and orally, which Don Jacinto observed, and through them and the mildness of his temperament, tranquility and favorable gains in the income were achieved in that office. This affair having been concluded, we departed for the great city of Cuzco along the route of the following posts.

CHAPTER XV

PROVINCES OF OMASUYOS, PACAGES, CHUCUYTO, PAUCAR-
COLLA, LAMPA, TINTA AND QUISPICANCHI. THE INDIAN *MI-
TAYOS*. THE WORKING OF THE MINES. ADVENTURES OF THE
BISHOP OF NUEVA VIZCAYA. THE LONGEVOUS INHABITANTS
OF COMBAPATA. CUZCO.

TRAVELERS who do not follow the postal route should
be advised that between Paucarcolla and Juliaca there
are two small rivers which, in times of high waters, are
crossed in boats with a detour of 1 league through Atuncolla.
Those who follow the posts have no need of this warning because the postilions will guide them through the places most
suitable, depending on the season and circumstances of weather. These rivulets, which are streams in dry weather and
voluminous rivers in the rainy reason, flow through deep beds
or stoneless gorges with an almost imperceptible slowness,
since the land is flat, wherefore no fatal accident will occur,
except in the case of notable carelessness.

The second post is situated in a small town named Tiay
Guanaco, meaning "Sit down, guanaco," the latter being an
animal which runs as fast as a deer. This name was left by one
of the Incas who, being in that place, received a message with
as much speed as if it had been brought by a guanaco. This
very fact proves that the posts were not always located at short
distances, as the Inca Garcilaso says,[1] since the Indians posted

[1] Inca Garcilaso de la Vega (1539-1616), a Peruvian mestizo, whose
Comentarios reales (1609-1617) is one of the best, although somewhat
idealized, works on the early history of the Americas. He describes the
Indian couriers, *chasquis*, who carried oral messages for the Inca along
established routes equipped with huts spaced equidistant for the change
of runners.

in relays did not understand the *quipus*, nor did they stop to form dispatches because in this case the runs would not have been so fast. The one with the speed of the guanaco must have been extraordinarily assiduous. The fact is that if all men were compared to dogs, the Indians would be the greyhounds, not, in reality, because their first start is so fast, but rather because of the ease and endurance with which they execute the ascents and descents of the narrow and perpendicular paths, thereby saving much distance on the road.

Before entering the province of Chucuyto one finds El Desaguadero, so named because the lagoon ends in that place where the overflowing and cascading waters of the large bed sink beneath the ground. To cross it there is a bridge, supported on reed boats, almost at the water's surface, of very easy passage, but dangerous in the event of a fall due to the large quantity of slime of great depth in which the most vigorous man will drown. The center of the bridge is the dividing line between the provinces of Pacages and Chucuyto, both of which are obliged to provide necessary reparations. The *mitayos* from those provinces who are going to Potosí to work in the mines of that great hill convene on the pampa of Pacages, where an amusing fair is held, inasmuch as some Indians take leave of their relatives and friends with joy, others with tears, and there they spend the prepaid allowance for the trip which they call *leguaje*. These numerous families, so called because each married Indian takes his wife and children with him, are divided— with their small tents which they transport on llamas and sometimes on small asses—into troops, it being very rare for them to have a mule or a horse since Indians are not inclined to use these animals on their extended trips. On such a long journey, these people perpetrate damage similar to that of the locust, because as the latter consumes the crops in the fields through which it passes, the former sustain themselves on cattle, killing cows and sheep for their aliment, not exempting potatoes when they are in season, all under the title of servants of the King, as if they were military troops in a foreign country. . . .

This province [Lampa] has five posts. Four are in large towns and the last one, which is the first one on the return trip, named Chungará, is situated on one side of the town of Santa Rosa, to which place the inspector ordered it moved, not only so that travelers may be supplied with necessary provisions but also to avoid the reciprocal tyrannies which are regularly committed in the unpopulated areas, feeling obliged, in his desire to be truthful, to warn that in these cases the Spaniards are always wronged, because the Indians, if they are not paid their advance salary and reimbursed to their satisfaction for their foodstuffs, do not supply provisions or mules, holding them back two or three days under pretext of their having strayed through the hills and ravines. If he is a Spaniard or a mestizo, he efficaciously charges the *mitayos,* in the presence of the traveler, to bring the mules before daybreak, and immediately, as if he were discussing another matter, he tells them in their own language to go on with their business and not bring the supplies for two days, or whatever time he whimsically decides, a trick in which the Indians are very clever and cunning.

It seems to me appropriate here to relate a funny story, told us by the inspector, of what happened to a certain bishop of Durango, in Nueva Vizcaya, in the viceroyalty of Mexico. This good prelate arrived for a visit to a mission (that is what the Jesuits call the large estates administered by just one priest and one coadjutor); he arrived, as I said, at one of these missions administered by a priest who, judging by his plumpness, could have been the head of a very large flock and, by his adroitness in all matters of commerce, the director of the largest consulate in the world; he was a very mature subject, particularly experienced in the science they call "courtly." He entertained the bishop and his retinue royally during an afternoon and evening, providing them with adequate supper at no cost, and for dessert he presented the bishop with a dozen Latin epigrams full of flattery which were much enjoyed by all. Chocolate was ready in large cups at dawn, since the bishop never warmed his seat for long during the course of a journey, in order that it might not become painful; but even the most saintly man always has one servant who can make his virtue equivocal. This servant pondered, in the presence of the priest and the bishop, over the weariness of the coach mules and the difficulty with which they would arrive at the spot where he was going to take his siesta, since there was no means of changing animals. The good priest—who I believe did not remove his huge spectacles even to sleep—slapped his forehead with his palm, at the same time ordering, in the presence of everyone, that six diligent riders go out to the fields and select the best draft mules, to go out to meet the bishop and present to him, in his name, the 12 best animals in order that he might continue his trip satisfactorily. The saintly bishop, although learned, was a simple soul, and he said he would accept them for use only until arriving at a certain estate where a friend of his had a supply of replacements. "This cannot be, Illustrious Sir," replied the priest, "because a mule which has served Your Lordship will never return to this estate." The good priest, seeing that his youths had already saddled their horses and readied their lassoes, went out to the corridor and told them in Mexican tongue that they should take to the bishop only two lean and useless mules, and that they should say that they had not been able to find more in the fields because the fat and serviceable animals had escaped.

Satisfied with the courtesy of the priest, the bishop took leave of him, got into his carriage with his chaplain and a page, and after having concluded his prayers, aided by his chaplain, he proceeded at a slow pace, praising the civility of the priest and of his religion in general. The small page was making great efforts to restrain his laughter, and the bishop, noting this, reprimanded him; but instead of complying, the youth broke into convulsive laughter, which gave the bishop reason to deduce some mystery. The boy wiped his nose and eyes to satisfy the bishop, but laughter was still showing from the windows of his heart, for which he could only say that the good priest was a very droll fellow. This bishop almost let loose a laugh, as the chaplain said, but gaining control of himself, he told the boy to explain to him openly the reason for his laughter, and the latter, composing himself a little, told him, still smiling and with tears trickling down his cheeks, that the fine priest had ordered the *cholos,* in their language, not to bring his lordship more than two skinny mules. The good bishop asked him if he knew the Mexican language, and he replied that he knew not a word, but that a little Indian who served him and to whom the priest paid no heed, had exposed the mystery to him. The bishop, fortified by his authority, again reprimanded the page and praised the reverend, but as he had arrived at the spot for his siesta and the offer of the priest was not in evidence, he began to doubt, until the youths arrived with the two lean mules; he dispatched them, ordering the *cholo* interpreter of the page to repeat the last order given to them by the reverend, which he put in writing for perpetual memory. The bishop, enlightened, said, in the after-dinner

conversation, that the simple country men seemed more useful to society than very clever men, because the former reveal
immediately their good will or evil intentions, while the latter
hide them beneath a heavy veil which cannot be penetrated by
the most acute sight and can be perceived only by chance, to
which he added, "The candor of these farmers is evident to all
of you, but I shall give just one example—old Menéndez, who,
being the only one who could give testimony on the imputation
of a false charge, replied the first, second, and third times,
'*Que no había tales carneros,*'[1] which is the same as saying that
it was a falsehood, an expression which no amount of exorcism
could make him change. This good man offered changes of
mules for the entire commission and their baggage as far as
Talamantes, an offer which he fulfilled doubly by providing the
necessary attendants; he gave us a country dinner, abundant
and elegant, and supplied the servants with all necessities, but
at the farewell he made no other demonstration than to remove
his hat, kiss my hand and say, 'Your Lordship, when you arrive
in Talamantes, *quitolis.*' I did not understand the term," the
bishop said, "but having such a good interpreter in the page's
cholo, I consulted him and he told me that the good old man was
only lending the mules as far as Talamantes, and that after that
his servants would return with them, which amounts to the
same as taking them away from me." The good bishop again
laughed and praised the ingenuity and simplicity of the farmer.
All of them are not so simple, because in that extensive kingdom there are farmers who live in great splendor. Enough
digression; let us again pick up the threads of our narrative.

After Chungará, or the town of Santa Rosa, one begins to
notice the rigors of the Vilcanota cordillera. Pucará is the town
nearest to its skirt and experiences most of the severity of its
storms and snowfalls. The latter cover all the streets in an
eighth of an hour, obstructing traffic, and snow even penetrates

---

[1] *Que no había tales carneros* (That there were no such sheep) is a saying commonly used to indicate the uncertainty of a matter.

the houses themselves, in the detached quarters such as the kitchen, servants' rooms, the patio and the corral. The storms are not of great duration, and for this reason the inhabitants have not taken the precautions necessary to avoid their ruin. As soon as the hail stops, the rain begins, and washing along the foundations, it forms precipitous streams which carry in their currents formidable pieces of ice capable of sweeping away anyone who tries to cross the streets on horseback. After Chungará or Santa Rosa there is a short ascent, and then one begins to descend without hazard, but with the inconveniences of the cordillera, which rarely fails to hurl hail, sleet, and sharp winds that pierce the body. Almost at the foot of the cordillera, or I should say at the skirt, since in reality one travels along the latter, are some small huts which seemed like palaces to us because they sheltered us from the cold; and in them we were able, in a short time, to eat something hot from the dried meats which we brought. It seems that those farms have been put there for profit, since their poor owners kept on the fire a large kettle of beans prepared in a country style, and in another stewpot some chunks of *chalona*, which is what they call the salted meat of the sheep, made in these countries from all those ewes which, due to their age or their sterility, show no promise of reproducing. We observed that poor travelers partake of this rustic food, and even the inspector ordered that his servants and the Indians accompanying him should be given a large bowlful so they might warm themselves and forget their hunger while the meal was being prepared. This place, with a slight variation, divides the jurisidiction of Lampa from that of Tinta since 4 leagues beyond, more or less, is the first post, named Lurucachi, which appertains to the aforementioned province of Tinta. Between Potosí and this place is cold country in which the pasture lands are exposed to destruction by the hard freezes, and in times of much rain dangerous mudholes are formed because of which it is necessary to make extended detours, not to travel at night, and to journey by day with an experienced guide from the area, since it happened many times to us—and we were traveling before the season of high waters—that we were detained an eighth of an hour by a small ditch before attempting to cross it, having observed that the mules, by not wanting to cross it, anticipated the danger. This is not an indefectible rule, due to the timidity and natural lack of confidence of these animals. The safest thing is to stop and observe the danger encountered by the guide or *baqueano*, as he is commonly called, who usually selects an animal of a skill comparable to his own. The principal part of the province of Lampa along the royal highway is crossed by these ditches which serve as watering places for the many small animals nourished on these plains, providing also a means of relieving their discomfort.

From Lurucachi to the great city of Cuzco one travels through temperate country, hot in parts, but without discomfort. . . . The town of Combapata is located on an elevation of the royal road in this district. Everyone vows that it is the most salubrious territory in all of Peru, and that by merely breathing its air men and women regain their health and recover in a short time from all sorts of illnesses. A very robust Spaniard of 80 years assured us that he had known Don Simón de Herrera, who was 145 years old, and Doña Tomasa Aballón, of 137 years, although Herrera accused her of trimming her age by at least 8 years; and they used to bet about which one could run the fastest. At the same time he knew four Indian women of the same age, a fact confirmed by the two aged Spaniards who had known them since a tender age. The town is small, and I believe it has no more than 100 inhabitants, counting boys and old men, and if in such a small population, six individuals averaging 140 years are found, it can compete with, and even surpass, in healthfulness, the memorable town of San Juan del Poyo in the kingdom of Galicia, since the 13 parishioners there did not reach an average of more than 116 years. Almost everyone in the town vouches for the agility of the Spaniards, since they used to bet on a race, which was a matter of walking fast and without crutches. Nothing was said about the Indian women, but it is customary and an accepted fact that they, as well as the men, continue until their death that common work necessary for their livelihood, preserving their limited talents. Don Lucas Luján, a miner from Aporoma, in the Carabaya province, who is 130 years old at the present time, goes about in wooden shoes and climbs with them into his mine. He reads and writes with considerable accuracy. We could relate a great many such examples in other countries which everyone generally considers unhealthful.

At a short distance from this town one enters the province of Urcos, better known as Quispicanchi. . . .

The town of Oropesa is suitable for the first post on the route to Cuzco or Quiquijana, inasmuch as it has good pastures in its environs, and within the town itself are stubbles of alfalfa, barley, and other products, so that the postmaster's mules may nourish themselves during the delay which may be occasioned by the slowness in the dispatch of mails, and so that travelers who come from Potosí may refresh their own mules and relieve the discomforts of continuous traveling. This post is only

5 leagues from Cuzco, on a road that is good in dry weather but very difficult in time of rain due to the many holes formed in its narrow lanes which divide the farms located on both sides, as well as separating them from the narrow ravine of Quiquijana. As soon as we were able to discern the roofs and towers of the city which is the largest in the great Peruvian empire, both in basic elements and fortunes, the inspector stopped and said to me, "There is the capital of your ancestors, Señor Concolorcorvo, very much improved by the Spaniards." But since I had left it at a very early age, I had no fixed idea of its buildings, entrances, or exits, and I remember only that my father lived in some very small lower quarters with an extended corral. At this moment several friends of the commissioner appeared, and with reciprocal joy and felicitations they introduced us to the place of my birth, the city of Cuzco.

CHAPTER XVI

CUZCO. DESCRIPTION OF THE CITY. DEFENSE OF THE CON-
QUISTADOR. CRUELTY OF THE INDIANS. THE WORKING OF THE
MINES. RESUMÉ OF THE CONQUESTS OF PERU AND MEXICO.
AUTHOR'S DEFENSE AND INSPECTOR'S OPINION.

WE Creoles who are natives of this city call it Cozco.
I do not know whether the variation in this word is
a thing of our own doing or the work of the
Spaniards. The inspector told me that the Indians had aided
considerably in the corruption of their own words, and to prove
it he cited the example of the word *maíz*. One day some of
Cortés' soldiers were seeking forage for their horses, and the
Indians, seeing that those extraordinary animals craved the
green grass, picked a large quantity of the tips from the plant
which today we call *maíz*, although it is also known as *trigo de
la tierra*, and handing over their small sheaves, they said "*Mabi,
señor*," which means, "Take it, sir." The Spaniards concluded
that they were speaking the name of that plant and its fruits,
and when there was nothing to feed the horses thereafter, the
soldiers always asked for *maíz* since the animals ate it with
great pleasure and they saw its good effect. Thenceforth the
Indians themselves continued to call the fruit *maíz*, whether it
was an ear of corn or kernels which had been shelled, wherefore they decided that this must be the true name for it in
Castilian.

Many superficial critics have labeled the early Spaniards
crude and stupid for not having constructed the city in
Andaguaylillas or on some other of the many flat plains nearby.
Others, in defending the early Spaniards, affirm in their favor
that they selected that high and craggy place for the city in

order to reserve the plains for pasture for the many horses they kept and for planting wheat, corn, and other food crops. In my estimation, both groups are in error; only those early Spaniards who followed the Indians can really know the explanation.

No one doubts that elevated sites are more healthful than those in the lowlands, and although strictly speaking Cuzco is not in a very high place, it overlooks the surrounding country which becomes flooded in the rainy season. The unevenness of the site, midway down the slope, permits the water to descend and clean the city of the human and animal filth which accumulates in the *guatanayes* (or gutters), streets, and public squares. The many materials which the Indians used in their temples and houses could not have been utilized in Andaguaylillas except at great expense of transportation and with the loss of several building foundations and large sections of the walls such as those seen now along the narrow streets, for all the streets built by my forefathers were probably similar to these, just as were those of all the other nations of the ancient world. If this great city had been established in Andaguaylillas or on some other plain nearby, not only would the first settlers have had a great waste of energy in transporting the materials and massive rocks which the Indians carved, but it would have been uninhabitable in ten years. In Cuzco one may see over 2,000 animals a day, wasting half of their food, since horses and mules trample down the alfalfa and barley which the inhabitants raise in great quantity. Besides the large number of people living in the city, which I believe exceeds 30,000, over 1,000 Indians enter daily from the surrounding provinces with their supplies and belongings, not to mention the mule drivers who come from other places. Thus men and animals eat and drink, and the resulting refuse is left in the city to be washed by the rains down the slope of the city through the *guatanayes* and outlets.

This word *guatanay* is equivalent to the Castilian *sequión*, or drainage ditch, which is made in large places for the flow of

perennial water or rain water which cleanses the cities. Lima has an infinite number of these, although they are badly distributed. In Mexico there are many well-placed ditches, but since the city is situated on such flat terrain, there is scarcely any flow of water, and it is necessary that they be cleaned almost daily by men who have been jailed for their crimes; this is a fitting punishment for them. Madrid, along with its other good appointments, has its sewers; Valladolid, its jetties which are constructed in the Esgueva River, just as many other heavily populated cities which need these provisions for cleanliness and sanitation. Flat terrain cannot make use of this convenience except at very great expense, and at the risk of exposing itself to flood at any time. In sum, it may be said that the city of Cuzco is very wisely located in the best possible site.

With all respect to its governor, there is no doubt that it could be better managed in times of peace, and I maintain that the early Spaniards who settled it in tumultuous days were men of sounder judgment than those of today. The central plaza, where the cathedral is erected, which was the temple and home of the Company of Jesus, is in perfect condition, and is surrounded by an arcade—except in that spot occupied by the cathedral and the seminary, which would be outstanding buildings even in Europe. The houses on the square are the worst in the city, as is true in almost the whole world, because the conquistadors and owners of these establishments tended to utilize them for established merchants, since it is they who best pay their rent. The same idea was held by the landlords on the small square, the Plazuela del Regocijo, so called to distinguish it from the Plaza Mayor, although from the beginning the former had a greater expanse, being rectangular, as can be seen if one takes away the islet made for the mint, but added later, for some reason, to the Church of the Merced, which has a sumptuous convent facing its main door. Cuzco has other plazas at regular distances on which the conquistadors built their palaces since they were outside the business district.

These great men were, and still are, unjustly persecuted by strangers as well as by their confreres. I do not wish to call the latter envious, but rather indiscreet for having declaimed so loudly against tyranny which was really only imagined, giving rise to the stories of begrudging outsiders who soon caused the whole world to be horrified at the cruelty of the Spaniards. The origin of this stems from the first discovery by Columbus of the island Hispanola, known today as Santo Domingo. On these islands Columbus did nothing more than establish commerce and friendly relations with the native princes and their vassals. Various commodities were exchanged without treachery, since gold was useless to the Indian, and he thought he was deceiving the Spaniard by giving him a pound of this precious metal in return for 100 pounds of iron in the form of shovels, picks, hoes, and other implements for working the ground. Columbus erected a small wooden shelter in which he left a handful of men to cultivate the friendship of the caciques of the area, leaving with them some supplies and merchandise which they might exchange for native products necessary for their survival until his return. The great hardships which Columbus experienced with his entire crew before he reached Spain are recorded in his own history as well as in others. Upon his return, he did not find a single one of the men he had left because they were sacrificed at the hands of the Indians.

When the Indians saw Columbus returning with more men and good officers—capable of killing a thousand Indians for every Spaniard—they spread the word that the Spaniards who were left there had perished at the hands of the Indian hordes rightly defending their honor and property. The Spaniards recognized the cruelty of the Indians and thence arose the distrust which they held for them, and their treatment of them as men who had to be restrained with rigor, threatening punishment for even the slightest offense so that the Spaniards would not be thrown into disorder and destroyed by the hordes. The pious ecclesiastics assigned by the great Charles I, King of Spain, considered this treatment inhumane, and consequently they wrote to the Court with pens dipped in blood, the contents of which letters were utilized by foreigners to fill their histories with reproach against the Spaniards and the first conquistadors.[1] A certain contemporary Frenchman averred that the Spaniards, to satisfy their greed, locked the Indians in the mines for seven or eight months without permitting them to see the light of

[1] The reference here is to the famous *Leyenda negra* which attributed to the Spaniards all manner of atrocities against the Indian. This legend, originating in the *Brevísima relación de la destrucción de las Indias* (1552) of Bartolomé de las Casas and kept alive by other Spanish clerics and historians, was considerably distorted in the writings of the envious English and Dutch during the seventeenth and eighteenth centuries. Don Alonso is speaking (here and in other passages in the text) not only of these critics, but also of the contemporary French and Spanish writers who criticized the Spanish colonial system. It is difficult to know to what works he refers, but he was obviously aware of the comments of Montesquieu and Voltaire on the Spanish treatment of the Indian. In addition, the eighteenth-century spirit of criticism and investigation prompted

day so that they might extract the gold and silver.

It is evident that the Indians never learned, and still do not know, how to work the mines for their benefit, and only when directed by Spaniards or joined by the intelligent mestizo miners are they able to extract the ore to fill their baskets, hampers, or bags of little weight. They could not perform their jobs without the assistance of the Spaniards and mestizos; but if, in the face of all this, our good neighbors said that the Spaniards who directed the Indians and were engaged in the hardest work themselves, such as swinging picks, used to leave the mines to go home to sleep and enjoy fresh air, I say that they were either wrong or they were lying for the sole purpose of presenting the Spaniards as cruel tyrants. But I would like to inquire of this nature-loving critic by what influence were these ferocious men converted into the humble creatures such as those he describes a few lines beyond, where he says that the contemporary Spaniards on the island use moderation with their slaves (he is speaking of Negroes bought from other nations) who, when sent on errands of only one-half leagues' distance, are told to go on horseback. This does not arise from a lack of critical ability in the French, but rather from their excess of malice, and the same may be said of the Italians and the English who are profiting most from the conquest of the Spaniards through their consumption of goods produced here in the provinces, the sale of which keeps the latter flourishing.

---

many expeditions to the New World by European scientists, whose published accounts included geographical, nautical, social, political, and cultural observations, many of which were not complimentary to the Spanish regime in America. It would be safe to conjecture that Don Alonso was familiar with at least three of such works: *Rélation du voyage de la mer du sud, aux côtes du Chili et du Pérou, fait pendant les années 1712, 1713, 1714,* by Amédée François Frézier (Paris, 1716); *Rélation abrégée d'un voyage fait dans l'intérieur de l'Amérique Méridionale* by Charles Marie de La Condamine (Paris, 1745); *Relación histórica del viaje a la América meridional* (1748) and *Noticias secretas de América* (1758) by Antonio de Ulloa (1716-1795) and Jorge Juan (1713-1773).

I was going to insert here, in summary form, all the essential facts about the Spanish conquest of the Americas, but the inspector, who knew my inclination to be profuse, cut out more than 700 pages which I had written defending the Spaniards and honoring the Indians of Cuzco since he deemed these matters inappropriate for a journalist, just as he prevented me from being excessive in the praises of my native land because he found me incapable of effecting it with the vigor and charm deserved by the place which was the principal seat of my Inca ancestors and the spot most revered by the Spanish conquistadors and principal settlers. The latter, who from the very beginning ennobled their city with sumptuous church buildings and convents, in which their piety and devotion to the true God was resplendent, and with palaces and public works where their magnanimity was revealed, have been accused of arrogance. The pious Spanish monarchs, perhaps poorly informed, stopped this by suppressing the *encomiendas,* but this is a matter not to be disputed, in which we must conform to the dictates of our superiors and follow the laws blindly. The location and size of this city naturally suggested that it should be the court of the Peruvian empire, but the great Pizarro established it in Lima, since its proximity to the sea and the port of Callao facilitated rapid communications with Chile and the continent.

"With your permission, Señor Don Alonso, I am going to strike a pair of blows at those foreigners who envy the Spanish glory. As soon as the Spaniards landed in Veracruz, they tried to . . ." "What did they try, my tiresome Inca?" asked the inspector. "To solicit the friendship of the inhabitants of that vast empire," I said, "and not being able to achieve it, it was necessary to take up arms in order to live among the multitudes of barbarians without harm to the men or horses. The Tlascaltecas, who comprised a large nation of such valor that they confronted and held in check all the power of the Mexican Moctezuma, were the first to resist the Spaniards formally until they

experienced their insuperable strength, and at the persuasion of
the old Xicotencal, peace was made without any hardship to the
Indians. Then Cortés sent his ambassadors to Moctezuma asking that he and a small number of Spaniards be received in the
Indian's court, and despite the refusal, Cortés did not utilize the
reinforcements offered by his supporters, the Tlascaltecas, who
were very anxious to punish the arrogance of the Mexicans.
Accompanied only by Spaniards, Cortés went to Mexico where
he was apparently received with courtesy, but being obliged
to restrain the pride of Pánfilo de Narváez, who was not complying with his orders, he left the great Pedro de Alvarado in
Mexico with a small escort, and when he returned, with twice
as many Spaniards, he found the Mexican court in rebellion.
There were several skirmishes, but even though 20 Indians
were killed for every Spaniard lost, it seems that from every
Indian who died, a thousand more were resurrected!

"The Spaniards and their horses were becoming weary from
the repeated encounters, but what made them doubt their survival even more was the unfortunate death of Moctezuma
which was caused by a blow from a stone hurled by one of his
own followers, because of which insolence grew and the risk
for the Spaniards increased. Therefore they resolved to abandon the city one night, but it was with great difficulty and effort,
since the Indians had destroyed the bridges, and from the flat
roofs men, women, and children hurled at them a barrage of
stones as thick as hail; and although it is true that the Spaniards
routed an army of over 80,000 Indians in Otumba, they came
out of this affray in Mexico so badly battered that they would
have perished had not they found asylum with the noble
Tlascaltecas. These patriots not only nursed, regaled, and con-
soled them, but they also enlisted a mighty army to avenge the
Spaniards and to seek their revenge against the Mexicans. The
command was entrusted to the younger Xicotencal who, although he disliked the Spaniards, was considered the most
valiant and bold, and was to fight under the command of

Cortés; but a few days after having laid siege to Mexico (to the delight of both Spaniards and Indians) the Indian youth retreated to Tlascala with a band of his men. Those noble and wise patriots, following the judgment of the righteous father of the young Xicotencal, took him prisoner so that Cortés could punish him in the military manner, and in the first council meeting, this revolutionary spirit was condemned to death by the order of both the Spanish and Indian leaders.

"The great city was vanquished, although it was defended to the last quarter with courage and tenacity. The King of Spain was declared monarch, since before the death of Moctezuma the electors had already named him emperor." "Of course," said the inspector, "there was some chicanery on the part of the Spaniards in this election, because in these empires elections are carried out only after the death of those who hold office." "But for the legitimate possession and continued inheritance of the Catholic Kings, it was sufficient to have the consent of the Tlascaltecas, since they had as much right to conquer as to be conquered by the Mexicans, as has happened all over the world." "What have you to say about the Peruvian empire, Señor Inca?" asked the inspector. "Since I spoke about the entry of the Spaniards into the Mexican empire, following the testimony of the illustrious Solís, I would deserve to be torn to bits if I did not say the same about what they did in Peru, as is related by the wise Herrera.[2]

"The latter states that as soon as the Spaniards set foot in the lands of Virú, they learned that there was in Caxamarca Manco Capac, a bastard ancestor of mine, who had revolted with half of Peru at his side, in an effort to dethrone his brother, the rightful emperor, who had his court in Cuzco. This discord did not disturb Pizarro; and so, with great haste, he dispatched his

[2] Antonio de Solís y Rivadeneira (1610-1686), author of *Historia de la conquista de Mexico* (1684) and Antonio de Herrera y Tordesillas (1549-1625) who wrote *Décadas o Historia general de los hechos de los castellanos en las islas y tierra del mar océano* (1601, 1615).

emissaries to the brother in Caxamarca, since he was closest. The latter formed a bad impression of the unexpected guests in spite of their bravery and strength, and he considered them as sent from heaven to do justice to his brother, the rightful lord; therefore, he abandoned the city and established camp, with all his riches and numerous army, in an advantageous spot a short distance away. This cowardly act inspired in Pizarro and all the Spaniards, who I believe numbered not more than 200, the courage to proceed with joy to occupy the city. Pizarro then went to Manco Capac to suggest that he return to his capital, escorted by guards, where he would be treated well and respected by the kind Spaniards, after leaving the bulk of his army in the field for the protection of the women and treasures. After much disputation, the Inca agreed to speak to Pizarro if he could be accompanied by 12,000 unarmed men, to which the Spaniard acceded, but having learned that the Indians carried concealed weapons, a contrivance of bad faith, he chose a means to be the aggressor instead of the victim. He posted all his men in the entrances and exits of the main square, and as soon as the Inca entered with his guards, the order was given to attack them and destroy them, except for the royal personage who was made prisoner.

"My relative, as all my relatives, was lacking in military skill and even courage, since he had abandoned the capital with an army of 80,000 men who could have fought the Spaniards 400 to 1. But leaving aside a host of reflections which could dispel traditions and anecdotes, I affirm the Manco Capac was a man of bad faith, a perfidious traitor, because when Pizarro proposed to him that he order his generals to disperse their troops and retire to their villages, he agreed to do it, but he did the exact opposite, justifying it by casting the blame on his *quipus*, and especially on the actions of his leaders. But what finally exasperated the Spaniards was the treacherous death which he ordered for his brother, the true Inca, who had left Cuzco to deal with Pizarro in good faith. The promise made by the tyrant, as the common Spanish call him, that he would provide for his ransom as much gold as could be contained in the quarters where he was lodged—which were as long and as wide as a present-day Spanish room—was sheer fantasy. The tale told by the Indians—that they buried that immense treasure in the heights of Guamanga when they learned of the death of their emperor—is the most extravagant chimera imaginable, because if the tyrant were master only of the lands and people between Quito and Piura, how did that gold get to the heights of Guamanga? I repeat, how many Indians carried the gold which Manco offered to the Spaniards? Where did he have these unlimited treasures? From what mines were they extracted? Why is it that all the barren mines of the precious metal were found in the domain of his brother, the rightful lord? If it were said that my fine ancestor had sought the gold in Chocó, in the province of Pataz, and in others in his empire, there would now seem to be some foundation for the promise made to the Spaniards who knew so little about the nature of the mines.

"Although the conquistadors could not be certain about the promise by Manco, they judged it to be deceitful, in view of his treachery in the orders he had given to his generals to maintain their armies and to arouse all the people in revolt against the Spaniards, and especially because of his perfidy against his legitimate and natural lord, whom he had killed in such a cruel manner; wherefore, the Spaniards considered it advisable to get rid of such a man capable of upsetting the entire empire and sacrificing in his hatred not only the Spaniards, but also the descendants of the true Inca.

"The empire began to be divided into several dependencies, but when Pizarro's companion in conquest, Almagro, arrived with an equal number of troops, or I should say, with as many troops as Pizarro had, and joined the latter in Caxamarca, they formed an army of 500 infantry and cavalry men, capable of blazing their way through the empire but not conquering it. This small army was reinforced by the troops sent into the realm by the great Pedro de Alvarado, who had left Guatemala with the idea of effecting a conquest of these extensive domains, but who had agreed to a friendly merger with Pizarro and Almagro, provided he receive financial aid to compensate for the expenses he had incurred.

"With such a feeble beginning, a conquest of more than 7 million Indians was carried out, with all of them taking up arms in the service of their Incas and chieftains for the defense of their homeland. We should not believe that this prodigious conquest was accomplished only by the bravery of the Spaniards—but if it were so, then let all the nations of the world admit that the Spaniards were the most valorous in the world, exceeding even the Romans, since the latter were larger in number when they besieged their city, and little by little they conquered their divided neighbors, more with cleverness than arms, frequently utilizing vile means. The Spaniards used no trickery to subdue my countrymen; they had no faithful and dependable auxiliary troops as did those who vanquished the great Mexican empire, nor were they aided by Spaniards from Europe. I do not mean to compare Pizarro and Almagro with Cortés, since there is no question that the latter was the greatest man. The Peruvian conquistadors served under his command, and although they could not agree with his principles, they imitated his valor and constancy, and in an equal time they could have conquered and pacified the entire realm if a disastrous civil war had not broken out among the Spaniards themselves. It was this that really ruined the conquistadors and snuffed out the splendor of the great city of Cuzco, my home, depriving the conquistadors and their descendants of 40 *encomiendas* which could have maintained a grandeur unequalled in the greatest court in the world."

"Proceed no further, Señor Inca," said the inspector, "because this is a matter for which there is no solution. It seems to me that you are attempting with your principles to prove that the Spanish conquest was just, legitimate, and perhaps the best founded of all those ever made in the world." "That is the opinion I hold," I replied, "based on the results in both empires, because if the Spaniards, following the system employed by other nations of the world, had occupied the main cities and ports of these great realms with good garrisons and had stocked large stores with a selection of trinkets and iron tools for the working of the mines and fields, at the same time distributing reputable workmen to provide instruction for their use, permitting freedom to the Incas, chieftains, and citizens to practice their abominable and sinful acts, then the Spanish monarchy would have been able to extract interests of considerable size from the Indies. My ancestors would have been more agreeable, and the envious foreigners would not have so many reasons to censure the conquistadors and the early or present-day settlers." "Stop!" cried the inspector. "It falls to my lot to defend the latter for their tyrannies, since I am better acquainted with both Americas, and my impartiality in this and other matters is quite evident to you.

"I shall not consider whether or not you spoke of the conquest with wisdom and candor. I do not doubt that it was beneficial to the Indians, because the Spaniards put an end to many of their errors and odious customs conflicting with Nature. At the time of your Incas, prisoners of war were sacrificed to inhuman gods, and the people ate the flesh of these victims with as much relish as they consumed that of animals. The Incas, chieftains, and other dignitaries and army officers reserved for themselves a large number of women, and since the latter numbered about the same as the men, it resulted that the commune had insufficient women for the propagation of the race and even less for carnal pleasure; consequently, the unnatural and bestial crimes which the Spaniards found in practice were very common. These were blotted out almost entirely through discipline and establishment of marriages at the proper time, imposing serious penalties on delinquents and punishing them in proportion to their mental abilities and physical state. For this reason the Holy Tribunal of the Inquisition ordered that the mestizos and mulattoes be treated with the same seriousness as the Spaniards, leaving the reprehension and punishment in the hands of the ecclesiastical vicars, just as it entrusted to the ordinary secular magistrates the punishment of the public sorcerers, who were nothing but imposters, making them wear the pointed hat so that the Indians might learn to despise their trickery and come to their senses.

"I could produce many examples of these measures provided by prudent officials, but I shall omit them so as not to prolong this diary which is beginning to bore even me; therefore, I shall pass on to the defense of the good Spaniards against the abuses published by foreigners concerning the tyranny with which the Indians were treated, in which many of our people concur out of ignorance, inexperience, and lack of knowledge about the kingdom. I shall divide the accusations for the sake of clarity—with the sole purpose of edifying those Spaniards unfamiliar with the subject—so they will not believe garrulous foreigners and especially those travelers who try to enhance their diaries by seeking fables and stories of extravagant acts inspired by Spaniards, which serve only to ridicule the memory of the latter among wise men."

CHAPTER XVII

ACCUSATIONS AGAINST THE SPANIARDS. THE *REPARTIMIEN-TOS* OF INDIANS. THE IMAGINARY TYRANNY OF THE CONQUIS-TADORS. THE SECOND ACCUSATION. THE SLAVERY OF THE INDIANS. THE TYRANNY IN THE WORKING OF THE *OBRAJES* OR WORKSHOPS.

The First Accusation or Imaginary Tyranny: Repartimientos

AFTER this empire was established in the house of the Kings of Castile and provincial judges were named under the title of *corregidor*, each one had assigned to him an annual salary of 1,000 assayed pesos for his support; and he was charged with administering justice to the Indians without exacting fees from them, with collecting taxes and handing them over to the royal treasury and with answering for shortages and false moneys, which is understood to include also coins which are very worn or have clipped edges. The state of the kingdom in the beginning, and even now, did not allow for salaries adequate for the many expenses incurred in some provinces, which average no less than 20 towns, separated by extended distances with roads generally rough and dangerous; wherefore the first *corregidores* established commerce among the Indians, under the name of *reparticiones*, in order to defray expenses with the profits and in order that the Indians and other persons without means or credit might supply themselves with the necessities for working the fields or mines and with clothing for themselves and their families, a practice permitted by this superior government and the royal *Audiencias* for more than 200 years; but since this commerce had no more than the consent of the government, it gave rise to infinite lawsuits and charges against the *corregidores*, all of which were lacking in civility (which depends more on temper than talent).

These disturbances gave the viceroys and tribunals reason to consult the supreme oracle about the means which should be taken to free their subjects from interminable lawsuits in which some were ruined, particularly those who entrusted their wealth to the *corregidores* and who had no part in the profits, either just or usurious. The Court in Madrid, with the information given in Lima and other parts and after consultation with justices and theologians, declared that in the future commerce of the *corregidores* in all effects necessary to the livelihood of the provinces—and especially in those of utility to the Indians —would be lawful, and that regulations should be made on the goods which were to be parceled out, reducing their prices, with great foresight, to 100 per cent profit, which means the value of the goods increased half again between the place it was bought and the place it was sold. This 100 per cent, which, ironically, among the Italians is considered a moderate profit, really is so in our case, because it must be understood that the 100 per cent is extended over a period of 5 years, which makes 20 per cent each year. This profit in the 5 years must be reduced by at least 25 percent, 4 per cent of which is paid in excise, plus the salaries of the deputy and the collectors, wages of caciques, and leakage in weights and measures, and losses due to insolvents or absentees, so that the 100 per cent, by a modest calculation, is reduced to 75 per cent, or 15 per cent each year, which is a standard profit for a private merchant selling for cash or on credit with a moderate term of payment; since although it is said that he loses on some goods, he also profits much more on others. I include the expenses of the *corregidores* in the taxes necessary for justice, and I omit the cost of negotiations in the Court, transportation costs from there to these domains, and the expense of freighting the articles to the provinces; but I can assure you that a *corregidor* who enters a province with a *repartimiento* of 100,000 pesos, proceeding justly according to regulations, cannot realize—if he pays interest of 5 per cent for the delay in his payments—more than 20,000 pesos in 7 years, considering the 2,000 spent at his entrance and departure.

Foreigners and even many Spaniards say that the *corregidores* do not follow regulations, and that they are excessive in their allotments and prices. This accusation, in general, is rash because I know that many have lowered their prices and have not been able to expend all the assigned quantity, not wishing to expose themselves to heated resistance. Don Felipe Barba de Cabrera, a person well-known in the city for over 40 years, was *corregidor* of the province of Pataz, his homeland, when His Honor the Marqués de Villagarcía was governor. Don Felipe had no *repartimiento* worthy of consideration except that of stamped silver, charging the miners that they show a preference to him in the sale of gold taken from their mines, but not interfering with the dealings which some had with private individuals, or showing hatred and indignation against them. His final success was as felicitous as his generous beginning, since he collected, without violence, all of his *repartimiento*, except for a quantity of a little over 2,000 pesos outstanding to a domestic clerk of his to whom was allowed the time extension he sought for paying without detriment. Other examples of this nature could be cited, but not many. *Quia apparent rari nantes in jurgite vasto.*

If all of us men conducted ourselves in exact conformity to the laws, errors in them would devolve and the legislators would find themselves obliged to reform the laws or to maintain a disorder prejudicial to the State, which seems an impossible thing, particularly in the Spanish domains where life is conducted with circumspect and seriousness. Spaniards, both European and American, are more docile and compliant with the law than the other Europeans and Americans who live on the islands. The latter sustain their rebellions for extended periods. Our people obey submissively, perform the incommodious acts with humility and respect; and although at one time or another a sudden flare-up has been incited, it is like a fire in a sleeping mat, of great illumination but of short duration. Just as the *monsieurs* boast of the honor of their language, since it is the one of most extensive use in this century in all Europe, with so many excellent works being written in it, so they ought to be tolerant of the criticism and wrong done to Spaniards by travelers who try, in their language, to defame such immediate neighbors as the Spaniards who mention them only with praise, receiving them in their country without repugnance and often with more than usual deference; but these *monsieurs*, milords, or illustrious Frenchmen, Englishmen, and Italians think only of debasing the Spaniards, publishing first in their pamphlets (which afterward become general history) follies and faults which are almost convincing to Spaniards of little intelligence, and give wise men an unjust concept, due to the lack of acquaintance with creative Americans who are usually occupied with their books and private meditations.

In the provinces in which the *repartimiento* is practiced by collecting in goods which are raised locally or are made in them such as baizes, the inferior *pañete*, sacks, and an infinite number of trifles including primitive objects having a fantastic price from which the Indians are not exempt, it seems at first glance— to those who regard things superficially—that the *corregidores* are tyrants because they distribute their effects at an exorbitant price, without paying heed to the kind they receive in payment or its value when sold for silver, after the many risks they run. All Spaniards agree that the worst offices of *corregidor* are those which collect in kind, whether or not the value of the latter attains a high price; but foreigners charge them with criminal action at the slightest provocation. I remember having read in certain accounts that the Spaniards in Chiloé sold 1 *vara* of native baize, which is worth 2 reales in Lima, for 2 pesos, and considering the distance alone, it could be sold in Paris for 50 *livres tournois*, which would pay the price for a large number of wire nails on which the Spaniards would reap great profit, particularly at the present time when each thousand is worth 2 reales.

Second Accusation Made against the Spaniards to Prove their Tyranny

It has been said repeatedly that the Spaniards made use of the Indians, treating them like slaves and even worse, because either they did not pay them or their stipend was so small that the Indians could scarcely support themselves on it. Lima is the most expensive place in all of Peru, and a helper of a brick-mason, whether he is a Negro or an Indian, earns 5 reales every day, being able to eat abundantly on 2 reales and have 3 reales left; but if the Indian or Negro chooses to drink up 8 reales worth of liquor and to take his meals in a tavern, of course the pay for six days will not suffice for food and drink for two.

The fact is that the first Spaniards, seeing that the Indians happily maintained themselves on a few grains of corn, like our chickens, and that eight Indians scarcely did as much work as two Spaniards, computed their salary at a very low figure. If we said all we know about this subject, it would be necessary to compose a thick volume. Foreigners are scattered throughout the kingdom, and we have not observed in them any more justice; they even consider us overindulgent.

The Third Accusation, the most Horrible which can be Imagined or Spoken of, is that concerning the Obrajes or Workshops

I confess that I have never read in any book about such tyrannies as the proprietors of the workshops commit against the wretched Indians. The Spaniards, without any experience, and even many ministers, informed by those falsely pious ones, have conceived great horror at merely hearing mention of the workshop, which seems to them more dark and gloomy than the cave of Trophonius, and they consider it similar to the mercury mines in Spain, about which the great Quevedo wrote the following stanza in the name of one forced laborer:

> Hidden away in a prison
> His Majesty keeps me concealed,
> Groping in a Norwegian alleyway
> With hangnails that have not healed.

The forced laborers in the workshops, or those who enter into them of necessity, need not grope with their nails because they are generally directed in them by very able men, the same as is happening, I believe, with those who go to work the mines in Guadalcanal. Our workshops are usually established in the best locales in the circumference of Cuzco and the immediate provinces, having agreeable climates. They are houses of considerable expanse and comfort. Their patios and inner patios are like small plazas surrounded by corridors, so that neither sun nor rain will cause discomfort to those working outside the shop rooms. The latter are well-proportioned, and between one loom and another is a distance adequate for making a small fire to roast or cook meat, which is provided; of similar comfort are all the other rooms for the spinners, carders, dyers, etc.

All those who work in these shops have an equal ration of food, the price of which is equitably regulated. I would like to ask European, African, and Asian gentlemen what food they provide to their forced laborers who work three times as hard as these. They will reply—and if they refuse, I will say it for them—that theirs have a ration of biscuit made from barley or rye flour, or by good fortune, some bread, which in Spain is called ammunition, made from poorly-ground wheat mixed with the chaff and often with the straw, from which mass one could build a strong wall, better than one made of mud. They rarely taste meat, and for a real treat of dried vegetables they are given a wooden bowl full of parboiled beans, without seasoning or relish other than that provided by their hunger.

Their bed, which is a heavy plank with a chain laid across for securing their feet, seems more like a torture rack than a resting place for the alleviation of the day's fatigue. No one has considered this kind of punishment of the natives as cruel or tyrannical within his own country, considering it necessary for restraining delinquents. Let us then consider the forced laborers in our mills, dividing them into two groups. The one is comprised of those guilty of various misdemeanors, the principal one being robbery, and the other, those put there so they may pay off their legitimate and confirmed debts since they have no means of payment other than the sweat of their labor in a house of coercion.

The first are placed in the shops for greater security, because the prisons in the Indian towns are generally dormitories or damp and lugubrious rooms of little security, from which those who wish to escape daily, a situation greatly aided by the Indians in order to be free from the obligation of guarding them

and supporting them, in case they are strangers or do not have relatives to give them what is necessary for their sustenance. The security of the workshops, their extension and healthfulness, to which is added also the means of support afforded by the work, suggested to the *corregidores* this means of securing them in these shops, shackling them in proportion to their crime so they might not escape—but the most severe amounts to two iron rings, girding the legs above the ankle, with a chain between, so light and fragile that any youth can break its links with two or three blows with a rock weighing one pound; therefore, it does not serve as an obstacle to his fleeing nor as a hindrance in performing his function. If he devotes himself to some task and does not have anything to eat, he is given regular ration of food. This usually amounts to dried beef, some dried vegetables, chile, maize, and sufficient firewood, water, and salt, with which these shops are well provided. If the delinquent applies himself to the work and fulfills his task, he is then considered a voluntary worker, is paid as such, and has his shackles removed.

Those imprisoned because of debts enter the workshop immediately because it is the intention that they pay their debt by this means. There are many tasks in the shops which require no skill, and they are the most rigorous work, but if the debtors are intelligent, the administrator places them in other less difficult jobs, in accordance with the needs of the workmen. This is regulated with equity, the best proof being that many willing workers pay off 1½ debts each week, others 1¼, and the slowest and most indolent gradually fulfill their obligations, but no blame is cast upon them, nor are they reprimanded; but they try to encourage those arrogant or lazy debtors who resist work, or do it poorly, with a whip, applied between the extremity of the back bone and the place where the flesh begins, or to speak more precisely, in the spot where boys are whipped, which reprimand is received by the lazy and those given to idleness like a game, causing them discomfort for only one-eighth of an hour in a whole week; and this constitutes the entire tyranny, which is so exaggerated, of the workshops and their superintendents. It is possible that in Europe, and even in Lima, they will not believe what I am going to say on the matter of food for the volunteer workmen and all those who complete their tasks, even though they may be forced laborers. To all of these is given, at least twice a week, an adequate supply of mutton—fat and *descansada*. In more than four workshops in the provinces adjoining Cuzco, I have seen large chunks, hanging between one loom and another, which could arouse a craving in men of the best tastes. It will seem perhaps to some persons, our own people as well as strangers, that all I have said is a poetic fiction to vindicate the proprietors from the tyrannies with which they are charged. I need not give satisfaction to the foreigners, and even less to the Spaniards living on this continent, because they can easily become enlightened—or else accuse me of being a flatterer and over-zealous defender of the principal men of Cuzco. I confess that I esteem these people highly because of their probity and generosity in the kind of treatment afforded their workers and subjects.

There is something deceitful in everything except milk, and even into that water may be poured; and sometimes a fish is found to prove it! We do not deny that the overseers make the profits off the laborers, supplying them with effects which are not worth half the price at which they are sold; but all this is nothing more than an artifice and a reciprocal fraud, to which no attention should be given; and if any circumspect is shown it is in favor of the workers and servants, because there is no precedent that they should pay their debts or loans, since the overseer is ever obliged to give them their adequate rations of food, to dress them with the cloth which they make, cure their illnesses, and provide all the ecclesiastical rights, including burial; wherefore, although the profit is made off these misguided creatures—and they deserve no other name than this—it is a profit which seems like a fantastic fortune only when it appears in the ledger.

If it were said that the proprietors of workshops are stupid men, maintaining such an offensive business, I would satisfy the charge saying that in this kingdom in every ten enforced laborers found in workshops, scarcely two may be counted who work willingly, and thus the proprietors of these shops, and even the lessees, sacrifice 7,000 or 8,000 pesos to keep the number of laborers adequate to maintain the shop in a state capable of realizing any profit. The latter scarcely reaches 20 per cent per year, in the event that the good cloth may be sold for cash silver at 3 reales a *vara,* which is impossible in the present state of the kingdom. In order to assure the maintenance of their shops at some profit, the proprietors deal with merchants handling goods from Europe, who will pay the price of the provinces, which is 3½ reales per *vara.* The usual agreement is that the proprietor receives half in effects—which are commonly called Castilian, although they are from all of Europe— and the other half in minted silver. The goods given by the merchants are generally those which they cannot sell because of their color or because some pieces of fabric are not currently in use, or because they offer a sizeable loss; and supposing, or I should say, being certain, that the merchant makes 40 per cent on these goods, and the proprietor gives them for the same price to the workers seeking supplies, either for their own use or to exchange them for silver in order to continue their excesses, the proprietor always earns 20 per cent, and if his mill produces 80,000 *varas* of baize and *pañete* annually, as is done in the largest mills, he earns 5,000 pesos, assuming that the production of each *vara* of cloth costs him no more than 2½ reales, which is the estimate made by the most intelligent men.

At the present time the shops in Cuzco are very short of means because trade with Europe is continuous, and the baizes from England are sold at a very low price, as are the linens and woolen products, which, since they are in abundance, debase the local product, to which is added the fact that in the environs of La Paz the flow of money is increasing (much of which is furnished by the interior provinces) and all this contributes to the decadence of a city which could be without dispute the greatest in the kingdom, because of its location, terrain, and products, surrounded by provinces that are the most fertile and abundant in produce, and in useful inhabitants—the Indians who labor at the cultivation of the land and in mechanical tasks, and bring the gold and silver from the most distant provinces.

CHAPTER XVIII

THE OPINION OF THE INSPECTOR CARRIÓ ON THE *REPARTI-MIENTOS*. THE *CORREGIDOR* AND THE INDIANS. THE INDO-LENCE OF THE INDIANS. THE OPINION OF THE AUTHOR. THE NAME CONCOLORCORVO. THE VIRTUES, QUALITIES AND CUS-TOMS OF THE INDIAN. THE CASTILIAN AND QUECHUA LANGUAGES.

YOU have already seen, Señor Inca, and you can see whenever you wish, the two greatest tyrannies com-mitted against the Indians by the present-day Spaniards, which are the principal ones demanding the attention of merci-ful men. Some believe that there must be merchants and dealers in mules who would manage the *repartimientos* at prices which are equitable, according to their concept; for example, the mules sold by the *corregidores* at 30 pesos each would be distributed for 20 by the men from Tucumán; and so it is with other products. I agree that some simple men would yield to the temptation to earn 5,000 pesos more on a thousand mules, but they would refuse the transaction, even when they would collect over a period of five years, because in addition to losing at least one trip, they would spend twice as much on their maintenance and paying the salary to the boys and caciques, because the distribution of 1,000 mules cannot be accomplished in less time than it takes for three or four sermons by the regular priests. There are many other objections which would take too long to explain and which could convince the diligent *corre-gidores* only with considerable difficulty.

"Finally, Señor Inca, I dare say that the *repartimientos* oper-ating under regulations are what support the Indians in their lands and their homes. Likewise, I dare to state that if it were absolutely forbidden to entrust the Indians with clothes, mules, and iron for tools for farm work, they could be ruined within ten years and would let themselves be eaten by lice, due to their lazy temperament and their inclination solely to drunkenness. I am tired of hearing some subjects praise a province and call it revitalized because it has paid off its *repartimiento* at the end of three years. This has happened many times with the highland Indians, but I should like to ask, what progress do these people make in the following two years? Perhaps they think that the Indians save money or increase their yokes of oxen or their supply of tools. If this is their idea, they are very much deceived, because in place of achieving this benefit as a result of having doubled the work in the three preceding years, through the efforts of the *corregidor* and his collectors, they have no other objective than that of drunkenness; and to maintain this state they sell their mule or cow, and frequently the tools used for working the fields, being content to sow only a little maize and a few potatoes which provide them with food and drink, and to guarantee the taxes so that the caciques and governors will not bother them or put them in the workshops which they abhor only because of their confinement.

"The opposite happens when the Indians are indebted to the *corregidor*. Then each town resembles a swarm of bees, and even the women and children spin wool and cotton on their way to church, so that their husbands can weave cloth. Everything is in motion and in this state abundance is perceived. The big farmer finds workmen and the shop foreman finds teasel and chamiso at a moderate price; and so it is with everything. The Indians have the same quality as mules in that they are ruined by very hard work, but they become very torpid and almost useless with too much idleness. For the Indian to preserve himself with any possessions, it is necessary to keep him in a continual movement proportionate to his strength; wherefore I would prefer to serve a province in which the Indians had paid the last peso to my predecessor the day I arrive than to find them revitalized, as they commonly say, for a period of one or two years, in which state I would consider them weakened in strength, accustomed to idleness and the vices springing from it."

The inspector was about to conclude his subject, about which he was talking, I knew, with aversion and distaste; but I had importuned him to suggest a solution to the several charges which Spaniards make reciprocally against each other about oppressing the Indians, taking away their possessions, and using them more harshly than if they were slaves. "Come now, Señor Inca. How many questions like that do you expect to ask me?" "More than two hundred," I replied. "Then go to the jail where there are plenty of idle birds of all kinds; there you will find a great variety of opinions, and you may accept those you deem best." "There is no idleness in jail," I answered, "because they need the time to scratch themselves and to kill their lice." "You are wrong," he told me, "because most of them eat lice, if they are Indians and mestizos. The Spaniards, tired of killing these loathsome animals, put them into a small tubular container, and when some man or woman passes near the bars and does not give them alms, with one puff they blow 200 lice on his back, and in less than a minute they are scattered from his neck over his entire body, causing unbearable ravage, because these starving creatures are going from a sterile pasture to one of abundance. But, to shorten the discussion, I should like to hear your candid opinion about these tyrannies and extortions. Speak now as a Spaniard, but do not forget the general skepticism of the Indians."

"In good time, Señor Don Alonso, but explain to me the meaning of skepticism." "This word," he said, "means universal doubt in all matters. The Indians doubt everything. I shall illustrate with two very different examples; the first illustrates what little faith they have, and the second, their scanty talent and excess of malice. Ask an Indian, instructed in the faith, if Jesus Christ is really present in the Sacred Host, and he replies, 'He probably is.' If he is asked whether a thousand sheep have been stolen from him, even though he has never had any sheep, he answers, 'They probably were.' Reconcile these two standards for me, Señor Concolorcorvo, and answer the first question I put to you." "I confess, sir," I said, "that the Indians in general have nothing worthy of being coveted by the Spaniards, because their entire wealth, speaking of the most prosperous ones, amounts to a yoke of oxen, a plow, a small hut in which they keep their meager harvest of corn and potatoes, along with all their furniture, which is scarcely worth 4 pesos, with some of them maintaining the mules provided by the *corregidor* to aid in transporting their belongings. The ordinary and lazy Indians, who occupy the larger part of the provinces, do not have one-fourth of these scanty possessions which are derived from application and work. Their house is reduced to a straw-covered hovel, called *ycho,* with a door which is entered with difficulty on all fours; their furniture corresponds, but if it were thrown into the street, it would just be picked up by another Indian servant in greater state of wretchedness. Therefore, I say that the Spaniards of this century . . ." "And all centuries," added the inspector. ". . . had no need, and I believe they never will have, to rob the Indians, since the latter, in general, think of nothing but their leisure and drunken orgies, which are followed by other brutal acts. I affirm that my countrymen are not the ones robbed, but rather they are the robbers of the Spaniards."

"Your critique is very fine," said the inspector, "but it pointed out to me that, in the time of the native monarchs and caciques, the Indians were in worse condition, because those princes and leaders kept them reduced to an oppressive servitude since they worked their land, with the strength of their arms, for their scarce food supplies, and never knew any meat other than that of the llama, vicuña, and alpaca, from the wool of which they wove their clothes. The Spaniards only did away with, or at least decreased, the abominable acts among these wretched people, and introduced the profitable use of cattle, horses, mules, and sheep, iron tools for working the fields and mines, nets and hooks for taking advantage of the products and gifts from the rivers and sea, as well as an endless number of other artifices and tools for working with less discomfort."

"With what nation," I asked, "would you compare the Indians, considering the configuration of the face, the color, and their customs?" "With themselves," replied the inspector. "I have traversed almost all of New Spain and this entire kingdom of Peru, and I have found no other difference than what one finds between hens' eggs. Anyone who has seen one Indian may consider he has seen them all; only in the paintings of your Inca ancestors, and even in you and others saying they are descended from the royal Inca house, have I observed more divergence; your faces resemble those of the Moors in the nose and mouth, although the latter have an ashen color, while you have that of a crow's wing." "Perhaps for that reason I was given the name Concolorcorvo." "Yes, Sir," he said. "I swear by the Battle of Almansa and the Peace of Nimega that I shall perpetuate that name in my house, as my forefathers did the name of Carlos, which is not as sonorous or meaningful. Concolorcorvo! What a resounding appelation, capable of stunning an army of great numbers, and of competing with the name of Manco Capac, which always struck me greatly, as did that of Miramamolín de Marruecos."[1]

"Do me the pleasure, Señor Don Alonso, of telling me something of the virtue, character, and circumstances of the Indians." "You could divulge this better, Señor Inca, depicting your inner state and inclinations, but not in a way that would cause you to turn pale (since you cannot blush). I say that the Indians are very suspicious in matters of faith and hope, and they are totally without charity, even toward their parents,

---

[1] The names of Manco Capac and Miramamolín de Marruecos are striking because of their cacophonous alliteration and because they were great figures in Inca history and chivalric literature.

wives, and children. The women are revengeful in the highest degree, even to the point of being inhuman, but we have also seen them stand up against armed men in order to defend their benefactors, the Spaniards, and, with more enthusiasm, their *compadres*. In the church and public processions they show much compassion with their tears and sobs, so that in their exterior acts they differ from men as greatly as the perceptible from the imperceptible, although both observe considerable silence, sobriety, and circumspect in the church, making two separate rows for the men and women, with a wide aisle between, so that those who wish may come in and sit where they choose, within the section designated for their sex; only the infants and very small children are permitted to be with the women. On feast days they all attend mass punctually, which is usually held at eleven o'clock in the morning, with the bells beginning to peal at eight so that those from afar may make ready, since at precisely ten o'clock the men are to be in the cemetery, dividing into tribal or family units, and the women inside the church; to these groups two Indian priests are assigned, who repeat to them all the exact doctrine, and at the time of entering the church, they call the names of all those on their lists, and to him who is absent without good reason, a fitting punishment is meted out: to the women, from the waist up, and below the waist for the men, at the hands of some Indian who; although he encounters the mother who gave birth to him, his wife, or his children, dispatches justice without showing charity or preference. I am going to draw this topic to a close by showing the exactness of the Indian. A certain *corregidor* ordered his Indian servants to give 100 lashes to one of his Negro slaves. They tied him securely to a post, and after having dealt him more than 80 blows, doubt arose as to whether they had given him 85 or 86. The Negro swore that he had counted 86. The Indians were of the opinion that they had done only 85, and so to ease their conscience, they started the count over again. The Negro spoke in defeasance, begging the Indians to take into account the 85 strokes of which they were certain; but they did not heed his pleas and dealt him the hundred over and above the 85; this is the proof of the great charity which they have for their fellowman!

"At dawn each day the children of both sexes go to the patio of the priest's house, or to that of his associate, where they are reviewed on the doctrines with great formality, the older children repeating them with exactness. I do not believe there is another nation in the world where Christian doctrine and the exterior aspects of religion are taught with more firmness than in the Spanish Americas, speaking now of areas where people live together, because truthfully, on the farms where large or small animals are raised, the shepherds are obliged to live in desolate places at great distances, and the same is true of some poor tillers of the soil, availing themselves of plots of land of little fertility on the slopes and in the ravines, who are lacking in spiritual nourishment and frequently die like animals, although it is not the fault of the clerics since the victims' relatives or companions do not inform them, either because of indolence or the lack of knowledge. This evil is almost irremediable in the sierra, because of the quality and location of the territories. These poor people, obliged to live in desolate areas, with no other companionship than that of the animals, are of necessity more crude, because besides not having intercourse with persons who speak the Castilian language, they scarcely understand signs and try to hide themselves from any Spaniard or mestizo who does not speak in their language, considering them barbarians, just as we consider them. Ovid expressed it thus, from his exile in Pontus, confessing that he was a barbarian in that land since no one understood him: *Barbarus hic ego sum quia non intelligor ulli.*"

"It seems, Señor Don Alonso, that in the preceding point you are praising the priests." "It is certain, Señor Inca, that the greater part of them fulfill their obligations in this matter; but so that you will not think that I flatter them or consider them perfect in all aspects, I am going to make an accusation against them, with all due respect to their great dignity, in a matter which is very delicate, both morally and politically. It is manifest that the Indians maintain some idolatries from their tradition which is kept alive through story and song in their language, as has happened in all the world. The worthy priests are usually men who are very wise in sacred writings, but since they generally do not know the Indian language, they solicit interpreters as their aides, on whom the title of *lenguaraz*, talkative one, as they are commonly referred to, is bestowed without their having any qualification other than a crude Latinity, a few definitions of meager moral examples, and whatever is dictated to them by natural reason. The priests explain the Scriptures to the Indians very poorly because they do not understand their language, and the aides equally poorly because they do not understand the Scriptures, not even literally from the Latin." "I have observed this," I told the inspector, "in a town where all the Indians were saying in the Our Father: 'Thy will be done, Lord, in Heaven as it is on earth.' Don Miguel Sierralta and his wife, who are the best linguists in the town of Guancavélica, assured me that they had heard a certain priest preach more than 20 heresies and crass errors in one sermon to the Indians in their town. I have been told the same by others.

"The damages ensuing in civil life are worthy of much regard, since through their stories and songs they preserve many idolatries and fantastic grandeurs of their ancestors, which result in their abhorring the Spaniards, regarding them as tyrants and prime cause of their misery, wherefore they have no scruples about robbing them when they can; and in mobs, in which usually 50 join against one, they commit deplorable depravities on the Spaniards, in which the indiscretion of certain stupid aides of priests and *corregidors'* cash-keepers usually figures. For these reasons and others which I pass over, the greatest effort should be made to make them forget entirely their native tongue. Only the priests can accomplish such a feat

with ease, merely by ordering that the doctrine be taught to the
children of both sexes in Castilian, which they will learn without resistance since they are indifferent about language. In this
way, without any effort, all children would be speaking Castilian at ten years of age; to this the requirement could be added
that they should always be spoken to and required to respond
in this language, calling attention to their solecisms as we do
with the gibberish of our own children and others. Except for a
few, the Indians who live in the unpopulated areas understand
and speak Castilian. In the time that I was *corregidor*, I observed that when the interpreter relayed a sentence to me, if
they agreed they said to me, '*Ao*, señor,' which is equivalent to
saying 'Yes, sir'; if they lowered their head considerably it was
an indication that they were satisfied, but when, due to the
malice or ignorance of the interpreter, he said something to me
contrary to their idea, without waiting for the interpreter to
conclude, they would say, '*Manan*,' at the same time affirming
it by moving their heads to the right and left, as we do.

"Let it not be thought that these were manifestations of half-
educated Indians. I insist that I have observed them in the most
barbaric Indians in various provinces and towns, which is clear
proof that almost all of them understand Castilian. All the
alcaldes, governors, *caciques*, overseers, and other ministers
which, in a province of 25 towns, number no less than 200
individuals, and in more than 1,000 who have been *alcaldes* or
councilmen, all express themselves competently in our language; but the most interesting thing is that when the common
people become drunk, which is day after day, they speak
Castilian in their assemblies and meetings, which is a marvel
comparable to that which took place in pagan days to those
who entered the cave of Trophonius, which sent forth prophets
and seers with the sacred vapors; it may be that the same thing
occurs, and no doubt it does, because it is true that the vapors
of Bacchus have the effect of instilling the gift of languages.

"No one can doubt that the Indians are much more adept

than the Negroes in all intellectual works. Almost every year more than 500 inexperienced Negroes, of harsh and crude speech, enter the kingdom, and with the exception of a few barbaric, or I should say fatuous, ones, none of them understands or makes himself understood sufficiently well in the space of one year; and their children, with no other contacts than with their masters, speak Castilian like our common people. The Negroes do not have interpreters, nor has there ever been any necessity. The Spaniards needed them at the beginning of the conquest to deal with the Indians and to be informed of their intentions and designs. Afterward, with the civil wars, they had no opportunity to teach their children Castilian, and since the latter were always in the care of their Indian mothers or maids, the mestizo children grew up speaking their language, and this was extended in all the sierra with issue, since even though schools for Castilian and Latin languages were established, they always retained an aftertaste of the foundation language, as is the case with you, into whose skull I have not been able to drive the idea that you should stop pronouncing and writing *llovía* and *lluver*, and an infinite number of other errors." "This is nothing, Señor Don Alonso, because I am a pure Indian." "Let's leave off this pure business until the mother who gave birth to you declares it, since it has nothing to do with the case in point; you had the same upbringing outside the home as the rest of the common Spanish highlanders, and you always served Europe and read only books written in Castilian; yet even though with your eyes you see it written *lluvía* and *llover*, you always say just the opposite, without giving us an argument dictated by logical reasoning, because if you extended this, you would say *llovía* from *llover* and *lluver* from *lluvia*."

"In Chuquisaca, Potosí, and Oruro, even the women speak Castilian very well in their public conversations and in their gatherings. In La Paz they speak Castilian competently in private conversations with men, but in their gatherings one hears only Aymará, which resembles greatly the Moorish language, in that the throat plays an important role. In their polished city of Cuzco, they speak Quechua, which is the softest language in the kingdom, but the principal ladies who speak Castilian very well manifest the passion they have for their first language, learned from their mothers, nurses and maids, because in their meetings, although attended (as the Romans would say) by barbarians, they speak Quechua among themselves at such speed that the eminent Creoles can scarcely understand it. The common Spaniards, who are so not only by birth and upbringing, are the most guilty of this lack of attention or etiquette, because having a very poor knowledge of Castilian, they are ashamed to express themselves in it and so expose themselves to the laughter of the jesters, who are in such abundance in the world. A certain Spanish lady, beautiful and well-dressed, was on the balcony of her house with a rose in her hand, when a speaker of nice words, who passed in her sight, wanted to flatter her with the following Spanish adage: *Bien sabe la rosa en que mano posa* (A rose well knows in what hand it rests), to which she replied with great satisfaction: *Qui rosa, qui no rosa, qui no te costó to plata.*[2] In the other provinces, from the slopes of Cuzco to Lima, proceding through Augaraes, Jaujinos, and Guarochiríes, the language in general is somewhat corrupted, but people understand each other very well."

---

[2] The sentence which the lady is attempting to say is: *Que rosa, que no rosa, que no te costó tu plata.* (Whether it is a rose or not, it did not cost you anything!)

CHAPTER XIX

CHRISTIAN DOCTRINE AMONG THE INDIANS. ERRORS RESULT-
ING FROM THE TEACHING OF QUECHUA. VICES OF THE
INDIANS. THEIR BRAVERY AND INDUSTRY. THE CONQUEST OF
THE CHACO. THE MANNER OF GOVERNING IT.

THE prime accusation made against the priests is that of
not putting all their zeal into introducing the Castilian
language through their teachings by the easy means
which I proposed. Only these ministers of the doctrine can accomplish this triumph, because the *corregidores*, who are sent to
govern 30 towns for five years, and ofttimes two years, do not
have the time nor the opportunity to establish a means so useful
to the Church and the State. The priests' aides, who generally
are ordained because of their language ability and who deal
most with the Indians, do not want them to speak another language, and they reprimand those who try to express themselves
in Castilian, calling them garrulous and pedantic, as the present
very worthy bishop of La Paz confessed to me. This method
considerably retards the progress of the Castilian language.
The members of the Company of Jesus, who were the principal
teachers in this kingdom for 150 years, tried, through a policy
prejudicial to the State, to keep the Indians from communicating with the Spaniards and from learning any other than their
native language, which the priests understood very well. I do
not wish to censure or refute their ideas nor to combat them,
and since they are now expatriated,[1] I should rather speak of

[1] When the 1767 royal decree of Charles III expelled Jesuits from Spain
and Spanish America, it is estimated that there were approximately 22,500
Jesuits administering to over 700,000 Indians in missions. In 1768 Alonso
Carrió de la Vandera was assigned to accompany a group of these priests
back to Europe where he deposited them with authorities in Cadiz.

general aims which their disciples and successors are continuing. Those good fathers affirmed that the Indians, by dealing with the Spaniards and learning their language, were being contaminated by and were engaging in horrible vices which they had never imagined. It cannot be doubted that some ministers of the gospel were speaking in bad faith on this point because, in all the histories written at the beginning of the conquest, many abominations, which the Spaniards never thought of—as I said before—were described; wherefore, the conquistadors may be charged only with declaring in their language the enormity of the sin and an abhorrence of those such as eating human flesh, sacrificing prisoners of war to their gods, worshiping monsters, tree trunks of horrendous shape, and ofttimes poisonous vermin.

"The plurality of women and incest, permitted by Indian law, were not vices of the Spaniards, nor were the bestial and unnatural crimes which they found common among the natives, and can be seen at the present time among those who have not been conquered. Infraction of the sixth, seventh, and eighth commandments of God was, and is, very common, as it is among the Spaniards and other peoples of the world, from which it may be inferred that the latter introduced into the kingdom no sin with which it was not already supplied twofold. If one speaks of execrations or curses, the Indians knew how to say *Supaypaguagua*, which means Son of the Devil, and as such God understood it; He was offended in one language as well as in another—unless one wishes to say that God understands only Castilian and punishes only those who offend Him with words from it. Drunkenness was found more widespread among the Indians than in any other part of the world, and the Spaniards alone seem to be blamed for having introduced it by a means more forceful than their customary use of brandy and wine. The priests would do a great service to God, to the King, and to the Indians if they would banish the Indian language from their curacies, substituting Castilian, charging their aides with this duty and ordering it of all ministers. The *corregidores*, their deputies and cash-keepers, and all those who travel through their curacies, would benefit notably, because the Indians, under pretext of not understanding Castilian, feign ignorance in many cases which gives rise to affrays and grievous quarrels. But enough about Indians."

"No, for the love of God," I said to him. "Do not take your leave without saying something of what you think about their bravery and industry." "As for the first, I say that they are similar to greyhounds which are capable of attacking a lion when in a pack, but alone they can scarcely conquer a hare, and no sooner is a drop of blood drawn on one than he considers himself dead. In the greatest commotion—provided it is not accompanied by drunkenness—as soon as they see one of their number dead, the rest flee, although they may number 50 to every 1 of our men." "Therefore," I replied, "with a very limited number of men, the Spaniards conquered more than 7 million Indians." "Your understanding is very meager, Señor Inca," the inspector said to me. "A conquest of a civilized kingdom, which is obliged to lose its inhabitants and expects no help from other powers, is effected by victory in two or three pitched battles, particularly if the leaders perish or are taken prisoner. The Spaniards, with the rout of the army of Otumba, accomplished little more than acquiring the reputation of being valiant, but they showed the Indians that peninsulars were mortal and vulnerable, as were their horses; but in the capture of Mexico, aided by the noble Tlascaltecas, they subjected that great empire of more than 40 million souls, because each prince, general, or cacique lent his support for fear of being defeated or crushed. If Darius had opposed Alexander the Great with 50,000 men under one or two good generals, even if they were defeated, the officials could have collected at least 20,000 men in the retreat, and Alexander, although he had not lost over 4,000 or 5,000, would have busied a part of his army in guarding the prisoners and baggage. Darius could have attacked a second, third, fourth, and fifth time with an equal army, which certainly would have wearied the valiant troops of Alexander and decreased their number in the skirmishes and in the very garrisons in the towns which they were conquering.

"Darius attacked Alexander as a conqueror and not as a warrior. He was of the opinion that Alexander should be frightened of the powerful army assembled and of the magnitude and trumpeting of his elephants. With this confidence he offered battle, and in one day he lost his life and a great empire, abandoning his treasures, including his wife and daughter, to the conquerer. The Chileans knew better how to conduct themselves with the Spaniards because, observing that they had always been defeated, even when they had four times as many combatants, and many times even with a hundred men to one, they changed their plans and method of fighting. They judged that the Spaniards were more skillful and valiant than they, and that they fought with better arms; but they knew that they were mortal and subject to human misery, and thus they resolved to offer them battle repeatedly, until they tired them, defeated them, and forced them to retire to their trenches, having lost some towns. These reflections prove that a large army of 200,000 men, even though they be veteran soldiers, confusedly lead by inexperienced officers, can be routed and put to flight by 30,000 well-disciplined soldiers under the command of wise and valorous leaders. But these matters are beyond the scope of our discourse and talent; so tell me, Señor Inca, if you have more to say or ask about your fellow countrymen."

"I ask, then, why the Spaniards, who conquered 7 million Indians and converted them to their customs and laws, cannot convert and subject the Indians from the Chaco and the mountains?" "This question would be better put to one of your Inca ancestors and caciques; but since they have accounted to God for their actions, whether good or bad, I shall assume the task of defending them, as well as that of enlightening those

Spaniards who believe that the Chaco and the extensive mountain area each can be conquered by a thousand men of the
militia, trained and directed by good officers. Of course, I confess that this number of men, at great expense, could march
through some provinces and territories, but the barbaric Indians, having no formal or rooted towns, would shift their location, and laugh at the vain efforts of the Spaniards, who, unable
to fortify the places, would abandon them; and the Indians
would again recover them at their pleasure and at a considerable loss to us, as you so judiciously said in your Part I.

"I consider barbaric those people who are not subject to laws
nor magistrates, living according to their whims, always following their passions. The Indians of the pampa and the inhabitants of the Chaco are of this nature. In New Spain, because
it was impossible to convert the barbaric Indians who inhabit
the unpopulated plains in the center of New Vizcaya—since it
is more than 100 leagues on the royal highway to the valley
of San Bartolomé del Parral—four fortresses were established,
at 25 leagues' distance one from the other, each with 50 soldiers
and the corresponding officers, it being a requirement that the
former be married and of an adequate age for reproduction.
These men used to escort the large herds of mules to the next
fortress each month, because those not arriving by the third
day, when the cordon was being formed, waited in the surrounding countryside until the following month; to avoid this
the muleteers used to take measures to accelerate their pace, or
to tarry in fertile and secure pasture lands. For this convoy no
payment was demanded, since the officers and soldiers were
well paid by the King, as they are now. The soldiers from the
first three fortresses never penetrated the interior to the right
nor to the left more than 2 leagues, in order to protect the fields
in which they kept their horses; but in the very fertile and
delightful valley of San Bartolomé, where there is a large town
by the same name, a volant company was maintained which
went out in platoons to reconnoiter the fields, for vast dis-

tances, under orders not to attack the Indians unless victory was certain; in case a large group was found convened, the location was observed and notice was given to all fortresses and soldiers, so that with combined forces they could attack and disperse them with the loss of only a few.

"They rarely took prisoners, and seldom did they permit any of these barbaric Indians inside the fortress, because the soldiers said they served no purpose other than eating their bread and stealing their horses, if any trust were placed in them. When the fortresses were scarcely 20 years old, each already composed a large town of mestizos and Spaniards of both sexes, with cultivated lands and pastures for the cattle; thus the fortress in this part increased so much that the Count of San Pedro de Alamo, whose large estate bordered on it, asked the governor that it be moved or eliminated because it was of no use in that place since it was free from attacks by Indians, who were less damaging to him than the multitude of mestizos and Spaniards who supported themselves off his estates; and finally he said that he would pledge himself to clean up the fields and convoy the herds with his own men, at a saving to the royal treasury of the 12,000 pesos it was costing annually. Since His Majesty had established and endowed these fortresses under the condition that they should be moved as soon as the country became more populated and the Indians had been eliminated, the count's petition was granted, and at the present time there is probably not any fortress in that extensive territory, but there are towns, the population proportionate to the fertility of the land and the supply of water, of which the countryside of New Vizcaya is almost barren. I shall conclude this matter by recounting a public event which was notorious in New Vizcaya.

"A certain captain of the volant company—whose first name I do not recall but his last was Berroterán, which the barbaric Indians pronounced Perroterán—abiding by the pious maxims of our King, which urged repeatedly that peace should be granted to the Indians when they request it, even if it be in the midst of battle, their defeat at hand, was several times deceived by the promises made to him by these Indians. They counted on the benignancy of our laws. Deceived, numerous times, as I said, by these infidels, he resolved to make war on them without clemency; and thus when the Indians asked for *paz*, peace, the good Cantabrian would construe it as *pan*, bread, replying that he would take some for himself and his soldiers; then he would engage them with more vehemence until he succeeded in terrifying and driving them from that entire territory; and it is said that at his hour of death, when the priest assisting him in a good departure asked him if he repented for having killed so many Indians, he only replied that he regretted leaving on this earth even one scoundrel without religion, faith, or principle who thought only of perfidy and deceit, living at the expense of the toil of the Spaniards and the sweat of the civilized Indians. The truth is that there is no other means of dealing with the Indians except defensively and by curtailing their numbers gradually by increasing our own. In New Mexico, which is 800 leagues from the capital, a small number of Spaniards, under the command of a governor, reside among a multitude of disputing nations without taking sides other than to ask a conquering nation to pardon the remains of a defeated army which sought their protection. This guiding principle causes them to be feared and loved by those barbarians who are less gross than those inhabiting the pampa and the Chaco."

"From all you have said I infer that you consider the Indians civil people." "If you are speaking of those Indians subject to the emperors of Mexico and Peru and their laws, bad or good, I say that they not only have been, and are, civil, but they are more obedient to their superiors than any other nation in the world. From the Chichas to the Piuranos I observed with particular solicitude their method of governing themselves. They obey punctiliously every officer from the councilman who holds the office of apparitor to the *corregidor*. They make their living from their crops and the raising of cattle without aspiring to be rich, although they have had some opportunities with the discovery of mines and ruins; but they are content to extract from them only some little support for their festivals and bacchanals. Some attribute this frugality to the fear that the Spaniards might strip them of those treasures, which are usually imaginary, or are founded, like the gold and silver mines, on the labor of many men and much expense. The Spaniards would be very happy if the Indians were wealthy so they could establish trade with them and reap benefits from their riches; but the pity is that at the greatest fair held by the Indians, which is at Cocharcas, to which more than 2,000 Indians from several provinces come, not one of them buys a real's worth from any Spaniard, because they do not take to the latter's merchandise; and so they proceed to the Indian shopkeepers who have the patience to sell them a quarter of a real's worth of needles, a quarter's worth of agave thread, and so on. The commerce of the Spaniards is transacted among themselves, including the mestizos and other half-breeds derived from the Indians up and down the range of mixture. The rare Indian taking some commodities is respected by the Spaniards, who generously offer him their goods on credit and do not disdain to be friendly with him and to seat him at their tables.

"No Spaniard is capable of deceiving an Indian, and if a Spaniard takes something away from an Indian by violent means, the latter will pursue him for justice to the end of his life. With all this, I am not saying, and I said this before, that there are no tyrannies, but that they cannot be regarded as such since they are reciprocal, due to the bad foundations established by the first conquistadors who conducted themselves according to the custom of the country."

CHAPTER XX

THE civilized Negroes in these dominions are infinitely more crude than the Indians. Let the good Inca take note of the differences in the dances, song, and music between one race and another. The instruments of the Indian are the flutes and some stringed instruments, which they play softly, just as they do their small tambourines. Their song is gentle, although it always touches on the sad. Their dances are more serious and measured, and have only one aspect which we consider ridiculous, which is the multitude of small bells, jangling rhythmically, that hang over the entire body, down as far as the soles of their feet. It is certain that the bells were introduced by the Spaniards on the breast leather of their horses, to exhilarate those noble animals and to confound the Indians, who, after discovering that they were not evil spirits, adopted them as tutelary of their dances and amusements. The diversions of the newly-imported Negroes are the most barbaric and gross that can be imagined. Their song is a howl. By merely seeing their musical instruments one can infer the disagreeableness of their sound. The jawbone of an ass, well-cleaned of flesh, with its loose teeth, constitutes their principal stringed instrument, which they scrape with the bone of a sheep, a spear, or some other hard stick, producing some high soprano sounds so annoying and disagreeable that they incite the burros to cover their ears or to run, even though they are the most stupid animals that exist and the least-easily frightened. In place of the pleasant tambourine of the Indians, the Negroes use a hollow log on the two ends of which they stretch a coarse skin. One Negro carries this drum, held above his head, while another walks behind with two sticks, shaped like stilts, in his hand, beating the hide with their ends, without order and for the sole purpose of making noise. The other instruments are equally polished, and their dances are reduced to swinging the belly and hips in an indecent fashion, accompanied by ridiculous gestures which bring to mind the festival to the devil held by the witches on their Sabbath; and finally, the amusements of the Negroes resemble those of the Indians only in that they all begin and end in drunken orgies. There is something of this, if we are to speak fairly, in all the functions of the common people in Spain, particularly at the conclusion of the sacred pilgrimages which sometimes end up in cudgel-swinging, as in the plays called *entremeses*, the difference being that in the latter they are make-believe, while in the former they are so real that their effects can be seen, because there are men who keep going with a club in the hand and an open gash in the head, spouting more blood than a penitent.

The Indians, as I said elsewhere, at the slightest blow on the head from which they see a little blood pour, consider themselves dead, because they fear that their soul which they believe, more firmly than Descartes, is located in the pineal gland, will be breathed from them. But leaving aside the civilization of the Indians, with respect to their laws, customs, and blind obedience to their superiors, it cannot be denied that they have an extraordinary ability in all arts, and even in science, to which a small number is dedicated—and would that it were even smaller, because the kingdom needs only workers and artisans since there are more than enough Spanish Creoles for letters, to which may be added the small number of Indians of recognized nobility. The common Indians are usually inclined toward those arts in which the body works very little; wherefore, for every blacksmith there are 20 painters, and for one stonecutter, 20 embroiderers of silk, silver, and gold. The multitude of skilled workmen existing in this city for the exercise of these crafts, plus the lace-makers, rope-makers, and all the rest, arrest the progress of excellence, because the Indian esteems only the finished product, and thus it seems to him more useful to devote himself to painting for one day for 2 reales, on which he can eat and drink to his satisfaction, than to earn 4 reales in the hard work with the saw, hammer, and all that which accompanies the craft of a bricklayer or a stonecutter; in this they could proceed wisely if they were sure of finding something to do until the last moments of their lives, and if they had no other obligation than the frugal maintenance of their person; but this error grows not out of their ignorance, but out of their indolence and cowardliness."

"The large part of these workers," I said to the inspector,

"are not pure Indians." "I confess," he replied, "that there are probably some counterfeit mestizos, but I dare say that 90 out of 100 are pure Indians. The Indian is not distinguished from the Spaniard in the configuration of his face, and thus when he devotes himself to serving one of us who treats him charitably, the first task is to teach him cleanliness; that is, that he wash his face, comb his hair and cut his nails, and that even if he keeps his own dress, with those measures and a clean shirt, although it be of coarse cotton, he will pass for a *cholo*, which is the same as being of a mestizo mixture. If he serves the Spaniard well, the latter dresses him and provides shoes, and in two months he is a mestizo in name. If the master is an honest man and is satisfied with a short term of service, he asks the Indian if he wants to learn some trade, and tells him to elect one to his liking; since the Indians, as I have said, never apply themselves voluntarily to tasks requiring physical labor, they select painting, sculpturing, and all those things relating to lace-making. The first two practices, those of painting and sculpture, are the most gainful for your countrymen because there is no lack of people of bad taste who are devoted to whatever is cheapest. The painters have support immediately, as do the sculptors, since some of them devote themselves to religious figures. Being skillful in forming a tonsure or a crown, along with other clear and desirable characteristics such as long robes, they bring out into the plaza, at a very low price, all the patriarchs and saints of the religion, putting their names below their feet. Their greatest difficulty is in the portrayal of living subjects, rational as well as irrational, but in painting the Sultan of Turkey or some animal from India, they put his name in the border to enlighten ignorant people, thus fulfilling their obligation to them.

"Among this multitude of daubers there are fair copyists with some talent, but they are so irresponsible that if they get a small payment of 3 or 4 pesos they do not touch their brushes for a week, and they come saying that their pallet, brush, and paints were stolen, so they may get another loan. Trusting in these tricks, they do not refrain from making settlements so lowly that they seem incredible; because of this some gentlemen of this city, in order to obtain pictures to their liking, confine these irresponsible ones in their houses, but if they relax the vigil on them for an instant, they disappear, only to appear in some town in the region where there is a festival; in these, and in the sculptors of the area, like the actors, you have, Señor Inca, another, but different, species of *gauderios* on foot. Their distinguishing mark is that they carry their waistcoat over the left shoulder, although this custom is more common among the residents of Guamanga. The embroiderers have their own particular brand of trickery, since they often disappear with the thread and the cloth. So it is that the man who paid for the materials usually does not get the finery for his horse, because it goes to another for half the price of its intrinsic value; and thus the cheating goes on ad infinitum. Everyone considers gypsies as crafty robbers, but I am sure that if they appeared in Cuzco or in Guamanga, they would have much to learn, and even more in Quito and Mexico, which are the two largest universities founded by Cacus.[1]

"The Indians who have settled in Lima, devoting themselves to employment in the mechanical skills and positions in the blanket-making industry, are the exception to that rule. Do not think you can remove many men and women from the Indian classification because they are of a lighter color because this comes from cleanliness and better treatment, aided by the mildness of the climate, and so their descendants pass for true mestizos, and many for Spaniards. I have not seen anything written dealing with the decrease in number of the Indians,

[1] *Cacus.* A celebrated mythological bandit who had his grotto in Mount Aventino. He was a giant and emitted smoke and fire from his mouth. Legend says he stole four pair of oxen from Hercules while the latter was asleep, and dragged them to his cave backwards so there would be no tracks. However, Hercules pursued him and strangled him for his crime.

and I have only heard that the brandy introduced by the Spaniards is the principal cause. I cannot deny that the excess of this beverage may be the cause of the death of a few hundred in this vast empire, but it is too much to suppose that 500 Indians, at the average age of 40, had perished each year due to its excessive use. The Indians usually marry between the ages of 15 and 20, when they have scarcely tasted brandy, and even if each one of the married men had no more than three children, there ought to be a sizeable increase among a people who do not journey outside their countries and have no destiny or state other than that of marriage. In the empire of Mexico, the Indians, not satisfied with the brandy introduced by the Spaniards, used, and still use, *mescal* and *chinguirito*, which are double the strength of the brandies of this kingdom, and cause the Spaniards who taste them violent headaches and great physical disorders, creating among them such a dislike that the mere smell of them causes illness. The Indians become drunk, as we have observed, and burst forth in delirium, and with all this the Indians are four times more fecund than those in this kingdom.

"Statisticians are astounded by the fact that there were 7 million Indians in this extended empire at the time of the arrival of Señor Toledo.[2] But if this is speaking only of those men paying taxes, the total number was almost unbelievable, since it amounted to 30 million souls, including those exempt by virtue of nobility and counting each taxpayer as having 3 dependents, a number which could not be supported in this kingdom, from Los Chichas to the valley of Piura. If at the present time there is scarcely 1 million, as some say, it is not known in what regions they live, nor from what products such a multitude supports itself. I have not seen remains of ruined towns which would correspond to even one-hundredth of this multitude of inhabitants, but rather they must have lived in the mountains, maintaining themselves on the fruits of the land;

[2] Francisco de Toledo, Viceroy of Peru, 1569-1582.

but supposing that 7 million Indians were of both sexes, including their children, it proves that in the greater part of this kingdom, made up of bleak tablelands, the women were of little fertility. Spain, which has scarcely one-fourth the territory which I have just indicated for this empire, continuously supports an equal number of Spaniards, not counting the infinite number of men who go to America, enlist in the armies and armadas and dedicate themselves to ecclesiastical offices and monasteries, none of which increase the State. It is considered the least populated country in all of Europe, and even so it exceeds by three times this kingdom, restricting myself now to the nation of Indians, known only as such.

"The Indian empire of Mexico, besides being infinitely more populated, has not had the occasion which this one has to corrupt the race with the entry of Europeans, and much less with that of Negroes. The latter are known only in small numbers between Veracruz and the capital because rarely do they go to the provinces of the interior where they are not needed, their being of little use in the cultivation of the fields and for the mills, due to the abundance of native Indians and mestizos and a few Spaniards who are obliged by necessity to apply themselves to these tasks. Its proximity to Europe entices many women to go to the Mexican empire, many of whom are Spanish, and their abundance makes the genre easily accessible for the general satisfaction of sensuality and the opportunity of marriage. From Lima to Jujuy, which is 500 leagues, one finds only a limited supply of Spanish women, with a particular paucity in Guancavélica, Guamanga, Cuzco, Paz, Oruro, and Chuquisaca, and in all other parts the Spaniards make their conquests of Negroes, mestizos, and other half-breeds among the Indian women, as did the first Spaniards, from which sprang the mestizos.

"These inevitable mixtures decrease even more the number of pure Indians, since these half-breeds have a color approximating white, and features without deformities, especially the

nose and lips. Everyone knows that sizeable groups of pure
Negroes of both sexes have been entering this kingdom for
over 150 years, particularly in the valleys between Piura and
Nasca, and although the farmers marry them, we see no increase in this race, despite their fecundity; this comes from the
fact that many Spaniards take Negro wives, from which union
are born mulattoes, whom their fathers try to set free. I believe
that if all those alive were restored to their mothers, neither the
Indian nor the Negro would suffer decline. *Intelligenti pauca.*
We do not deny that the mines consume a large number of
Indians, but this is not caused by the work they have in the
silver and mercury mines, but rather from the libertinage in
which they live, voluntary nocturnal revelries, and other excesses to which an absolute cure can be applied. The contact
with mercury, and with the rock which produces it, is the
same, or has the same effect, as any other metal or crude ore;
but let us suppose that every year 2,000 more Indians die in the
mines than in their homes while engaging in work more in accord with Nature.

"This number is really quite small compared to the multitude
of Indians who were registered in the times of Señor Toledo.
Some people assert that at the present time there are no more
than 1 million Indians of all sexes and ages, referring now to
this kingdom, and if from this number were subtracted the
900,000 women, children, old people, and those exempt from
taxes, and there were only 100,000 married men whose wives,
like land that lies fallow, bear children only every two years, it
would still result in an increase of 50,000 every year, and consequently in 100 years the Indian population would increase
by 5 million, because these people are not destroyed, even in
war, nor do they hide themselves away in the ecclesiastical
state; neither have we seen plagues, as in Africa, which do away
with millions of souls in just one season of the year. All these
observations prove clearly that the Indians of this kingdom
have never been prolific, because we see no vestiges of towns,

nor signs that the armies which the Incas led, and constituted all their power, were very numerous. The severe climate of the tablelands produces only scant pasture for the cattle, along with some potatoes. The ravines are small, reduced almost to gullies through which passes the water descending from the mountains at the skirt of which corn and barley are planted, as well as some vegetables of little worth. The well-cultivated valleys could support a number of additional people in the gold and silver mines, and in the only mercury mine; but if there were no miners to consume the products there would be less work in the valleys, because the proprietors would become lax in their cultivating or would receive new settlers, taxed in an amount that they could not pay in silver because of the lack of an outlet for their surplus products; and all those who live in sterile regions would be ruined as they are limited to just one crop a year which might be lost due to damage by the weather.

"We must confess that the Spaniards occupy a stretch of territory, not needed by the Indians, which is very fertile for raising sugar cane and alfalfa; but the larger part of this uncultivated terrain has been made fruitful by the Spaniards constructing ditches and bringing from great distances water which many Indian day-laborers have shared, and are sharing, so that the Indians gained, rather than lost, in the improvement of these lands in the deep ravines and sandy valleys. Their caciques, bosses, and overseers are much to blame for the decrease of the Indians because, pursuing the collection of royal tributes, they take it upon themselves to pay the taxes assigned to those who die, in order then to avail themselves of the lands which the King assigned to the dead taxpayers, either annexing them to their own lands, if they are neighboring, or selling them to some Spanish or mestizo farmer; and the natives are left without land, obliged to associate themselves with the farmers or to go to the large cities to find means of sustenance, which is usually prejudicial to the State because these vagabonds usually maintain a state of celibacy, exercising all manner of vices, until, because of them or their debts, they die at an early age or conclude their education in the workshop as in Europe in the outposts or the galleys. Many other causes could be pointed out for the diminution of the Indians, Señor Concolorcorvo, from the state in which our ancestors found them, but time would be lost, and if you wish to accompany me to Lima, prepare to leave in two days, because although this present city is so agreeable to foreigners, due to the generosity of the citizens and the public and private diversions in its beautiful estates, which are opened to any respectable man, I must leave it to proceed to my destination."

"I am ready," I said to him, "to follow you to Lima, to which I made my first and only trip when I left Cuzco with the intention of going to Spain to make inquiry about my uncle who, although an Indian, achieved the good fortune of dying in the honorable service of a gentleman on the council of the present Señor Charles III—may God perpetuate him—thanks to Señor Fernando VI—who enjoys immortal glory—because the Catholic Kings of Spain have never forgotten those descended from the Incas, even though the line may be transversal or doubtful; and if I, in reality, did not continue beyond Buenos Aires in my intention to place myself at the feet of the King, it was because of having received news of the death of my uncle and because many judicious Spaniards told me that my papers were so water-soaked and filled with erasures that they could not be read in the Court, although in reality they were in as fine condition as those of my good uncle." "There is no longer any help for that, Señor Inca, because not all Telemachuses are fortunate enough to have a Mentor guiding them; and now since you are anxious to return to Lima to inform yourself better about its grandeur, make preparations." "But shall we leave unmentioned much of the story of Cuzco?" "Have no worries," the inspector said to me, "because since it is necessary that we stop in Guamanga, you will have ample opportunity to write about the magnificence of the great Corpus

Christi festival and the amusements from the first day of the year through the last of the carnival preceding Shrovetide." "Those are my thoughts exactly," I said to him, "because I would commit a grave injustice and be considered a poor patriot if I failed to publish these grandeurs which you probably have not observed even in Lima itself." "Speak softly, *pasito*, as I always say, *aparte* as the Spanish comedians say, or *tout bas* as the French express it, because if the mulattoes of Lima hear it, they will put you in the harp, which amounts to being suspended by your hands, tied behind your back, a punishment they use in political matters." "Mulattoes and mules are all the same: they pretend to be gentle in order to give a kick when they wish." "You imitate your countrymen very well without great effort. Let us jump on to Guamanga," the inspector said to me, "by way of the successive posts; but first take your leave of the postal administrator of this great city." "It is right that we should do so," I said to him, "and that we should give a short description of his person and circumstances." "Take care," said the inspector, "because if you make a slip you can count on being seasoned with cudgels, as the natives of Extremadura say."

"Do not worry about that because their anger soon passes." "Do not count on it, Señor Concolorcorvo, because these crude fellows hand out their beatings as prettily when they are of good humor as when they are angered; do what you wish, but take my advice." "Very well," I replied. "Señor Don Ignacio Fernández de la Ceval is as tall as I am, more or less, and I measure 3 *varas*: one and one-half in front and the same behind. I confess that his hair is much finer than mine, but not as thick. Our coloring is different, since mine is that of a crow and his, of a swan. His eyes, somewhat dull, are different than mine, which seem like those of a hawk, and we are similar only in the size and particular charm of our faces for frightening children. His mouth is rent from ear to ear, while mine, although not so large, is adorned on both halves with blobber lips so fine that they compete with those of the King of Monicongo. His talent cannot be compared to mine because I have none whereas Don Ignacio is very clairvoyant; and finally, he is a man of integrity with the tenacity to overcome obstacles and to run the risk of hardship and grief in order to carry out the laws and ordinances dealing with income from the mails, as was the situation at the beginning of his administration; this is the principal administration of those added in this kingdom, since it receives and dispatches at the same time, in just three days, the mail from the general route from Lima to Buenos Aires, with the obligations to handle the commissions of gold, silver, and parcels, with which much care must be exercised; therefore, Don Ignacio earns well the salary of 1,200 pesos temporarily granted to him annually by His Excellency Señor Don Manuel de Amat, present viceroy of these kingdoms and subdelegate for the income from the mails."

"These last phrases," the inspector said to me, "exonerate you from the cudgel, because you proceeded in a fashion contrary to that used by surgeons who cleanse and soften the skin before applying the lancet or scissors."

"We all thought," I said to the inspector, "that by now you would have equipped yourself with boots and spurs for the departure—as I said before."

CHAPTER XXI

THE exit from Cuzco to Lima is difficult since the modern Spaniards abandoned the Inca causeway, an act in which they are really culpable, since even though these causeways were annoying to their beasts of burden, they could easily have been made into wide and unobstructed highways, reinforcing them with rubble and rocks from the old causeways.

. . .

All the countryside up to Guamanga is composed of hills, gorges, ravines, and some plains, in which are situated the canebrakes and sugar mills of the provinces of Abancay and Andaguaylas. The first has a formidable hill because in times of rain large ridges are formed in which the mules scarcely find a place to put their feet. This is a journey demanding alertness, in which the couriers are slowed down—just as in the preceding region in which the pack mules have made holes in the loose and muddy earth—where one cannot use his spurs or accelerate his pace without danger of a very great fall. At the conclusion of the descent one finds the great

Bridge of Abancay, or Pachachaca, Speaking with Impropriety

This is the third architecturally-constructed bridge seen since leaving Chuquisaca, with a single arch which rests on the two cliffs on either bank, dividing the provinces of Abancay and Andaguaylas. This bridge is among the first, or perhaps the first, built at the beginning of the conquest, to provide passage to Cuzco, and from this city to the other provinces beyond, since it crossed a large river which separated them. The bridge was made following all the rules of art, as it shows at the present time. It has been made famous, and it will be forever, by the two celebrated battles won near it by the royalists, but it is worthy of note that such a famous bridge has been abandoned and will soon fall into a state of ruin if repairs are not made. . . .

After crossing the bridge one enters the province of Andaguaylas, all of which is composed of hills, ravines, and hot gullies, where there are canebrakes and sugar mills populating the hillsides. It appears that the owners of these farms are men of little frugality, or that the farms, in reality, do not pay for themselves, because they call the canebrakes *engañaverales* and the sugar mills *trampiches*.[1] This entire region, like Abancay, is very hot and luxuriant, with the exception of some elevations; and while passing through it, the inspector, pointing out a high hill, told me that at its skirt was the memorable church dedicated to the Holy Virgin in her Sovereign Image, named Cocharcas—so called because once when a pious pilgrim was passing through the area with a statue of the Virgin, as is the custom with many of my countrymen, its weight became so great that it overburdened him, and when he related this to the ecclesiastics and farmers of the province, the excessive weight of the image was declared a miracle, as if the sacred statue were making it known that it wished to make this spot its home. Of course, the event made a great impression on those devout people because a magnificent church was built for simple devotion on a plain of the first descent, since a desert area would be inappropriate. At the same time a large plaza

---

[1] The attitude of the farmers is seen in this play with words. The *caña-* of the word *cañaveral*, canebrake, is changed to *engaña*, deceit, and *trapiche*, sugar mill, is altered to include the word *trampa*, trick.

was constructed, surrounded by shops, and in the middle a fountain was placed, issuing water only during the fair which is held from the day of Holy Name of Mary until the end of its octave—four days before and four days after—attended by all the Indians as well as the people from Guamanga, Cuzco, and the surrounding, and often distant, provinces. All these fine people convene to celebrate the eight-day festival contentiously, and besides the program of the church, which is extensive, there are large illuminations of natural and artificial fires during the eve and night of the day itself.

Two priests from the Company of Jesus used to come for the octave—paid to preach the gospel in the church and in the plaza and to exhort penance, as is the custom in the missions. The merchants usually set up their booths at the surrounding doorsteps, while some small mestizo farmers station themselves in the middle of the plaza; and all do a small amount of business because this fair constitutes more a festival than a business opportunity, wherefore only from Guamanga do any Spanish or mestizo shopkeepers come, trusting they will sell to the Spanish farmers, secular as well as ecclesiastical, from the surrounding area, since the little business done by the Indians is done with their fellow men. It has been disclosed that during the octave one clearly sees the miracle of the tree of the Virgin being covered with leaves at a time when the others in the hills are bare. This miraculous tree is rooted at the water trough, which, during the year, waters the small plantations that the Indians have in the surrounding heights; but four days before the fair they turn it into the trough so that all those attending may avail themselves of its waters. It is the tree that drinks from it beforehand; consequently its leaves revive, and it is covered with them at the end of 20 days, as would happen to any other tree that could obtain such beneficence. It is merely that the common people do not see the watering of said tree, nor do they reflect on the fact that springtime is already making its entry into these countries. Intelligent people, in place of this apparent miracle, substitute another concerning the *cholo* horse thieves from Guamanga—saying the Virgin effects a miracle with them alone, since although they come to her sanctuary on foot, they return to their homes on horseback.

The post which was always in Ocros was wisely established in Hivias because the one in Uripa became more convenient. All the territory between Zurite and Cangallo is of hot climate and infested with mosquitoes which are very vexing, particularly between nine in the morning and four in the afternoon, wherefore travelers should take measures to avoid their annoyance, especially in the journeys from Apurima and Quebrada de Pampas. In the latter there are many tunas which tempt the sweet-toothed travelers and cause intermittent fevers. The waters of the Pampas River, or whatever passes through this place, are turbid and somewhat salty, which excite more than quench the thirst. The inspector told me that they did harm only to those who gorge themselves, and that the two times he had lodged there of necessity, he had only experienced damage to his saddle mules from the multitude of bats which, attaching themselves to the back of the animal's neck, suck the blood and leave a wound with considerable swelling. The lead mules free themselves from these impertinent creatures, for as soon as they feel them, they roll over and pass their feet over their necks, by which they succeed in killing some, or at least in frightening them away, and thus they pass on to the inexperienced animals. From a slight elevation we could make out La Tartaria and Las Guatatas which occupy half the body of the great city of

Guamanga

This city is the residence of the bishop of this diocese, having an adequate cathedral situated in the main plaza, with several canons who are very obedient in the Divine Offices and worship of the church, and even more so in the generosity with which they pass out the leftovers of their rich canonicates—imitating the pastor—to the many poor people in the city and its small common land. It is very similar to the city of Chuquisaca, but it exceeds the latter in mildness of climate. Its common land is small and barren, but some noble men have farms in the province of Andaguaylas, from the products of which they support themselves frugally. People of means and lustre have been lacking in this region the last few years. The household of the Marqués de Valdelirios, joined to that of Cruzate with the marquisate of Feria, is now absent, and will soon establish itself in Lima. The Marqués de Mosobamba, as well as the heir of the house of Tellos, moved to the province of Andaguaylas to reestablish their farms which were half ruined. With the death of Oblitas and Boza, their large farms were divided among their children and grandchildren, which division is not illustrious; nor is that partition which was made of the great wealth left by Señora Doña Tomasa de la Fuente and Señora Doña Isabel Maysondo, who supported a large part of the inhabitants of this city with their sizeable alms. By this I do not wish to discount the existing nobility nor their charity and generosity. The poor, noble families only arouse the public to pity, often exposing themselves to scorn. Rich nobility is the asylum of the rebuffed and wretched people.

Two days before we arrived in this city, the administrator of the post died, and the inspector temporarily named Don Pablo Verdeguer, a European who is married to Señora Doña Francisca Gálvez—a lady of an illustrious family of which there are many in this city. While the inspector bids farewell to the many friends he has here, I shall fulfill the obligation of an illustrious gentleman from Cuzco, making a sketch of the two greatest festivals, divine and profane, which are celebrated in Cuzco.

CHAPTER XXII

IN all the Catholic world the great festival of God begins
in the month of June and concludes after eight days. In the
poorest town in all of Spain and the Indies these days are
celebrated with jocular solemnity. This solemnity is observed
in the churches, during the celebration of the Divine Offices as
well as in the processions which are accompanied by the ecclesiastical capitularies in lavish adornments following the
sacred communities, with the distinctive marks of their ranks
and insignia of the Holy Tribunal of the Inquisition. Then follows the secular council and all the nobility in their best attire.
These three double rows carry their lighted candles of the
finest wax, and they observe a fitting solemnity. The sacred
monstrance is borne by the bishop, or in case he is incapable,
by the dean, and the poles of the pallium or canopy are handled
by the most worthy ecclesiastics, or in some places by the
seculars. A short distance behind, in the center of these three
rows are several priests, incensing the Lord; and the devout
ladies throw perfumed flowers or scented water from their
balconies, out of respect for the Saint of Saints. All the streets
through which it passes are covered with awnings; the balconies, doors, and windows are hung with the finest embellish-
ments, and the walls filled with paintings and the most exquisite
mirrors; at short intervals are sumptuous altars where the
bishop stops and deposits the sacred monstrance so they can
kneel down and worship the Lord, while the priests chant their

prayers in which the people join, expressing themselves in their own way, although it is always pious and edifying. So the entire course of the procession is a continuous altar, and up to the end of the first three rows reigns a solemnity and a silence in which only holy praise is heard.

The second part of the procession is really comical, but it seems to me that it is in emulation of the most remote antiquity, for which it cannot be considered as a ridiculous—and certainly not a superstitious—obsequiousness; the dances of the Indians who come from all the nearby parishes and provinces are very serious in substance, because these people are so by nature. Their principal adornments are of solid silver, which they rent from several mestizos who earn their living in this business (as is also the case with the paintings, mirrors, engravings, and sconces). The dragons and giant figures, although they have no connection with the rites of the Catholic church, are approved for common use in the most respectable cities and towns in Spain because they contribute to the gaiety of the town and its respect for the great festival. This festival in Cuzco is repeated by the Indians in all the parishes, and each in turn contributes to the magnificence of the others; and even the Spaniards view with pleasure these festivals, particularly those put on with ecstatic joy by the Indians.

Profane Festival

This begins at the first of the year when the *alcaldes* and other magistrates are elected. Ladies and gallants provide themselves beforehand with costly liveries and horses richly trapped. Exquisite sweets, made of sugar and the best fruits in the entire kingdom, from their own harvests, are the specialty of the principal ladies, as is the making of drinks, cold and hot. The latter are kept in their bottle-cases all year for regaling the disciples of Bacchus, and the cold ones are prepared by merely having the ice necessary for cooling them brought in the previous day;

in this they are very wasteful. The fiestas, at most, are reduced to bullfights which last from the first day of the year through Shrove Tuesday, with an intermission of a few days which are not holidays in the law courts. The expense of these bullfights is defrayed by the four *alcaldes*, aided, I believe, by the royal *alférez*. Their cost becomes profuse because, in addition to sending refreshments to all the ladies and gentlemen in the large Regocijo Plaza, they also send many trays of ices and large platters of sweets to those who could not come to the balconies of this great plaza, where there is a bull on a rope at all times which, as soon as he relaxes from the first impetuousness, is turned loose in the other streets, for the amusement of the people; a particular bull is sent to many distinguished persons so they may be entertained and enjoy his capers from the balconies of their houses. There are no professional bullfighters, and the only ones who hazard a try immediately are a few majordomos of farms, on fast horses, and many boys on foot, usually Indians, who correspond to the bullfighter's assistants in Spain.

Several bulls come out adorned with silk, silver, and gold, and with many delicate silver stars attached to the surface of their skin; these are most unfortunate because everyone tries to kill them in order to reap the spoils. All the nobility of Cuzco goes to the plaza on fine horses, richly trapped in velvet embroidered with gold and silver in relief. The gentlemen's clothes are of the finest cloth made in Lyons, France, and in this country, but they cover this elegance with a cloak they call a poncho, made of alpaca wool in strips of several colors—really crude garments for functions of so much splendor. These gentlemen form their squads, accompanying the *corregidor* and *alcaldes*, and station themselves at the street intersections to see the bullfights and to run from one place to another to defend themselves from the assaults, to see the animal's cunning, as well as to greet the ladies and to collect their favors in the form of sugar plums and scented water, thrown from the balconies, to which each responds according to his polish; but the usual thing is supply oneself with a large bag of plump bonbons to throw at the people on the balconies, who respond with like ammunition or grape shot, which the commoners pick up from the ground and sell back to the gentlemen. At the end of the function, which is when the bell is sounded for the Angelus, they turn loose three or four bulls with rockets attached and shoot off fireworks; with the waving of ladies' handkerchiefs and several flags from the balconies, a *vitoreo* or cheer of pleasant confusion is heard—although it somewhat resembles the *tiroteo* or shooting of geese in Andalucía, since contusions, wounds and a few deaths result from both! At night there are delightful serenades in the houses of the *corregidor* and *alcalde*, concluding with sumptuous banquets, until the last night before Lent, when everyone retires almost at dawn on Ash Wednesday.

The inspector commended my description, but it did not seem proper to him that I should compare the *vitoreo* with the *tiroteo*, because the latter is a term used only by bullies of the lower ranks when they lay hands on their small arms, which they call *titeres*; and just as other people say *chamusquina* for a quarrel, they say *tiroteo*, a term which the great Quevedo used in his famous *Xácaras*, because such a word is used only by the gypsies. Contusions, which become abscesses, result from the blows received from the stub-horned bulls, and the Indians, in their drunken revelries, blindly submit in order to see the blunt-horned beasts. The noise and glare caused by the artificial fires, the sound of the drums and clarions, and the shouts of the people madden those proud animals; and with their snout and head they throw *cholos* in the air with the same ease that a hurricane lifts straw from the ground. They do not feel the bruises until the following day when 10 or 12 appear in the hospital, because the rise of the liquor in their barometers does not stop the circulation of the blood.

An endless number of festivals are celebrated in this great

city, but none equals this one, which would be infinitely more magnificent if it were moved to the octaves of San Juan and San Pedro, when the rains have passed; two months earlier the fields are filled with tasty grasses, bulls, and fat and vigorous horses, and the calmness of the sky would invite the gentlemen to throw away their ponchos and capes in order to show off their costly attire, and to avoid many slips and dangerous falls of horses, as well as a great many other inconveniences resulting from the heavy and incessant rain in the months of January and February that I have experienced whenever I attended these festivals. But in the carnival everyone is crazed, wherefore it is fruitless to try to persuade the nobility of Cuzco to preserve good judgment on those days. It is now time to leave Guamanga and proceed to Guancavélica, passing the posts mentioned in the following chapter.

CHAPTER XXIII

ROUTE FROM GUAMANGA TO GUANCAVÉLICA. THE TOWN
OF GUANCAVÉLICA. THE MERCURY MINE.

ONE-HALF league from Guamanga is a deep ravine called the Quebrada Honda which has a perpendicular descent of one-half league, and an ascent of the same distance, with narrow pathways; but the inspector told me that he had never seen water in its bottom. Anyone situated in the bottom, and looking toward the sky, would have the solution to Vergil's problem since scarcely the 3 *varas* of sky of his thinking can be seen. I shall copy the two distichs, with the same liberty that many others have done it:

Dic quibus interris, et eris mihi magnus Apollo
Tres pateat Coeli spatium non amplius ulnas.

Vergil knew very little about problems when he proposed this one as such, or else in his Mantua, or in all of Italy, there were no deep and narrow ravines such as are common in all of America. But let us suppose that there are none, or that there was just one from which he got his information. Is it possible that there are no high chimneys? If I were his little shepherd, I would certainly laugh considerably at his question, although you should know very well that we Indians laugh scarcely three times in our lives." "Very well," said the inspector, "carry on. This whole journey is over annoying roads on which one dares not spur his horse due to the many stones and precipices."

"The journey from Guanta to Parcos, although it is only 10 leagues, cannot be done in one day with a double load without a change of mules, because after leaving Guanta, a very hot territory, until one crosses the Huarpa River, whether by bridge

or ford, the animals are covered with sweat and are extremely
exhausted. The steep hill of Marcas, which has 2 leagues of
difficult road, dangerous for men and horses, continues
incontinenti. The mules cannot take four steps without stopping
to rest. Many fall exhausted, and the most vigorous can
scarcely get their loads to the first plain by nightfall; merely to
unharness them and to allow their sweat to dry requires a wait
of two or three hours, and while they roll around and search
for the scarce grass, more than six hours pass. The remainder
of the road to Parcos, although it is uphill, skirts along slopes
of medium height, making it accessible. In this journey alone
the couriers fall behind more than 10 hours, and the only
remedy is to place a post in Marcas, or to pay the master at
Guanta for a replacement that could go unloaded, in harness,
to the foot of the hill to receive the cargo quickly, while the
mules which departed from Guanta loaded proceed to go up the
hill free of burden and to rest at the summit before concluding
the trip to Parcos. The postmaster of this spot makes his trip to
Guanta speedily and without hardship to his mules—the first
because he takes only cargoes of little weight, and the second
because the mules do not work so hard on the descent.

.   .   .

Guancavélica

This memorable town, as would be expected owing to the
chance discovery of the large mercury mine, is situated between
this high hill and another of the same magnitude, and has adequate streets and ordinary houses. It has always been governed
by very distinguished persons, as I was told by the inspector
who met Señor Sola, of His Majesty's Council; Señores Leyva
and Vega, also members of the Council; and Señor Ulloa, captain in the navy, to whom the town owes the ease with which
traffic moves in its streets; and the present-day Señor Jáuregui,
former president of Chuquisaca, who built, at his own expense,

a single-arch stone bridge across the deep ravine which provides a bed for a stream that joins the Grande River; with the heavy rains this stream detained the mule drivers, or exposed them to great dangers, particularly those from Ica, who transport brandy in clay jugs. These governors have effected many other public works, particularly in the mine, which is a huge subterranean town with streets, pillars, and arches for the sake of safety. Merely the description of this mine would fill a volume larger than my itinerary—and if a description of the apparatus and ovens in which the metal is converted to vapor and, in turn, to mercury, were added, a bulky volume would be consumed."

"That description would be very fruitless, Concolorcorvo, since so many wise men have already done it. I am certain that Señor Sola presented a model of the mine of Guancavélica in pure silver to the King, with all the construction done up to his time; and each governor has sent to Spain and the superior government a sketch of the mine and the farms of the subjects who work them, along with the conditions affecting increase or decrease of fineness of metal and their causes." "That cannot be," I replied, "because it depends more on chance than on human reasoning." "You are mistaken," he answered; "let us speak no more of this matter."

And then he added: "There is not a town in all the world more peacefully governed than Guancavélica, because one wise man rules alone, with an assistant very subordinate to his orders, without any *alcaldes*, solicitors, or attorneys. All lawsuits are settled within a day, and thus little is written but much progress is made in civil causes. Only one notary, who serves the entire province, resides in this town, but he performs only in criminal cases of consequence, and in the writing of bills of sale and contracts. All else is settled by the prudent governor, without judicial clamor, and thus not as many tricks and appeals are seen as in the rest of the kingdom."

. . .

CHAPTER XXIV

THE TRIP TO LIMA THROUGH COTAY. THE RAVINES AND HILLS.
WATERS OF STONE. THE FARMS. THE ROPE BRIDGES.
THE POSTMASTERS.

ONE leaves Guancavélica by a small bridge on the eastern edge of town, crossing a stream that joins the Grande River, and follows the banks of the latter downstream along a somewhat rocky slope which is wide and without peril. To avoid this slight annoyance in dry weather one crosses it two or three times, to take advantage of the plain and the firm terrain in the turns of the river, until he again picks up the slope; and in the space of 2½ leagues is the river they call Mal Paso, which has a narrow passway of stone slabs which can easily be repaired. It is common opinion that the waters of this river turn into stones at the outskirts of the town. The inspector laughs at this, and merely informed me that among the multitude of people drinking this water he had not seen a town in which they were suffering less from kidney stones.

Four leagues beyond is the bridge of Jáuregui, of which I spoke before, from which it is 5 leagues to Cotay on good road between snow-covered sierras, although in the rainy season there may be some mudholes of little depth since the terrain is somewhat rocky.

The place named Cotay is of considerable expanse, through which runs a stream that stops the mule drivers in times of high water, particularly between nine in the morning and four in the afternoon, when the sun is melting the snow. One league downstream from our route is a natural bridge formed by two

cliffs, of which some avail themselves; and in this case, one
may enter and leave by the Condorsenca road—in which there
are some mudholes in the rainy season and which has two
rather perpendicular slopes at the ends—but without danger of
loss of cargo. The river flows from the east to the west, and on
the bank on this side is the usual lodging house of the muleteers,
on a small hill of easy access. There are also three or four
large, dilapidated stone houses which are roofed over when
bishops or governors spend the night in them; this is the best
place for a post, since it is a sheltered spot, and the housing
is already half constructed.

.   .   .

The town of Viña has 250 mules dedicated solely to the
miserable task of transporting fruit from the ravine of Lunaguaná to the town of Guancavélica, whereby each one earns
scarcely 8 reales of profit in two weeks, and the owners anx-
iously desire to utilize them in the service of the mails and
travelers. The populace of this town alone, with great pleasure
and profit, will put a post here and in Turpu, adopting measures
to keep the slope on their territory in good repair and free from
dangers, for their own utility, up to the place called Llangas.

It is 7 leagues from this town to that spot, all downhill,
through a ravine, with some passes and cave-ins (of little
danger at the moment) which could easily be repaired because
there are enough thick trees nearby to supply sufficient wood.
At the descent to Llangas are some disturbing and rather dangerous drop-offs, easy to repair since they are of earth and loose
stone.

The descent ends in Llangas, which has sufficient land for
many fields of alfalfa which they do not water from the Viñas
River, although they have the irrigation ditches open, because
little alfalfa is consumed. Here it joins the Grande River which
is commonly called the Cañete. One-half league beyond is its

rope bridge which is under the care of the Indians from the town of Tupe, in the province of Yauyos, to whom the bridge-keeper pays 26 pesos per year besides allowing free passage of all their cattle. Its entrance and exit are very good, and loaded mules and men on horseback may cross it. The road is good and suitable for trotting, as is that up to the town of Lunagauná, which is at a distance of 6 leagues, populated all along with farms and little villages abounding in all necessities —and especially in very intelligent Indians who speak only Castilian and are distinguished from the Spaniards in color only. They offer their houses generously and sell their food-stuffs at the regulated price without resistance. They keep their bridges from one bank to the other well-repaired and solid so that loaded mules may pass without difficulty at a slight charge, which money is applied to the construction of their churches.

· · ·

From this place [the Asia estate] to Chilca it is 8 leagues, and at 3 leagues is the town of Mala, having some fields of alfalfa and pasture, and a river which is swollen in the rainy season—but there are skillful guides who lead the couriers of the King and parcel post across safely and quickly; only with travelers do they use fraud, concealing or destroying the ford for their own advantage. This river has, on a detour of 2 or 3 leagues, a rope bridge which is in a somewhat abandoned state, but could easily be restored by the Indians of Coillo, charging them the same per load as is charged in the ravine at Luna-guaná, which is 1 real for each.

Chilca, the principal town of the province of Cañete, has many mules but is able to support very few near to the town since the earth is nitrous, with a scarcity of water and few pasture lands. The greater part of their carriage and commerce is done outside the province. Nevertheless, those in the town designated for trips to Lima are sufficient to repair the general road, with which the town of Mala could help them very much, since both are inhabited by intelligent Indians and merchants.

From Chilca to Lurín it is 7 leagues with some sandy spots of little concern. Here are more than enough mules because there is an abundance of pasture all year long; wherefore there is so much traffic to Lima that mules are encountered at all hours in the market named Mamacona, which is the only annoying sandy area, much exaggerated by a certain inexperienced informant. From this town to Lima it is 6 leagues, although the King's couriers have paid for 5. There are men who know how to do nothing but contradict and oppose all ideas which are not their own. "These men," said the inspector, "are called green books by the keen-witted Gracián."[1] "What does that mean?" I asked; and he replied that they were those who think they bring honor to themselves by dishonoring and condemning others. "The mules," he continued, "reared in the mountains on solid ground, become exhausted in the sandy valleys; and quite the opposite, those from these valleys are fatigued in climbing the high hills, and they usually bruise their feet, which is the equivalent of *mal del vaso*. There is not a day in the year in which mules from the two coasts do not enter Lima, carrying loads which are heavier than those brought from the mountains. They make double trips, yet are more vigorous when they arrive. But why belabor the point, since most of the crude muleteers who come down from Cuzco and return with a double load, go and come through these sandy valleys, which are considered insurmountable by that rigid censurer whom I know not and care not to know."

The general administrator of the mails knows very well that those from Piura and Arequipa, in spite of the sandy areas and the great distances, arrive more quickly than do those from Cuzco, wherefore it is unforutnate that the inspector prefers this route to the present old one which is being followed.

It is supposed that the income from the post houses will de-

[1] Baltasar Gracián y Morales (1601-1658) whose *El héroe* (1637) and *El discreto* (1646) present a portrait of the ideal gentleman of the seventeenth century.

fray their expenses, but this is a childish and very malicious observation because the income has never supported, nor does it now support, any house; and one is needed much less on this route than elsewhere because all the postmasters have a ranch or a house where they live, which they open up, not only to couriers who stop for just one or two hours, but also to travelers who wish to make longer stopovers. The other claim made— that the residents of the valley of Jauja and the province of Tarma are lacking in communications—is a trick to frighten unknowing persons. First, because with muleteers and travelers leaving these two provinces for Lima every day, the residents send with them their correspondence which is of little consequence; but supposing that a fixed and determined communication with these two provinces were a necessary thing, then nothing would be easier than to send a *cañari*, financed by them or by the income—with one Indian going from each place, with his packet, to Oroya and then alternating for the trip to Lima through the San Mateo ravine. The commerce in the interior of these two provinces rarely passes through Guancavélica, which is closer to Lima and on a less craggy road; wherefore they could also elect that town for the sending of their letters, so that their correspondence might remain there, along with those which could be sent to the other provinces, and those from Lima could be transported by ordinary courier who would pass rapidly through the heights of Viña; thus the *cañaris* would have only the trip to Guancavélica, and with the delay of just one delivery per year they would receive their replies— from Lima as well as from the more remote provinces—very punctually.

In conclusion, one may deviate from the route from Lunaguaná, because there are several ravines which are perhaps more accessible than the one which leads toward the town of Viña; and even after this town there is another ravine called Abajo, or El León, but he should follow the road which is designated, since it is always more suitable and accessible than

that through Guarochiríes and Angaraes. The bishops, governors, and distinguished people always make their visits along
the coast as far as Lunaguaná and Viña, which is proof of its
greater convenience and the great civility of its inhabitants
who, when compared to the Guarochiríes, are the same, although in a different way, as the present-day Frenchmen compared to the old Gauls or the Athenians to the Lacedemonians.

To conclude this itinerary, I should advise that it is not an
infallible rule to consider as the best route the one followed by
distinguished persons and people of means, because all these
persons select the two best seasons of the year. For the mails,
which of necessity travel on fixed days, a route must be selected
which has no obstacles in any season. An unexpected landslide
may be remedied by a short detour or a temporary repair,
but the rapid current of a river without bridge or barges—although it is not present for a period of more than two months of
the year—is sufficient cause to abandon a flat route, which is
liable to sever the line of communications and to cause great
setbacks in the kingdom. The trip from Lima to Arequipa has
over 8 large rivers with a clearly-outlined ford, but the mails
have never experienced any considerable delay; and although
the inspector prefers the route through Lunaguaná (since only
the two rivers Lurín and Mala must be forded) he recommends
that the slopes up to Viña and its heights be examined closely
in severely rainy weather, and particularly the large lagoon
named Turpu and the river of Cotay, as well as the slopes of
the two cordilleras which he traversed in the middle of May
when the rains had passed and the snow all melted.

The small stipend paid to the postmasters slows down the
trips considerably, because the replacement mules do not pay
for themselves and they cannot maintain horses at the stake in
the corrals. The transporting of commissions of gold and silver
and other packages of utility to commerce and to private individuals causes much delay to correspondence. The rough road,
as a matter of fact, is that between Lima and Cuzco, and yet

several private individuals and couriers have made it in 7 days, covering more than 26 leagues each 24 hours, allowing some stops for rest. I say that if the run were split at Guamanga, the trip could be made in 5 days, because any man of average endurance can stand 2½ days without rest, and all things belonging to him will advance from Cuzco to Buenos Aires at a speed which is faster in proportion to the better condition of the road, provided he pay well the posts along the way. I conclude this diary with a joke about a man from Tucumán.

A certain Englishman in Buenos Aires bet that he could have a letter in Córdoba, which is 150 leagues away (although the inspector computes it to be only 146) in 48 hours, which by the first computation means 75 leagues in 24 hours, or more than 3 per hour; and he set the wager at 4,000 pesos. Several merchants were astonished at the amount, without thinking about the means which the Englishman could take in order to make the trip, until they called the *Corredor Cordobés*, the Cordovan Runner, who had the best reputation for that run, but had never done it in less than 3½ days. When he had presented himself, he asked that the Englishman appear so he could accept the challenge. When he arrived, he broke up his tobacco, rolled a cigarette with great tranquility, and without saying a word, awaited the Englishman, filling the entire room with smoke. The bystanders stood in suspense. The Englishman, who was a man of detail, arrived very soon, and the gentleman from Tucumán received him with rustic courtesy and, blowing two puffs in his face, told him that those gentlemen had informed him of all that had transpired. The Englishman confirmed his bet, believing that the merchants would support him, but the fine fellow from Tucumán very serenely said that neither he nor all his ancestors, nor his entire present generation, had 4,000 pesos, but that if he wanted to bet 20 *pesillos* (that is what they say to indicate a small quantity), he was ready to risk that amount.

The Englishman, irritated, shouted the following words: "*Sols, sols, sanibavichi canifestan!*" which is an execration or an oath of contempt. The man from Tucumán understood well from the gestures and calmly replied, "Listen, my English friend, do you think that here, even though we are a poor lot, we do not understand your *trafacías?*" Among them that word *trafacías* means not only wickedness and deceit, but also cunning and sharpness, and he added that he, with his sons and grandsons, dared to make the same trip in even shorter time for 500 pesos. The residents of Buenos Aires understood the mystery, and there is no need to explain it to those from Peru.

Quia intelligentibus pauca.

. . .

CHAPTER XXV: THE SECOND RUN FROM CUZCO TO THE IMPERIAL CITY OF POTOSÍ. THE RUN FROM POTOSÍ TO SAN MIGUEL DEL TUCUMÁN. THAT FROM TUCUMÁN TO BUENOS AIRES. has been omitted as of no present interest or significance. It is a short section listing the provinces along the postal runs.

Translator's Note

CHAPTER XXVI

A BRIEF COMPARISON OF THE CITIES OF LIMA AND CUZCO.
CHARACTERISTIC ASPECTS. THE RESIDENTS OF LIMA AND MEX-
ICO. THE DRESS OF THE LIMA WOMEN. REASONS FOR THEIR
VITALITY. SINGULAR FEATURES. WEDDING BEDS, CRADLES,
AND HOUSEHOLD FURNISHINGS.

I ATTEMPTED to write a description of Lima, but the inspector told me it was an undertaking which many intellectual giants had been unable to accomplish, and that it
would be ludicrous for a pygmy to undertake it. "But, Señor
inspector, is it possible that I should end such a detailed itinerary without saying anything about Lima?" "Yes, Señor Inca,
because this is not a matter for you, but rather for me, since my
commission ends here. Señor Don Jorge Juan," he added, "Don
Antonio de Ulloa, and the greatest cosmographer in the kingdom, Doctor Don Cosme Bueno, described the singular aspects
of this city with the quill from a swan, and you cannot add anything of importance with your goose quill." "Nevertheless," I
replied, "please tell me what difference there is between this
city and that in which I was born." "I suppose, Señor Inca," he
answered, "that you are devoted to Cuzco, your homeland, and
you want me to say that it surpasses Lima in all aspects, but
you are mistaken because, leaving aside its location and its
common lands, you must have observed that the King maintains
a viceroy in splendor in this great capital with an assignation
from the King which is equivalent to all the income from the
family estates in Cuzco. It has, as well, three military units
financed by the Crown: a well-equipped and well-paid cavalry,
an infantry, and halberdiers—who serve not only for ostentation and splendor, but also for the personal security and peace

among the large population—to which is added a complete *Audiencia,* courts of higher accounting and of the Royal Inquisition, a university, a theater for plays, and public parks near the city, which are not found in Cuzco or in any other city in the kingdom.

"Lima supports 250 carriages and more than a thousand calashes, which are different from the former only in that they have two wheels, are pulled by a mule, and are more subject to being upset. There is nothing of this in your great city. In the matter of clothing, one is as foolish as the other, the only difference being in the matter of tastes, size of families and commerce, in which Lima greatly surpasses Cuzco. In this city there are many titles of marquis and count, and an even greater number of gentlemen belonging to the orders of Santiago and Calatrava, who, with the exception of one or two, have sufficient income to maintain themselves with splendor, to which are added many first-sons and gentlemen who support themselves with their farms and other respectable businesses, giving luster to the city. I have no doubt that in the city of your birth, as in the others of this vast viceroyalty, there are illustrious families, but the total of all of them does not match that of this city, where little notice is given to the conquistadors, for although there was no lack of noble families among them, such families increased as the conquest became firmly established.

With the selection of men for the tribunals and other honorable positions, there came to this capital from Spain many second-sons of illustrious families, some already married and others who acquired the state here, and even many of those who were destined for the interior provinces came to establish themselves here in the capital, as has happened in the courts all over the world. Many subjects who came from Spain for the sole purpose of seeking a fortune kept their nobility concealed until they acquired their fortune and could maintain their luster in such an expensive place where luxury is too well established.

In Cuzco and the other cities in the sierra and part of the valleys, the only costly items are dress and the household furnishings which maintain their splendor for centuries. The most important lady in Cuzco has five or six maid servants, serving her well, on whose clothing she scarcely spends as much as is spent here on one Negro servant of average account. In this city, without considering the farms, there are 1½ million pesos squandered, because generally speaking, there is not a slave who saves his master as much money as is spent on him. Their infirmities, genuine or feigned, are not only expensive to the masters because of the medicine, physician, or surgeon, but also due to their absence and lack of service. Every Negro child born in one of these houses costs the master over 700 pesos before he reaches an age when he may be put into service. This evil situation has no remedy as long as they are products of legitimate marriages, but it could be remedied in part by reducing the male servants to a smaller number, as is happening everywhere in the world.

The multitude of servants adds to the confusion of the household, invites anxiety, obstructs service, and causes the children of the family to become lazy so that they can scarcely dress themselves at the age of 12, besides other difficulties which I shall pass over. This present situation, along with the expensive clothing which is provided from the cradle onward, due to the overindulgence of some mothers, are two bleeding sores which are noticeably draining the wealth.

"I have no doubt, Señor Concolorcorvo, that you, since you have seen only the exteriors and roofs, or I should say flat roofs, of the houses, probably think that the one in which I live is the best in the city, since it has the coat of arms above the main door and three or four rooms of considerable size. This house, in its present state, should be considered as one of the fourth-class houses, that is, there are many others which are three times better. The residents of Lima do not fancy the adorning of the doorways with embossments and large coats of arms which add beauty in the large cities. The tile roofs here are useless, due to the lack of rain, which may be considered a serious lack for clearing their skies and cleaning their streets, for although a number of ditches cross the streets, pure water does not flow in them; since they are of little depth and the water is scarce, they hold only excrement and urine, which are prejudicial to health and ruinous to the buildings as is publicly known to all. The great palace of the viceroy, viewed from the façade, appears to be a town hall such as those in the two Castilles, but its interior shows the grandeur of the person inhabiting it. The same is true of other houses belonging to distinguished people, as you will see in time.

"The nobility of Lima is not debatable, unless it can be in the rest of the world as well, because every year we are seeing Creoles inherit some of the oldest seigniories and primogenitures of Spain. I do not give examples so as not to offend those families on which I have no definite information and because it is not my intention to offer a defense for them. The present viceroy, His Excellency Señor Don Manuel de Amat y Junient, greatly enhanced the city with parks and other public works of advantage to the State. I cannot make mention of them all, for it would be necessary to write a large, bulky volume and to have another pen, but no one can deny that his genius and ingenuity are, and have been, superior to that of all viceroys in matters of culture and good taste.

"The people of talent of Lima seem to be outstanding in all the kingdom. This stems from their having an earlier and more permanent cultivation of the mind. A child from this city expresses himself well at the age of four, while highlanders can scarcely express themselves in Castilian at eight, making many solecisms, which comes from the fact that they are studying two languages at once: Castilian and their native tongue, which is the most common at home among the nurses, maids, and mothers; and thus, when they go to the Spanish school, which is usually taught by an ignorant man, instead of 'Give me a glass of cold water,' they say, 'A glass of cold water give me' (which corresponds to *Uno chiri apamuy*), considered gross and stupid by ignorant persons. The Biscayans (I speak of the common ones) use the same word order and, for this reason, understand Quechua much better.

"I protest to you, Señor Inca, that for 40 years I have been observing the peculiarities of the talented Creoles in both Americas, and comparing them in general, I find them no different from the peninsulars. The comparison which has been made up to the present between the Creoles from Lima and those from Spain who take up residence here is unjust. Here the white youth is rare who does not devote himself to learning from an early age, while rare is the one who comes from Spain with even the slightest superficial knowledge, except for those publicly employed for letters. It is notorious that the outstanding are not always selected, because in addition to the fact that they, trusting in their merits, can always find positions in Spain, they do not wish to risk their lives in a long sea voyage and change of climate, or in having no patrons with whom to locate satisfactorily here. If the stage were changed, that is, if all vocations were made available in Lima, one would clearly see that proportionately there were as many learned men as on the peninsula and that any city in Spain comparable to this one would be matched in creative talent, good judgment and literary production, without considering the several giants in this area, so rare that one scarcely finds two in one century—like the great Peralta, the Lima son so well-known in all of Europe, who was praised so highly by the most beautiful and critical pen Galicia has produced in this century.[1]

"In keeping with this, I am going to satisfy the Peruvians

[1] The critic mentioned here is Padre Benito Jerónimo Feijóo (1676-1764) the Spanish encyclopedist whose essays on all phases of eighteenth-century life are collected in his *Teatro crítico universal* (1726-1739) and *Cartas eruditas y curiosas* (1742-1760). His praises of Peralta are found in *Españoles americanos* (Vol. IV, *Teatro crítico . . .*).

and the other Creoles from the Mexican empire, whence sprang
the common opinion concerning the weakening or short duration of mental soundness necessary for continuing learning
after 40 or 50 years of age. Mexico City is the antipode of Lima.
The air of the latter is extremely damp while that of Mexico is
dry and thin. The soil of Lima, by nature, begs to be dry, and if
any damage is experienced, it is from the dampness brought
by the ditches interwoven among the streets and houses. To
find water in Lima it is necessary to dig down 200 *varas*. In
Mexico water is found at less than 1 *vara*, but the effect of the
air is such that lower rooms are protected from dampness by a
flooring less than 1 palm high. Products are kept in the store-
houses for many years without noticing moisture, and sugar,
which becomes damp in Lima in storerooms on the upper floors,
dries out so much on the ground floor in Mexico that it becomes
like flint. Metals keep their luster for many years, while in Lima
they lose it in a short time; and so it is with other things which
happen due to the humidity or dryness of the air. The atmos-
phere of Mexico City is impregnated with salt, because all its
environs are filled with this substance. There is a kind of salt,
with the appearance of brown soil, called *tequesquite,* which the
natives say spoils and rots the teeth, covering them with a black
tartar; and thus it is rare to find a set of teeth which preserves
its white luster. Almost all Mexicans of both sexes experience
this destruction from a very early age, which is complicated by
continuous catarrh. Convulsions are so common that rarely did
I enter a church of some congregation without seeing a man or
woman suffering from them, falling on the floor as if he were
struck by epilepsy, accompanied by twisting the throat and
mouth until the latter kissed the ear. The first aid offered by bystanders is to wrap the victim in their capes, which are capable
of suffocating a strong man, but this temporary remedy has
been seen and proved effective.

"Syphilis is as common as the catarrh, but it is easily cured.
Matlasague, which is an intestinal fever, causes great destruc-

tion, especially among the Indians. Pneumonia is very dangerous and to be feared, but especially bad is the evacuation from
both orifices of the body at the same time, which the Mexicans,
with great propriety, call *miserere*; in conclusion, Mexico City
is probably the most sickly place among all the cities in the
world. The Europeans, and even the Creoles born and reared to
a robust age in the interior provinces, do not suffer, or rather,
they resist, the malignant influences of the place for a long
time.

"Without a change of clothes, the Mexicans are as dis-
tinguishable from the Peruvians as women are from men. In
general they are of a very delicate complexion. Rarely is one
found with a complete set of teeth at 15, and almost everyone
wears a white handkerchief covering his mouth from ear to ear,
some to protect themselves from the air, others to cover their
inkwell mouths, as they say with propriety among themselves,
and even the most polished ladies are not exempt from this
misery; but since this imperfection is so common, these ladies
are as sought after by their own men and by foreigners as all
other women in the world, because they are as neat and discreet
as the ladies from Lima, although the latter surpass them in
manner of speaking and in the bloom of the complexion, which
springs from their keeping their teeth until old age, and from
the mildness of the air and climate which is conducive to keeping the skin more smooth and pliant. The ladies from Lima
prefer the color of jasmine to that of roses on their faces, and
thus they use less vermilion than any other women in the world.

"The Mexican ladies can shine in the four corners of the
earth, as soon as they relinquish their natural teeth in favor of
a good supply of ivory ones, which are now in use, to make
their speech more smooth and sonorous in order to compete
with the ladies of Lima, scoffing at their *tequesquite,* and aided
by their reddish color, long hair, airy gait, and other charms.
If Mexico boasts of having a mill in every house, the ladies
of Lima match it with their fulling-mills, which serve the same

purposes, except that cocoa cannot be ground in them. If there is one syringe in every house in Mexico (I am not speaking of the poor ones), here there are two in every house of average decency and probity, and in addition, each one has an apothecary bag for the succor of sudden illnesses. There may be some truth in the story of the sedate and serious José Ruiz de la Cámara, who was acquainted with an old Mexican woman who knew nine effective remedies for curing hemorrhoids, but here the most untalented woman knows more remedies for all kinds of illnesses than Hippocrates and Galen together. The women of Lima and Mexico acquire this knowledge out of necessity, since they live in morbific places." "It seems to me," I replied to the inspector, "that the ladies of Lima contract many infirmities due to the little protection afforded their feet and the dampness they receive through them." "You are mistaken, Señor Concolorcorvo," the inspector answered. "The Indian women and other common people go barefooted, as do poor people in many other parts of the world, and they do not contract illness as a result. The young ladies are not of a different nature. They are raised with this fragile footwear, and from a very early age they wear dresses above the ankle, resembling imperial curtains, and they wrap themselves up in the same fashion as those accustomed to a capitular cloak or a collegiate cassock. However, their shoes have two bad features, or I should say, three. The first is that they give an extraordinary shape to their feet, for which they can be pardoned since it is the native style. The second is the costliness of these shoes, due to their short duration and their exquisite embroidery, and the third is the dust which they pick up, gaining entry through the huge hallways, balconies, and windows which open from them for the exhalation of vapors of their prisoners!

"The Mexican women dress and wear shoes in the style of Europe, as I have been told, for in my time they used clothing of a mestizo fashion which from the waist up imitated somewhat the dress of the Indian women, with the *güipil* and the *quisquémel, tobagillas* (blouses in the summer and shawls in the winter) which correspond here to the printed cottons newly discovered among the young ladies (loose garments in the summer and mantillas of frizzed baize in the winter). To make a worthy comparison between the ladies of Lima and Mexico it would be necessary to compose a lengthy discourse, but I cannot pass over one particular quality of the Mexicans. They make better use of a few servants. They speak to them very little and very slowly, and in gatherings: *Loquantur arcana per digitos*; they are the most clever pantomimists in the world, but I have noticed that their gestures do not follow any general rule, because I have observed that some servants who returned to service in a house confessed that they still did not understand the signs of their mistress because they varied from those used before."

"I am amazed," I said to the inspector, "at the ability and skill of the Mexican ladies who succeed in expressing themselves and being understood by means of gestures. I confess that from the time I was born I have never heard that word but now, according to what you have said, I understand that this word indicates those movements of the hand and face with which newborn babies and deaf mutes express themselves, which is understood by those who deal with them; it is a pity that the ladies of Lima do not introduce this language into their houses, in order to relieve themselves of so much shouting." "The women of Lima, Señor Inca, are as skilled as the Mexicans, and, generally speaking, as able as all the others in the world, but these ladies are served by the most base people in the human race, particularly with reference to the men. The men servants in the rest of the world study the best method of serving, but here the greatest skill is devoted to studying how to serve little and badly. The most prudent and long-suffering lady becomes impatient three or four times every day, in spite of having been reared from the cradle among these people, who, besides being gross by nature, are debased by the forced servitude; this evil is almost irremediable unless steps are taken to deny the many aids given to the Spanish and mestizo women through displaced charity. I know very well that people of good judgment will be of my opinion, and with a little reflection, the dandies would adopt my way of thinking and would not maintain a sizeable number of hypocrites and idlers without any qualifications other than that of having a white face. My digression is becoming prolix and it is time to return to our discourse.

"Mexican youth is so devoted to learning from an early age that it greatly surpasses that of Lima. As soon as they learn to write poorly and to translate Latin even worse, they are put in the many schools which exist so they may practice the science of *ergo*. All the collegians in Mexico attend the university in the morning and afternoon, and it is a pleasure to see these collegians, walking in two rows in the streets, some arguing while others are reviewing their lessons. In the university the little fellows are invited to resume their syllogisms. There is no entertainment in the colleges other than studying and debating, and even in the doorways of the assessor's office and in the barbershop, one hears nothing but *concedo majorem, nego minorem, distingo consequens,* and *contra ita argumentor,* with all the other jargon used by dialecticians, so that there is not a section in the whole of that great city where one does not hear this noise, despite that made by the many carriages, and hawkers of almanacs, novenas and other printed matter, as well as those who sell sweets and other dainty tidbits.

"With this continual studying, cases of rheumatism and catarrh increase, being more common among people who devote themselves to studying and nocturnal meditation, and for this reason the most industrious subjects find it impossible to continue these rigorous tasks after 50 years of age, much less to write articles of importance. They themselves have made this known, and are doing it now, saying that their minds are fleeting. Anyone would believe it to see their pale and lean appearance and the mouth void of teeth and molars; therefore they only produce works which need little incubation, like a sermon or the description of a festival, along with some witty poems and pictures which enliven their imagination. This, Señor Inca, has been the reason for attributing to the Spanish Americans a weakening of mental faculties which does not exist even in the Mexican Creoles of lazy and valetudinary life. I communicated with many of the latter in Mexico, and I found them of sound judgment and witty in their conversations; at the same time I observed that this great city had many lawyers and doctors working continuously, the greater part of them being Creoles from that city. Lawyers at least have to search through books, peruse records, dictate petitions, and prepare defenses in the royal tribunal. For all this they must exhaust their reasoning just as the doctors, who are the most studious men, or at least they should be, since these men command the gallows and the scalpel. From all this it may be deduced that a considerable portion of the Creoles of Mexico preserve sufficient vigor and strength of brain for study and deep cogitation."

"If this is true, Señor Don Alonso," I replied, "then what was the basis for the opinion that Spanish Americans lost their soundness of faculties at the age of 50 or 60?" "The same," he replied, "as that held by Quevedo in writing the following verses:

> A desire since childhood I have stressed,
> And before, if that could be,
> A doctor without gloves to see,
> A lawyer who sans beard was blessed,
> A poet that was neatly dressed,
> A Creole giving money at his will,
> And I say this not for sake of ill.

"This is not true," said the inspector, "because in America, contrary to the satire against Creoles, they are not only gen-

erous, but wasteful. It is a fact that the natives of Peru are the
most frugal in all the Americas, and even so they have squandered large fortunes in a short time, not only in their own
country, but also in Spain and other parts of Europe, as is well
known.

"No one is ignorant of the results of the generosities of youth.
Men of good judgment who support themselves in an honorable fashion, are considered the world over as greedy men who
labor to lay up riches. Usually, Señor Inca, these are not the
avaricious men of whom the Scriptures speak, but rather men
of great benefit to the State. It is they who restore the maidens,
succor widows and the poor with debts, and support the hos-
pitals. The generous people, so celebrated in the world, are
nothing more than those who squander what the world produces, and usually the fruits of someone else's toil. Their entire generosity amounts to enlarging their retinue and languish-
ing in vain pursuits, leaving their family and descendants a
patrimony of wind.

"But, to return to our subject, I would like to ask: What harm
is done the Spanish Americans by saying that just as their
mental faculties excel, so they weaken at 60 years of age, or
50, as some have said? Señor Feijóo denies that mental soundness excels, but he concedes that its application does, which is
the same thing. He affirms that many Creoles graduate as doctors in both branches of law at the age of 20. Before graduating,
it is natural for them to have been teachers in the sciences
which they studied, as is common in America, without being
professors. It is natural that for the remaining 30 years they
should be engaged in public instruction and a continuation of
their studies. If European Spaniards (and I say the same about
other countries) begin their major study at the age of 20, when
the Americans are already graduated, or capable of graduating
as doctors, it is natural that because of their slower study they
cannot be graduated until the age of 35, speaking of those of
average talent, and they cannot serve the world of letters more

than 25 years, while the Creoles may serve 30, because after 70 years of age, there are few who devote themselves to public instruction, either because it causes them great annoyance or because they are occupied in the secular or ecclesiastical ministry. If Americans know as much at the age of 50 as Europeans do at 70, and are as useful because of their teaching and writing, they should be more applauded, just as that worker who produces in one day a statue of a perfection equal to that of another who executes it in two. It is a fact that there are countries in which the strength of the brain is preserved longer than in others, and in this matter there is a great difference between Lima and Mexico. In Mexico the lightness and dryness of the air, and other influences, dull the brain and cause insomnia. The opposite is true in Lima, because its heavy and damp air strengthens the brain and induces sleep, thus leaving mental powers nimble for pursuing the tasks of cogitation. The Mexicans cannot but weaken themselves greatly with their frequent baths in hot water.

"Do you have any other questions, Señor Inca?" "I should like to ask first," I said to him, "if you consider shameful the dress of the women of Lima, and the rest of this kingdom of Peru." "You are one of those poor devils," he said to me, "of which there are so many in this kingdom and in other parts of the world. The native dress of common usage is not shameful. The portraits of the great Catholic princesses give us an idea of the customs of the countries. These great ladies are the models of honesty, and yet they bare their arms to the elbow and their neck and bosom so far as to show the beginning of that place from which comes our first nourishment. The high fit of the waist is allowed on the dresses which they call 'courtly', because for ordinary days, when they have no need to display costly necklaces on their bosoms, they use kerchiefs of the finest chiffon, which cover the low neckline. This same style is observed, although more rigorously, by persons of grandeur and is imitated by the honorable common people. Those who go to extremes in this formality are considered indecent and shameful, and are censured by people of good judgment. From the waist down the European ladies are covered to the ankles, and only public dancers bare their calves to show the adroitness of their movements, but they take precaution to wear stockings of plain black satin so as not to shock the public.

"The ladies of Lima and the others living between Piura and Potosí—and the same is true of the common people, except the Indian and newly-recruited Negro women—follow a style contrary to that of Europeans, Mexicans, and the ladies of Buenos Aires; that is, whereas the latter display the greatest luster from the neck to the bosom, with adornments on their arms and wrists, the ladies from Lima conceal this splendor with a veil, not at all transparent, when it is hot, and in cold weather they cover themselves with a double muffler, which in reality is very extravagant. All their splendor is based on the lower parts, from their garter to the soles of their feet. Nothing certain is known about the origin of this dress, but I believe they were trying to imitate paintings made of angels. The more formal and decent ladies of this region show half their ankle. The bizarre or showy women use a tier of crimped cloth, baring the lower calf, while those whom the public considers shameful (and with sufficient reason, for they are that) raise their underskirts to the knee in the fashion of the imperial drape. These women treat ladies of good judgment as old-fashioned, and the young ones who imitate them, as fools. These are much lauded by the people of little judgment, and the aforementioned ladies are applauded by persons of honor and talent, and especially by men and women of virtue.

"Are there other questions, Señor Inca?" "Yes, Señor," I replied, "and I could go on until Judgment Day if God would grant us as long a life as He did to Elias and Enoch. My second inquiry is: whether the inhabitants of Mexico and Lima, which you consider the most sickly courts in the Spanish American empire, live as long as those in other countries in these domains." "I would say so." "And how do you account for this?" I asked. He replied that the same indisposition of the countries obliged their inhabitants to exercise more precaution with their food. "I have had little experience in Mexico, for although I was in that extensive empire for 10 years, and in Mexico City for more than 5, I did not consider it such a serious matter, but I recall having communicated with many old people of both sexes, 70 years old and of sound mind. I came to Lima in 1746, when I was 30 years old, and although in the first 4 years I busied myself with general ideas and those fantasies in which young men engage at that age, I realized later that in Lima there are a great many old people, perhaps more than in other countries which are considered salubrious.

"I have reflected that in those unhealthy countries of America the women outlive the men. Those women not born in the sign of the Crab regularly die of old age, and maintain their faculties up to 80 years. I could give more than 24 examples of ladies over 80 years old, in this capital alone. The lady of whom you heard mention this morning is one of the most illustrious, and her children, grandchildren, and great grandchildren, by whom she is surrounded, affirm that she is 86 and that she has a sister in La Encarnación known for her sound judgment and virtue." "I know of whom you speak," I replied, "because in this house much mention was made of Señora N (I cannot give her name because the ladies of Lima, like all the rest in the world, do not relish having their years counted until after their death). This noble lady, of such advanced age, maintains her soundness of mind, just as many other aged women, reads and writes precisely without spectacles, and holds conversations filled with witty remarks; but since the latter are directed toward praise of old customs and censure of the modern, the young women consider them a plague common to old ladies!

"Not many years ago a distinguished subject died in this capital, a Creole of Lima, known for his old nobility and learning, and even more for his jocular temperament; and in the last days of his life, which I deduce was after having passed his ninetieth birthday, he struck upon the idea of vituperating everything in this country and praising everything from the peninsula, so that one day a great grandson told him that nothing remained for him to say except that the Sacred Host from Spain was better than that consecrated here, to which the old man replied without vacillation, 'Yes, grandson, because over there they are made with better flour.' This is really a shocking reply if it is not taken in the jocular style with which he was trying to reprimand his descendant. Contemporary of this Señor Bermúdez, a Creole, was another similar gentleman, named Mendoza, a European, who maintained his jocose temperament until the last moments of his life. When the final unction was being administered to him, he noticed that one of those acolytes who usually assist the priest was looking with terror at his pale countenance, sunken eyes, and sharp nose, whereupon he made such a grotesque grimace that the boy, throwing the candle on the bed, took to his heels, screaming as though a specter had tried to swallow him. The priest who was aiding the man in a good death asked a little later if he felt he was dying, and he replied in a tremulous voice that since he had never died before, he could not reliably answer. People of little judgment attribute such acts to a lack of soundness of mind, but they really reveal that the mind is clear until the last moments of life. I would say such people are victims of ignorance.

"Do you have any more questions, Señor Crab,[2] because I am getting annoyed." "Oh, yes, Señor; I would like to know if you have seen anything singular in this city which distinguishes it from the rest you have seen in the dominions of our Monarch." "A rare offer! I suppose," he said, "that you, Señor Crab, do not wish to hear bagatelles, but things of great sig-

---

[2] The inspector is undoubtedly suggesting here that Concolorcorvo, in his persistent questions, is like the crab whose claw seldom frees its prey once it has been grasped.

nificance." " *Ao,* Señor." "Well then consider these two aspects: the first is the grandeur of the wedding beds and the second the cradles and furnishings for the newly-born infants in opulent homes. The first are almost *ad pompam,* and the second *ad usum.*" "What comprises these sumptuous beds, cradles, and furnishings?" To this he replied, "The bed clothes are the most exquisite woven in the best mills in Europe. Draperies at the head and foot are made of scarlet damask no less, decorated with the finest golden braid and fringes made in Milan. The bedspreads, adorned in the same fashion, are of the richest silk stuff woven in Lyons, France. The sheets and pillows are the finest linen made in Cambray, adorned with the widest and most delicate laces and inlays woven in Flanders, to which is added a large cloth, similarly decorated and so transparent that through it one may perceive the splendor of the pillows, which on the upper part, have scarcely one span of Dutch batiste. The cradle and furnishings of the child are of the same stuff, without mentioning the jewels for adorning the infant, who is usually bedecked with brilliant stones, which I consider a single expense because they also serve for the other children, except those which are filched by the nurses and servants. So Creoles from houses of average opulence can boast of having been reared in better diapers than the princes of Europe and even those around the Great Turk with all his seraglio."

"It would delight me to see this grandeur and to touch those laces . . ." I said to the inspector. "It would not be difficult for you to see them, but they would not permit you to touch them with those coal-miner hands, for fear you might spot them or leave them smelling like dried potatoes." "A Negress smelling like a barnyard is worse, and I have seen such making up these beds." "But not beds as elegant as these, Señor Concolorcorvo. These are made and unmade by young ladies who live on nectar and ambrosia." "Then how is it," I asked, "that I have seen many ladies from Lima eating cracklings, tripe, cheese stew, corn pap, and other things eaten by my countrymen?" "Those,

Señor Inca, are ladies from Arcadia, who are accustomed to pastoral food and dances to the music of the Satyr's pipes; but these whom I mentioned are nymphs, from Parnassus, presided over by the sacred Apollo, who maintain themselves, as I said, only on nectar and ambrosia, like the gods. Their amusements are provided by lofty compositions in prose and verse, and when one of them wishes to wander over the entire terrestial sphere in one hour, she mounts Pegasus, who is ever ready and grazing near the sacred choir."

CHAPTER XXVII

JUDGMENT OF THE INSPECTOR CONCERNING THE HISTORICAL
ITINERARY OF THE AUTHOR. A COMPARISON BETWEEN THE
EMPIRES OF PERU AND MEXICO. ANECDOTE OF THE FOUR P'S
OF LIMA. CONCLUSION.

B Y the waters of Styx! (which is the strongest oath uttered by the gods of my ancestors, as I have been told), I understand nothing of Arcadia and Parnassus, nor *antaño* and *hogaño, allende* and *aquende*,[1] and many other terms, fables and figures which you blew at me; I fear they have been invented in your mind so these residents of Lima can make fun of a poor highlander, who is an Indian to boot." "Be not so distrustful," the inspector said, "because these gentlemen are tolerant and capable of digesting greater scraps." "Do not be so sure, Señor Don Alonso," I replied; "these men of genius are very clairvoyant and of a cunning spirit; they do not pardon the slightest faux pas." "*Eh bien*, monsieur Concolorcorvo; let us suppose that in the drawing rooms and social gatherings your great historical itinerary is criticized, on the basis of this part, and that it is discovered that your efforts were fruitless and the entire work is not worth a rush. What will you care about that after having sold your copies at a good price? Utter insults against and commend to the devil any work or composition about which people do not speak badly. None has been issued up to now suiting everyone's taste, and there are an endless number of people who, not being capable themselves of composing six lines in octavo, find defects in the sen-

---

[1] *Antaño, hogaño, allende* and *aquende* are colloquial or obsolete expressions employed by the inspector in preceding chapters, meaning: long ago, this present year, on the other side and on this side.

tences of the most skilled writer. All this is chaff for the author. If you succeed in reaping the cost of its printing, which I seriously doubt (even if La Robada shows you special favor out of respect for me and my friendship of long standing), you still gain much by spreading your name through the extensive dominions of Spain more solidly than Guzmán de Alfarache and Estebanillo González,[2] who are celebrated, although in a different sense, by so many wise men and ignoramuses."

I had resolved to ask the inspector more questions, but since he swore to me by the Battle of Almansa and by the Peace of Nimega, which are the only things upon which he swears (imitating Zerquera), that he would give me just one more answer, leaving me at the fourth question of this last interrogatory, I put my hand to my head to ponder the means of ending this trip and my historical itinerary. It was my intention to find out if this capital of the Peruvian empire could be compared to that of Mexico. I proposed this to him and he replied: *Alta petis Phaeton*. I know not in what language he was speaking, for I understand only Quechua, and poorly at that, and Castilian even worse; but he expressed himself in these terms: "The Creoles of these two courts, which are the largest in the two empires of Mexico and Peru, compete in grandeur. The Mexicans say 'from Mexico to the sky, and in the sky a small window or balcony from which Heaven is viewed'; that is the height to which enthusiasm and exaggeration can go. The residents of Lima offer in opposition to this grandeur their four P's, to which they could add with reason their fresh fish or products of the sea, which the Mexicans are lacking because of their greater distance from the sea—from 2 to 80 leagues through hot and humid country; it is by chance that the pickled

---

[2] Guzmán de Alfarache and Estebanillo González are heroes of picaresque novels widely read in the Spanish-speaking world of the seventeenth and eighteenth centuries: *Guzman de Alfarache* (1599) by Mateo Alemán and *Vida y hechos de Estebanillo González* (1646), the author of which is unknown.

fish from Vera Cruz arrive in Mexico City in a condition fit to be eaten without detriment to the health and disgust to the palate.

"So that you, Señor Inca, may put an end to such a wearisome trip, conclude it with a humorous joke played by a Guatemalan *gachupín* on certain *chapetones* of Lima.[3] To avoid all equivocation and unhappy feelings, it is necessary to state that outside of Lima all those people who have ever lived in this capital, whether they be Creoles or Europeans, are called *limeños*, residents of Lima. In New Spain they are designated as *peruleros*, Peruvians, and they keep this name even in their homelands on the peninsula; thus in Madrid, my brother-in-law, I, and other Creoles are known as both *peruleros* and *limeños*. Six or eight of these were in Guatemala at the time when the kingdom was governed by the illustrious Araujo y Pardo brothers, *peruleros* in whose court were *chapetones* or *gachupines*, as they say abroad. This Guatemalan *gachupín* observed the many praises made of Lima by the *chapetones*, but at the same time he noticed that they had not mentioned the important four P's, and one night he ordered these letters to be placed in red ochre on the main door of the archbishop's palace, along with a note challenging the *chapetones* to decipher their meaning, with a penalty of 100 pesos for buying the drinks if they did not produce the true meaning, and a promise that he would pay in the event he was defeated. The *peruleros* received the information, and immediately each one offered to accept the challenge and to decipher the enigma. The judges named for the decision by the Guatemalan were the Araujo brothers (governor and president of the royal *Audiencia*) and the archbishop in whose house the gathering was to take place. The *chapetones* were certain of the victory; on this fact the *gachupín* based his hope of winning. On the day of the assem-

---

[3] *Gachupín* and *chapetón* are names given to natives of Spain who live in the New World. *Gachupín* is used more in the Mexican empire, while *chapetón* is a word native to Peru.

bly, all the *chapetones* gathered in advance in the house of the archbishop. The Guatemalan let himself be coaxed, pretending to be afraid; but at last he entered and took a back seat, like a convicted criminal. The *limeños* ordered that the challenge be read and ratified by the *gachupín*, who said that he was ready to pay the penalty for his animosity, but that the *limeños* must all ratify their acceptance, to which they all gladly agreed, each one trying to play the role of oracle by himself. The president, being the most clairvoyant, showed, with his false laughter, some lack of confidence in the victory of his compatriots, but he finally ordered that the oldest should speak on behalf of all and with full authority.

This fine fellow was about 50 years old. His physiognomy showed a continuous abstinence, but his dress indicated something quite different. On his hat he wore a band of Chinese ribbon, with a square of *paraos* (merchant ships of Chinese style), and to secure the ends, a large golden buckle adorned with brilliant stones. He protected his neck with a kerchief of fine cambric embroidered in black silk, with some cutwork at intervals and very delicate lace on the edge. The cape, although somewhat worn, was of the most exquisite blue cloth from Carcassonne, embroidered in gold which, due to the ravages of the climate, had turned to a silver color. His jacket, or *valenciana*, which covered him to the knees, was of blue velvet with more than 2,000 eyelets and as many buttons of gold thread (which was more likely silver, according to the *contraste* or assayer). The waistcoat did not reach the length of the jacket, but it contained pockets in each of which 1,000 ordinary pieces of La Mancha lace easily fit. It was of tapestry of blended colors, but its background was not clearly discernible. His trousers were of red velvet, fitting very tightly, and they ended above the knee with a garter, of three fingers' width, of gold braid, with three buttons of the same stuff instead of the fourteen customarily used today. His stockings were scarlet, the best made in Laguna, and his shoes of polished cordovan, with a double sole. The buckles were of gold, as was his tobacco pouch, the two together weighing probably a couple of pounds. On the fingers of his right hand he wore six or seven exquisite rings, and in the buttonhole of his waistcoat, a gold chain with a toothpick and lugs having other adornments which could compete with the watch chains currently used by the ladies. His outer shirt showed, by its unusual whiteness, that it was of the finest fabric, and his cap, which covered his ears, of Dutch batiste with three rows of Quito braid, embroidered with costly cutwork, and edged with fluted lace from Flanders, two fingers wide, which would seem to the moderns today like a beautiful and costly *coroza* or paper hat worn as a mark of infamy. His companions presented themselves dressed in like manner, which was the current style in their land, and thus they were recognized in New Spain just as the Hungarians are in France."

"I swear again by the waters of the Styx, Señor Don Alonso, that I understand very little of the picture of my countryman's clothes which you have painted." "And what concern is that of mine?" he replied. "In the year 46 of this century, a year remembered because of the great earthquake, I came to this capital where I still found this manner of dress in vogue. If it is considered ridiculous at the present time, at least one cannot refrain from confessing that this dress was expensive, and at that time it displayed the opulence of the owners and the general spirit instilled by style. All the cultured nations of the world have varied their styles and manners of dress, and all seem, at the present time, extravagant and even ridiculous. The time will come when the modes of dress now current will be criticized and considered ridiculous, despite the fact that currently the dress of men is much reformed and more economical, in imitation of the royal house of Señor Don Carlos III—may God perpetuate him—and the measures taken in this kingdom by His Excellency Señor Don Manuel de Amat y Junient.

"The dean of the Peruvians was a serious man of few words. As soon as the two governors, judges, and presidents of the

assembly gave the signal, he arose, and touching his cap with
his right hand, began his harangue in the following manner:
'Sirs, the enigma proposed by our countryman, the *gachupín*,
and the challenge which he made, prove the little knowledge
he has of the events occurring across the ocean, and show that
he considers us *chapetones* as men who think only of our own
interests without attending to the singular aspects of our
country. We have full knowledge of everything, even though
we are foreigners. It causes me considerable shame to decipher
an enigma so public that even the boys in Lima know it. In
conclusion, the four P's affixed to the door of this archbishop's
palace by the *gachupín* mean nothing more, as Your Excel-
lencies know, than *Pila, Puente, Pan* and *Peines;* that is, Fountain, Bridge, Bread, and Combs, in which Lima surpasses the
arrogant Mexico City.' The entire congress chanted victory for
the Peruvians, and in short order they would have thrown the
Guatemalan from the assembly for his stupidity, and without
hearing him they would have condemned him to the ransom of
the drinks; but the archbishop, after consultation with the president, sounded the bell indicating that the *gachupín* be heard,
and with this signal and that made by both presidents, putting
a finger to their mouth: *Conticuere omnes, intentique ora
tenuerunt.* Thereupon the *gachupín* offered his defense in these
words:
    " 'I have no doubt, sirs, that if I were in Athens, where the
wise men passed judgment and the common people made the
decisions, they would pass sentence against me and all would
consider me a courageous madman, as do the gentlemen from
Lima; but inasmuch as I am in a gathering where two men, wise
and impartial, despite their patriotism, are to pass judgment,
I am certain to attain the victory which my opponents already
claim as their own, with the applause of all the bystanders. I
cannot deny that the men from Lima explained themselves in
the full sense of what my four P's mean in their country, but I
should like to ask these gentlemen if they regard me so stupid

as to ask a thing so well known. Are there not, by chance, other four P's in the world? I find them in Guatemala, and these gentlemen should seek them in this city, yea, even in this very house of the archbishop on whose door I affixed them.' The *chapetones* cried out again, and a second time the archbishop sounded his bell. The *gachupín* then declared that the four P's of his enigma stood for *Pedro*, *Pardo*, *Paulino* and *Perulero*, which were the four words connoting the archbishop: Pedro, Pardo, Pauline and Peruvian. The president stretched out on the bench in convulsive laughter, and the archbishop doubled up without being able to restrain himself. The *chapetones* likewise laughed, and confessing to have lost the battle, rendered homage by buying the drinks, whereupon the assemblage disbanded, and this weary, historical journey comes to an end.

Canendo, et ludendo retuli vera.

F I N

Appendix

RESUMEN DEL NUMERO DE ALMAS, QUE EXISTIAN EL AñO DE 1770 en la Ciudad de la SSma. Trinidad , y Puerto de Sta. Maria de Buenos Ayres, con la Razon de los que nacieron, y murieron en dicho año, fegun confta de los Libros Parroquiales , y la que dieron las Comunidades de Religiofos de ambos Sexos, y demas.

PARROQUIAS.......N. DE ALMAS....NACIDOS.....MUERTOS

	N. DE ALMAS	NACIDOS	MUERTOS
CATHEDRAL	8146	523	316
S. NICOLAS	5176	344	185
LA CONCEPCION	3529	318	158
MONTSERRAT	2468	184	096
LA PIEDAD	1746	151	091
	21065	1520	846

CLERIGOS................... 077
REGULARES,yMONJAS

STO DOMINGO...·........ 101
S. FRANCISCO.............. 164
LA MERCED................086
RECOL. DE S. FRANC....046 } 942 defte n. Murieron...085
BETHLEMITAS............088
CAPUCHINAS.............040
CATHALINAS...............072

HUERFANOS............099
PRESIDARIOS...............101
CARCEL.........................068

Nacidos..........1520
Muertos.........0931

Aumento........0589

Total.....22007

DIVISION DEL NUMERO DE ALMAS, QUE CONSTA ARRIBA.

03639 Hombres Efpañoles, en que fe incluyen 1854. Europeos, los 1398 de la Peninfula à56, Eftrangeros, y 1785 Criollos

04508 Mugeres Efpañolas...

03985 Niños de ambos fexos

05712 Oficiales, y Soldados de Tropa Reglada, Clerigos, Frayles , Monjas, y Dependientes de unos, y de otros; Prefos, Prefidarios, Indios, Negros, y Mulatos, libres de ambos fexos , y de todas edades.

04163 Efclavos Negros, y Mulatos, de ambos fexos , y de todas edades.

22007 De los 3639 Hombres Efpañoles, eftàn comptàs las Milicias de efta Ciud. en la forma fig.

024 Compañias de Caballería de Vecinos de à 50 Hombres, fin Oficiales, Sargentos, y Cabos
09 Dichas de Forafteros de Infantería de à 77 Hombres, Idem.
01 De Artilleros Provinciales de 100 Hombres.
08 Tambien hay 8 Compañias de Indios , y Meftizos de à 50 Hombres. Idem
08 Dichas de Mulatos libres , de Caballería Idem
y 03 De Infantería de Negros libres. Idem

53 Hacen 53 Compañias ; las 40 de Caballería, y 13 de Infantería.

ESPAñOLES CASADOS.

Europeos.........0942 y el refto de 912 Solteros
Criollos ....1058 y el refto de 727 Idem.

2000   1639

DISTANCE TABLES

CHAPTER III

From Buenos Aires to Carcarañal

	leagues		leagues
From Buenos Aires to Luján	14	To India Muerta	16
To Areco	10	To Esquina de la	
To Arrecife	10	Guardia o Carcarañal	24
To Pergamino	10		—
			84

CHAPTER IV

District of Córdoba

	leagues		leagues
From Esquina de la Guardia		To Puestos de Ferreira	3
to Cabeza de Tigre	7	To Ampira	10
To Saladillo de Ruy Díaz	5	To Río Segundo	5
To Esquina de Castillo	9	To Córdoba	9
To Fraile Muerto	2	To Sinsacate	14
To Esquina de Colman	8	To La Dormida	16
To Esquina del Paso de		To Urahuerta	10
Ferreira	3	To Cachi	7
To Tío Pugio	5		—
			113

Santiago del Estero

	leagues		leagues
From Cachi to Portezuelo	9	To Chañar Pugio	14
To Ambargasta	7	To Santiago del Estero	8
To Ayuncha	30	To Vinará	20
			—
			88

CHAPTER V

The District of San Miguel del Tucumán

	leagues		leagues
From Vinará to Mancopa	13	To Río de Tapia	7
To San Miguel del Tucumán	7	To Pozo del Pescado	14
			—
			41

CHAPTER VI

The District of Salta

	leagues		leagues
From Pozo del Pescado to		To the Fortress of Cobos	16
Rosario	13	To Salta	9
To the Concha Estate	10	To Tres Cruces	9
To the Pasaje River	15		—
			72

CHAPTER VIII

The District of Jujuy

	leagues		leagues
From Tres Cruces to La		To Humahuaca	11
Cabaña	3	To La Cueva	8
To Jujuy	6	To Cangrejos Grandes	12
To Guajara	10	To La Quiaca	9
To Los Hornillos	7		—
			66

CHAPTER IX

Route from Buenos Aires

	leagues		leagues
From Buenos Aires to Saladillo de Ruy Díaz: 8 posts	96	To the Pass at La Lagunilla	1
From Saladillo to Paso	2	To the Pass at Las Lajas	9
To El Sauce frontier	24	To El Morro	10
To La Carreta Quemada	13	To the city of San Luis de Loyola	25
To San José	6	To Cieneguita de Corocorto	37
To the Cuarto River	4	To Médano Grande	2
To the edge of La Lagunilla	3	To the Turn-off for Ciénaga	26
		To the city of Mendoza	6

Posts: 22. Leagues: 264

CHAPTER X

Los Chichas Province

	leagues		leagues
From La Quiaca to Mojos	7	To Escara	4
To Suipacha	8	To Quirve	6
To La Ramada	12		
To Santiago de Cotagaita	8		

Posts: 6. Leagues: 45

CHAPTER XIII

The Provinces of Porco, Poopo, and Oruro

	leagues		leagues
Porco		To Las Peñas	4
From Potosí to Yocalla	10	To Yruma	4
To La Leña	6	To the Intermediate Venta	4
To Lagunillas	6		
		Oruro	
Poopo		To Oruro	9
To Vilcapugio	8		
To Ancato	5		

Posts: 9. Leagues: 56

CHAPTER XIV

Provinces of Poopo and Sicafica

	leagues		leagues
Poopo		To Ayoayo	8
From Oruro to Caracollo	8	To Caxamarca	5
		To La Ventanilla	6
Sicafica		To La Paz	4
To Panduro	5		—
To Sicafica	8	Posts: 7. Leagues: 44	

CHAPTER XV

Provinces of Omasuyos, Pacages, Chucuyto, Paucarcolla, Lampa, Tinta and Quispicanchi

	leagues		leagues
Omasuyos		*Lampa*	
From La Paz to Laja	7	To Juliaca	6
		To Nicasio	6
Pacages		To Pucará	6
To Tiay Guanaco	7	To Ayaviri	6
To Guaqui	4	To Chungará	9
To Cepita	7		
		Tinta	
Chucuyto		To Lurucachi	9
To Pomata	7	To Caccha: Omitting the	
To Julí	4	distance to Sicuani	6
To Ylave	5		
To Acora	5	*Quispicanchi*	
To Chucuyto	3	To Quiquijaca: Omitting the	
		distance to Checacupi	10
Paucarcolla		To Oropesa: Omitting the	
To Puno	4	distance to Urcos	8
To Paucarcolla	2	To Cuzco	5

Posts: 21. Leagues: 126

CHAPTER XXI

Provinces of Cuzco, Abancay, Andaguaylas, Guanta, Vilcaguamán and Guamanga

	leagues		leagues
Cuzco		To Pincos	6
From Cuzco to Zurite	7	To Andaguaylas	6
		To Uripa	6
Abancay			
To Limatambo	6	*Guanta, Vilcaguamán,*	
To Marcaguasi	4	*and Guamanga*	
To Curaguasi	6	To Hivias	10
To Tambo Urco	6	To Cangallo Tambo	8
		To Guamanga, the Capital	
Andaguaylas		City	6
To Cochacajas	6		—
		Posts: 12. Leagues: 77	

CHAPTER XXIII

Route from Guamanga to Guancavélica

	leagues		leagues
Guanta		To Paucará	7
From Guamanga to Guanta	6	To Guancavélica	6
Angaraes			—
To Parcos	10	Posts: 4. Leagues: 29	

CHAPTERS XXIII-XXIV

Route from Guancavélica to Lima, through Cotay

	leagues		leagues
From Guancavélica to Cotay	9	To Asia	7
To Turpu	6	To Chilca	8
To Viña	8	To Lurín	7
To Llangas	7	To Lima	6
To Lunaguaná	6		—
To Gualcará	6	Posts: 10. Leagues: 70	

GLOSSARY OF SPANISH WORDS

Ají   The red Indian dwarf pepper; chili pepper.

Alcalde   An officer corresponding to mayor or head of the town council.

Alférez   A military rank, used in both Spanish army and navy, corresponding to ensign or lieutenant. *Alférez real*   Royal Ensign, chief municipal officer in Peru and Bolivia.

Aloja   A fermented liquor made from carob beans, corn or fruits. Also known as *chicha*.

Arroba   A weight measure of about 25 pounds.

Audiencia   A tribunal, appointed by the Crown, which was the unit of civil government in the colonies.

Bola   A burrowing animal of the armadillo family.

Bolas   A kind of weapon consisting of balls of stone or iron, attached to the ends of a thong or cord, used for hurling at and entangling an animal.

Cacique   An Indian chieftan.

Cañari   An Indian runner; a native of the Cañari tribe of Peru.

Cordillera   A mountain range. The Andes.

Coroza   A pointed hat, made of paper and worn by criminals as a sign of their guilt.

Corregidor   A provincial governor.

Chañar (Also *chañal*)   A medium-sized leguminous tree, native to Chile and the River Plate region. Confections are made from its fruit and its wood is used for construction.

Chicha   A fermented drink made from corn and fruits.

Chinguirito   A rum-like drink made from the lees of sugar.

Cholo   A title of contempt which the whites gave to the Indians of a baser sort and to native servants.

Chuño   Powdered dry potatoes from which soup is made.

Encomienda   A trusteeship system in which an allotment of Indians was assigned to a landowner for work on his lands or in his mines.

Fanega   A measure of weight, equalling approximately one hundredweight.

Gauderios   A term used to designate the inhabitants of the pampas before the word *gaucho* came into use.

Güipil (Var. of *Huipil*)   A low-necked, sleeveless blouse, of hip length and richly embroidered. Worn by the Aztec Indian women.

Lanzas   Duty paid to Spanish government by grandees in lieu of military service.

Maestre de campo   A high-ranking official of the militia who was in charge of a number of troops.

Magno   A fruit, in northern Chile, from which bread is made. In Peru the word is used to designate a plant whose stem was used to produce red dye.

Mescal (Also *mezcal*)   An intoxicating liquor made from the maguey plant.

Mistela   Flavored brandy; a drink made with wine, water, sugar, and cinnamon.

Mitayo   An Indian forced laborer.

Mulita   An Uruguayan armadillo.

Pañete   A kind of cloth of low quality.

Peso   A silver coin, equal to 8 reales and thus often called "a piece of eight."

Pimentón   Red pepper.

Quipus   Cords of different colors, with knots of varying size and location, used by the Inca Indians to record memorable events and to keep accounts.

Quirquincho   A burrowing animal of the armadillo family.

Quisquémel   A kind of shawl, with an opening for the head, worn by the Aztec women.

Real   A Spanish coin, usually of silver, which in Spain was the equivalent of 34 *maravedís*. Its value has varied with the place and epoch.

Regidor   A town councilman.

Repartición   An allotment.

Repartimiento   A system of labor designed to replace the forced labor of the Indian in the *encomienda* system. Indians were forced to work, but were paid. However, it amounted to bondage for the native, for the landowner frequently loaned him money in advance or sold him necessities on credit, thereby keeping him in a state of perpetual debt and peonage.

Residencia   Among the Jesuits, a house of residence not yet formed into a college.

Saladillo (Dim. of *salado*)   A name given to land rendered barren by too large a portion of saline particles.

Vara   A measure of length corresponding to approximately 33 inches.

Zapallo (Also *sapallo*)   A species of squash or pumpkin.

11-12 13-14 15-16 17 18-20 21-23 24 25-26 47-28 49-30

31 1-10 11 12-13 14 15-17 18-19 20 21-22 23 24-27 28 29-2

3-4-5-6-7-8-9-10-11 12 13-14-15-16 17-18-19-20-21-22 23 24-25 26-27

18-19 20 21 22-23-24 25-26 27-28 29 30 31 1-2 3-4 5-6 7 8 9 10 11

11-14 20 21 22 23

11-12 13-14 15-18 19 20-21 22 23-24 25 26 27-28 29-30

31 1 2-3 4 5 6-9 10 11 12 13 14 15-18 19-20 21-3 24 25-26 27

13-14 15 16 17-18 19 20 21-22 23-26 27 28 29 30 31-3 4 5 6 7

8-9-10-11-12-13 14-15 16 17 18 19 20 21 22 23

10-11 (2-18) 15-16 17-18 19-20 21-21 23-24 25-26 27
X   X   X   X X

28 29-30 1-2 3-4 5 (6-8) 9-10-11-12 (13-15) 16-17-18-19-20 -21-22 23 -24
X   XX X X   X   X   X   X   X

(28-29) (28-3) 4-5-6 7-8 9-10 11-12-13-14 15 16-17-18 -19-20 -21-22 23-24
                                           X

G 3-4   (M) 28 X   F X 30
L 2-2   29-30   (S-T 31-3)
LP 1-4   (P-T) 1-2 XX   W,R,F,S,C
C 2-4   3-4   S, S 9-8
BA 3   (M) 5 X   M,T 9-14
RT 3   6-8

T 2   9
S 2   10
SP 2   11
B 2   (M) 12
                13-15
                F 16 X
                S 17
                (S) 18 X
                19
                20 X
                21 X
                Th 22
                23 X
                24 SC
                25 C
                M 26 XP